Second Corinthians, Chapters VII to end, Galatians and Philippians Volume 47

EXPOSITIONS OF HOLY SCRIPTURE

EXPOSITIONS OF HOLY SCRIPTURE

ALEXANDER MACLAREN, D. D., Litt. D.

SECOND CORINTHIANS
Chaps. VII to End
GALATIANS AND PHILIPPIANS

HODDER & STOUGHTON

NEW YORK

GEORGE H. DORAN COMPANY

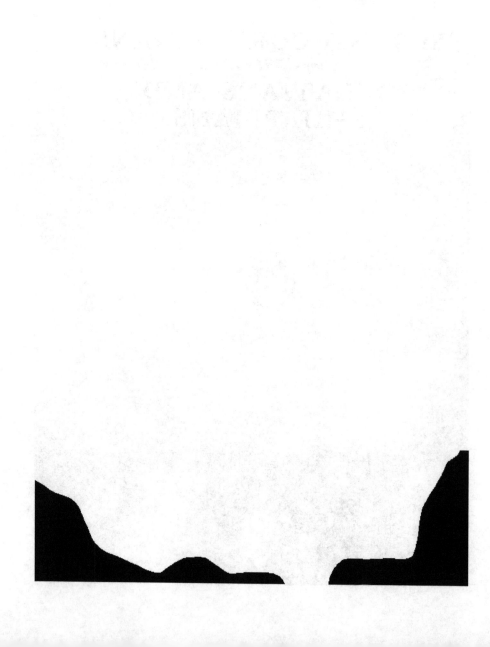

CONTENTS

II. CORINTHIANS

II. CORINTHIANS

GALATIANS

CONTENTS

PHILIPPIANS

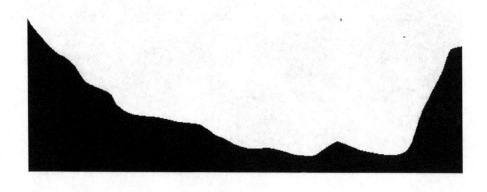

II. CORINTHIANS

HOPE AND HOLINESS

Having therefore these promises . . . let us cleanse ourselves from all filthiness of the flesh and spirit, perfecting holiness in the fear of God.'—2 COR. vii. 1.

IT is often made a charge against professing Christians that their religion has very little to do with common morality. The taunt has sharpened multitudes of gibes and been echoed in all sorts of tones: it is very often too true and perfectly just, but if ever it is, let it be distinctly understood that it is not so because of Christian men's religion but in spite of it. Their bitterest enemy does not condemn them half so emphatically as their own religion does: the sharpest censure of others is not so sharp as the rebukes of the New Testament. If there is one thing which it insists upon more than another, it is that religion without morality is nothing—that the one test to which, after all, every man must submit is, what sort of character has he and how has he behaved—is he pure or foul? All high-wn pretension, all fervid emotion has at last to face tion which little children ask, 'W₂ he a good

very truths on which so often fervid imaginations
have built up a mystical piety that had little to do
with the common rules of right and wrong. But Paul
keeps true to the intensely practical purpose of his
preaching and brings his heroes down to the prosaic
earth with the homely common sense of this far-
reaching exhortation, which he gives as the fitting
conclusion for such celestial visions.

I. A Christian life should be a life of constant self-
purifying.

This epistle is addressed to the church of God which
is at Corinth with all the *saints* which are in all Achaia.

Looking out over that wide region, Paul saw
scattered over godless masses a little dispersed company to each of whom the sacred name of Saint
applied. They had been deeply stained with the vices
of their age and place, and after a black list of criminals
he had had to say to them 'such were some of you,'
and he lays his finger on the miracle that had changed
them and hesitates not to say of them all, 'But ye are
washed, but ye are sanctified, but ye are justified in
the name of the Lord Jesus and by the Spirit of our
God.'

The first thing, then, that every Christian has is a
cleansing which accompanies forgiveness, and however
his garment may have been 'spotted by the flesh,' it
is 'washed and made white in the blood of the Lamb.'
Strange cleansing by which black stains melt out of
garments plunged in red blood! With the cleansi
of forgiveness and justification comes, wherever th
come, the gift of the Holy Spirit—a new life sprin
up within the old life, and untouched by any co
with its evils. These gifts belong u
of the Christian life

their possession only the receptiveness of faith. They admit of no co-operation of human effort, and to possess them men have only to 'take the things that are freely given to them of God.' But of the subsequent stages of the Christian life, the laborious and constant effort to develop and apply that free gift is as essential as, in the earliest stage, it is worse than useless. The gift received has to be wrought into the very substance of the soul, and to be wrought out in all the endless varieties of life and conduct. Christians are cleansed to begin with, but they have still daily to cleanse themselves: the leaven is hid in the three measures of meal, but ''tis a life-long task till the lump be leavened,' and no man, even though he has the life that was in Jesus within him, will grow up 'into the measure of the stature of the fulness of Christ' unless, by patient and persistent effort, he is ever pressing on to 'the things that are before' and daily striving to draw nearer to the prize of his high calling. We are cleansed, but we have still to cleanse ourselves.

Yet another paradox attaches to the Christian life, inasmuch as God cleanses us, but we have to cleanse ourselves. The great truth that the spirit of God in a man is the fontal source of all his goodness, and that Christ's righteousness is given to us, is no pillow on which to rest an idle head, but should rather be a et-call to effort which is thereby made certain of ss. If we were left to the task of self-purifying own effort we might well fling it up as im- It is impulse after purity, and the vision of what purity is, and imparts the power of attaining it, strengthening at once our dim sight and stirring our feeble desires and energising our crippled limbs, then we can 'run with patience the race that is set before us.'

We must note the thoroughness of the cleansing which the Apostle here enjoins. What is to be got rid of is not this or that defect or vice, but 'all filthiness of flesh and spirit.' The former, of course, refers primarily to sins of impurity which in the eyes of the Grçeks of Corinth were scarcely sins at all, and the latter to a state of mind when fancy, imagination, and memory were enlisted in the service of evil. Both are rampant in our day as they were in Corinth. Much modern literature and the new gospel of 'Art for Art's sake' minister to both, and every man carries in himself inclinations to either. It is no partial cleansing with which Paul would have us to be satisfied: '*all*' filthiness is to be cast out. Like careful housewives who are never content to cease their scrubbing while a speck remains upon furniture, Christian men are to regard their work as unfinished as long as the least trace of the unclean thing remains in their flesh or in their spirit. The ideal may be far from being realised at any moment, but it is at the peril of the whole sincerity and peacefulness of their lives if they, in the smallest degree, lower the perfection of their ideal in deference to the imperfection of their realisation of it.

It must be abundantly clear from our own experience that any such cleansing is a very long process. character is made, whether it be good or bad, but a slow building up: no man becomes most wicked at once, and no man is sanctified by a wish or jump. As long as men are in a world so aboun with temptation, 'he that is washed' will need daily to 'wash his feet' that have been stained in the foul ways of life, if he is to be 'clean every whit.'

As long as the spirit is imprisoned in the body and has it for its instrument there will be need for much effort at purifying. We must be content to overcome one foe at a time, and however strong may be the pilgrim's spirit in us, we must be content to take one step at a time, and to advance by very slow degrees. Nor is it to be forgotten that as we get nearer what we ought to be, we should be more conscious of the things in which we are not what we ought to be. The nearer we get to Jesus Christ, the more will our consciences be enlightened as to the particulars in which we are still distant from Him. A speck on a polished shield will show plain that would never have been seen on a rusty one. The saint who is nearest God will think more of his sins than the man who is furthest from him. So new work of purifying will open before us as we grow more pure, and this will last as long as life itself.

II. The Christian life is to be not merely a continual getting rid of evil, but a continual becoming good.

Paul here draws a distinction between cleansing ourselves from filthiness and perfecting holiness, and these two, though closely connected and capable of g regarded as being but the positive and negative of one process, are in reality different, though ctice the former is never achieved without the or the lat accomplished the and more, to God, and to receive into himself more and more of God.

The purifying which Paul has been enjoining will only be successful in the measure of our consecration, and the consecration will only be genuine in the measure of our purifying. Herein lies the broad and blessed distinction between the world's morality and Christian ethics. The former fails just because it lacks the attitude towards a Person who is the very foundation of Christian morality, and changes a hard and impossible law into love. There is no more futile waste of breath than that of teachers of morality who have no message but Be good! Be good! and no motive by which to urge it but the pleasures of virtue and the disadvantages of vice, but when the vagueness of the abstract thought of goodness solidifies into a living Person and that Person makes his appeal first to our hearts and bids us love him, and then opens before us the unstained light of his own character and beseeches us to be like him, the repellent becomes attractive: the impossible becomes possible, and 'if ye love Me keep My commandments' becomes a constraining power and a victorious impulse in our lives.

III. The Christian life of purifying and consecration is to be animated by hope and fear.

The Apostle seems to connect hope more immediately with the cleansing, and holiness with the fear of God, but probably both hope and fear are in his mind as th... double foundation on which both purity and consec... tion are to rest, or the double emotion which is ... produce them both. These promises refer directl... the immediately preceding words, 'I will be a F... unto you and ye shall be My sons and dau... which all the blessings which God can give ...

can receive are fused together in one lustrous and all-comprehensive whole. So all the great truths of the Gospel and all the blessed emotions of sonship which can spring up in a human heart are intended to find their practical result in holy and pure living. For this end God has spoken to us out of the thick darkness; for this end Christ has come into our darkness; for this end He has lived; for this end He died; for this end He rose again; for this end He sends His Spirit and administers the providence of the world. The purpose of all the Divine activity as regards us men is not merely to make us happy, but to make us happy in order that we may be good. He whom what he calls his religion has only saved from the wrath of God and the fear of hell has not learned the alphabet of religion. Unless God's promises evoke men's goodness it will be of little avail that they seem to quicken their hope. Joyful confidence in our sonship is only warranted in the measure in which we are like our Father. Hope often deludes and makes men dreamy and unpractical. It generally paints pictures far lovelier than the realities, and without any of their shadows; it is too often the stimulus and ally of ignoble lives, and seldom stirs to heroism or endurance, but its many defects are not due to itself but to its false choice of objects on which to fix. The hope which is lifted from trailing along the earth and twining round creatures and which rises to grasp these promises ought to be, in the measure of its reality is the ally of all endurance and noble self-sacrifice. Its vision

hope set on Jesus and fear directed towards God. It
is in the fear of God that holiness is to be perfected
There is a fear which has no torment. Yet more, there
is no love in sons or daughters without fear. The
reverential awe with which God's children draw near
to God has in it nothing slavish and no terror. Their
love is not only joyful but lowly. The worshipping
gaze upon His Divine majesty, the reverential and
adoring contemplation of His ineffable holiness, and
the poignant consciousness, after all effort, of the
distance between us and Him will bow the hearts that
love Him most in lowliest prostration before Him.
These two, hope and fear, confidence and awe, are
like the poles on which the whole round world turns
and are united here in one result. They who 'set their
hope in God' must 'not forget the works of God but
keep His commandments'; they who 'call Him Father,'
'who without respect of persons judgeth' must 'pass
the time of their sojourning here in fear,' and their
hopes and their fears must drive the wheels of life,
purify them from all filthiness and perfect them in
all holiness.

SORROW ACCORDING TO GOD

'Godly sorrow worketh repentance to salvation not to be repented of: but
the sorrow of the world worketh death.'—2 COR. vii. 10.

VERY near the close of his missionary career the
Apostle Paul summed up his preaching as being
directed to enforcing two points, 'Repentance towa
God, and faith in our Lord Jesus Christ.' These
repe tance and faith, ought never to be se
in t ht, as they are inseparable in ct.

repentance is impossible without faith, true faith cannot exist without repentance.

Yet the two are separated very often, even by earnest Christian teachers. The tendency of this day is to say a great deal about faith, and not nearly enough in proportion about repentance; and the effect is to obscure the very idea of faith, and not seldom to preach 'Peace! peace! when there is no peace.' A gospel which is always talking about faith, and scarcely ever talking about sin and repentance, is denuded, indeed, of some of its most unwelcome characteristics, but is also deprived of most of its power, and it may very easily become an ally of unrighteousness, and an indulgence to sin. The reproach that the Christian doctrine of salvation through faith is immoral in its substance derives most of its force from forgetting that 'repentance towards God' is as real a condition of salvation as is 'faith in our Lord Jesus Christ.' We have here the Apostle's deliverance about one of these twin thoughts. We have three stages — the root, the stem, the fruit; sorrow, repentance, salvation. But there is a right and a wrong kind of sorrow for sin. The right kind breeds repentance, and thence reaches salvation; the wrong kind breeds nothing, and so ends in death.

Let us then trace these stages, not forgetting that this is not a complete statement of the case, and needs be supplemented in the spirit of the words which I e already quoted, by the other part of the insepar-ble, 'faith towards our Lord Jesus Christ.'

ness, lie at the foundation of all true Christianity. Now I do not insist upon any uniformity of experience in people, any more than I should insist that all their bodies should be of one shape or of one proportion. Human lives are infinitely different, human dispositions are subtly varied, and because neither the one nor the other are ever reproduced exactly in any two people, therefore the religious experience of no two souls can ever be precisely alike.

We have no right to ask—and much harm has been done by asking—for an impossible uniformity of religious experience, any more than we have a right to expect that all voices shall be pitched in one key, or all plants flower in the same month, or after the same fashion. You can print off as many copies as you like, for instance, of a drawing of a flower on a printing-press, and they shall all be alike, petal for petal, leaf for leaf, shade for shade; but no two hand-drawn copies will be so precisely alike, still less will any two of the real buds that blow on the bush. Life produces resemblance with differences; it is machinery that makes facsimiles.

So we insist on no pedantic or unreal uniformity; and yet, whilst leaving the widest scope for divergencies of individual character and experience, and not asking that a man all diseased and blotched with the leprosy of sin for half a lifetime, and a little child that has grown up at its mother's knee, 'in the nurture and admonition of the Lord,' and so has been k 'innocent of much transgression,' shall have the s experience; yet Scripture, as it seems to me, and nature of the case do unite in asserting that there certa elements which, in varying proportion found in all true Christian e

these an indispensable one — and in a very large
number, if not in the majority of cases, a fundamental
one—is this which my text calls 'godly sorrow.'

Dear brethren, surely a reasonable consideration of
the facts of our conduct and character point to that as
the attitude that becomes us. Does it not? I do not
charge you with crimes in the eye of the law. I do
not suppose that many of you are living in flagrant
disregard of the elementary principles of common
every-day morality. Some are, no doubt. There are,
no doubt, unclean men here; there are some who eat
and drink more than is good for them, habitually;
there are, no doubt, men and women who are living
in avarice and worldliness, and doing things which the
ordinary conscience of the populace points to as faults
and blemishes. But I come to you respectable people
that can say: 'I am not as other men are, unjust,
adulterers, or even as this publican'; and pray you,
dear friends, to look at your character all round, in the
light of the righteousness and love of God, and to
plead to the indictment which charges you with neglect
of many a duty and with sin against Him. How do
you plead, 'guilty or not guilty, sinful or not sinful?'
Be honest with yourselves, and the answer will not be
far to seek.

Notice how my text draws a broad distinction
between the right and the wrong kind of sorrow for
'Godly sorrow' is, literally rendered, 'sorrow
according to God,' which may either
s ref

there is another kind of sorrow, which the Apostle
calls the 'sorrow of the world,' which is devoid of that
reference to God. Here we have the characteristic
difference between the Christian way of looking at
our own faults and shortcomings, and the sorrow of
the world, which has got no blessing in it, and will
never lead to anything like righteousness and peace.
It is just this—one has reference to God, puts its sin
by His side, sees its blackness relieved against the
'fierce light' of the Great White Throne, and the other
has not that reference.

To expand that for a moment,—there are plenty of
us who, when our sin is behind us, and its bitter fruits
are in our hands, are sorry enough for our faults. A
man that is lying in the hospital a wreck, with the
sins of his youth gnawing the flesh off his bones, is
often enough sorry that he did not live more soberly
and chastely and temperately in the past days. That
fraudulent bankrupt who has not got his discharge
and has lost his reputation, and can get nobody to
lend him money enough to start him in business again,
as he hangs about the streets, slouching in his rags, is
sorry enough that he did not keep the straight road.
The 'sorrow of the world' has no thought about God
in it at all. The consequences of sin set many a man's
teeth on edge who does not feel any compunction for
the wrong that he did. My brethren, is that the
position of any that are listening to me now?

Again, men are often sorry for their conduct without thinking of it as sin against God. Crime mean
the transgression of man's law, wrong means th
transgression of conscience's law, sin is the tra
of God's law. Some of us would per
'I have done crime.' We are all

quite ready to say: 'I have done wrong many a time'; but there are some of us who hesitate to take the other step, and say: 'I have done sin.' Sin has, for its correlative, God. If there is no God there is no sin. There may be faults, there may be failures, there may be transgressions, breaches of the moral law, things done inconsistent with man's nature and constitution, and so on; but if there be a God, then we have personal relations to that Person and His law; and when we break His law it is more than crime; it is more than fault; it is more than transgression; it is more than wrong; it is sin. It is when you lift the shutter off conscience, and let the light of God rush in upon your hearts and consciences, that you have the wholesome sorrow that worketh repentance and salvation and life.

Oh, dear friends, I do beseech you to lay these simple thoughts to heart. Remember, I urge no rigid uniformity of experience or character, but I do say that unless a man has learned to see his sin in the light of God, and in the light of God to weep over it, he has yet to know 'the strait gate that leadeth unto life.'

I believe that a very large amount of the superficiality and easy-goingness of the Christianity of to-day comes just from this, that so many who call themselves Christians have never once got a glimpse of themselves as they really are. I remember once ⸚ring over the edge of the crater of Vesuvius, and ⸚ng down into the pit, all swirling with sulphurous

Have you ever lo⸚d into your ⸚rts, in ⸚n, and s⸚ t⸚ ⸚thi⸚ ⸚ and

or amount or length of time during which this sorrow
shall be felt. If, on the one hand, it is essential, on
the other hand there are a great many people who
ought to be walking in the light and the liberty of
God's Gospel who bring darkness and clouds over
themselves by the anxious scrutinising question: 'Is
my sorrow deep enough?' Deep enough! What for?
What is the use of sorrow for sin? To lead a man to
repentance and to faith. If you have as much sorrow
as leads you to penitence and trust you have enough.
It is not your sorrow that is going to wash away your
sin, it is Christ's blood. So let no man trouble himself
about the question, Have I sorrow enough? The one
question is: 'Has my sorrow led me to cast myself on
Christ?'

II. Still further, look now for a moment at the next
stage here. 'Godly sorrow worketh repentance.'

What is repentance? No doubt many of you would
answer that it is 'sorrow for sin,' but clearly this text
of ours draws a distinction between the two. There
are very few of the great key-words of Christianity
that have suffered more violent and unkind treatment, and have been more obscured by misunderstandings, than this great word. It has been weakened
down into penitence, which in the ordinary accepta-
tion, means simply the emotion that I have already
been speaking about, viz., a regretful sense of my own
evil. And it has been still further docked and
degraded, both in its syllables and in its substance,
into *penance*. But the 'repentance' of the New
Testament and of the Old Testament—one of the tw
conditions of salvation—is neither sorrow for sin
and satisfaction, but it is,
y expresses, a change of purpo

regard to the sin for which a man mourns. I cannot now expand and elaborate this idea as I should like, but let me remind you of one or two passages in Scripture which may show that the right notion of the word is not sorrow but changed attitude and purpose in regard to my sin.

We find passages, some of which ascribe and some deny repentance to the Divine nature. But if there be a repentance which is possible for the Divine nature, it obviously cannot mean sorrow for sin, but must signify a change of purpose. In the Epistle to the Romans we read, 'The gifts and calling of God are without repentance,' which clearly means without change of purpose on His part. And I read in the story of the mission of the Prophet Jonah, that 'the Lord repented of the evil which He had said He would do unto them, and He did it not.' Here, again, the idea of repentance is clearly and distinctly that of a change of purpose. So fix this on your minds, and lay it on your hearts, dear friends, that the repentance of the New Testament is not idle tears nor the twitchings of a vain regret, but the resolute turning away of the sinful heart from its sins. It is 'repentance toward God,' the turning from the sin to the Father, and that is what leads to salvation. The sorrow is separated from the repentance in idea, however closely they may be intertwined in fact. The sorrow is one thing, and repentance which it works is another.

notice that this change of purpose and break

the question is: Does it make any difference in his attitude? Is he standing, after the tempest of sorrow has swept over him, with his face in the same direction as before; or has it whirled him clean round, and set him in the other direction? The one kind of sorrow, which measures my sin by the side of the brightness and purity of God, vindicates itself as true, because it makes me hate my evil and turn away from it. The other, which is of the world, passes over me like the empty wind through an archway, it whistles for a moment and is gone, and there is nothing left to show that it was ever there. The one comes like one of those brooks in tropical countries, dry and white for half the year, and then there is a rush of muddy waters, fierce but transient, and leaving no results behind. My brother! when your conscience pricks, which of these two things does it do? After the prick, is the word of command that your Will issues 'Right about face!' or is it 'As you were'? Godly sorrow worketh a change of attitude, purpose, mind; the sorrow of the world leaves a man standing where he was. Ask yourselves the question: Which of the two are you familiar with?

Again, the true means of evoking true repentance is the contemplation of the Cross. Law and the fear of hell may startle into sorrow, and even lead to some kind of repentance. But it is the great power of Christ's love and sacrifice which will really melt the heart into true repentance. You may hammer ice to pieces, but it is ice still. You may bray a fool in a mortar, and his folly will not depart from him. Drea of punishment may pulverise the heart, but not chan it; and each fragment, like the smallest bits of magnet, will have the same characteristics as whole mass. But 'the goodness of God leads to repentance,' as the prodigal is conquered and sees the true hideousness of the swine's trough, when he bethinks himself of the father's love. I beseech you to put yourselves under the influence of that great love, and look on that Cross till your hearts melt.

III. We come to the last stage here. Salvation is the issue of repentance. 'Godly sorrow worketh re pentance unto salvation not to be repented of.'

What is the connection between repentance and salvation? Two sentences will answer the question. You cannot get salvation without repentance. You do not get salvation by repentance.

You cannot get the salvation of God unless you shake off your sin. It is no use preaching to a man, 'Faith, Faith, Faith!' unless you preach along with it, 'Break off your iniquities.' 'Let the wicked forsake his way and the unrighteous man his thoughts, and let him turn unto the Lord.' The nature of the case forbids it. It is a clear contradiction in terms, and an absolute impossibility in fact, that God should save a man with the salvation which consists in the deliverance from sin, whilst that man is holding to his sin. Unless, therefore, you have not merely sorrow, but repent- ce, which is turning away from sin with resolute ose, as a man would turn from a serpent, you ot enter into the Kingdom of Heaven.

t you do not get salvation for your repentance. case of b   te   it is no ca   of   by

Not my penitence, but Christ's death, is the ground of
the salvation of every one that is saved at all. Yet
repentance is an indispensable condition of salvation.

What is the connection between repentance and
faith? There can be no true repentance without trust
in Christ. There can be no true trust in Christ without
the forsaking of my sin. Repentance without faith,
in so far as it is possible, is one long misery; like the
pains of those poor Hindoo devotees that will go all
the way from Cape Comorin to the shrine of Jugger-
naut, and measure every foot of the road with the
length of their own bodies in the dust. Men will do
anything, and willingly make any sacrifice, rather
than open their eyes to see this, — that repentance,
clasped hand in hand with Faith, leads the guiltiest
soul into the forgiving presence of the crucified Christ,
from whom peace flows into the darkest heart.

On the other hand, faith without repentance is not
possible, in any deep sense. But in so far as it is
possible, it produces a superficial Christianity which
vaguely trusts to Christ without knowing exactly
what it is trusting Him for, or why it needs Him; and
which has a great deal to say about what I may call
the less important parts of the Christian system, and
nothing to say about its vital centre; which preaches
a morality which is not a living power to create;
which practises a religion which is neither a joy nor a
security. The old word of the Master has a deep truth
in it: 'These are they which heard the word, and anon
with joy received it.' Having no sorrow, no penitence,
no deep consciousness of sin, 'they have no root in
themselves, and in time of temptation they fall away.
If there is to be a profound, an all-pervading,
transforming-sin, and devil-conquering faith, it

be a faith rooted deep in penitence and sorrow for
sin.

Dear brethren, if, by God's grace, my poor words
have touched your consciences at all, I beseech you, do
not trifle with the budding conviction! Do not seek
to have the wound skinned over. Take care that you
do not let it all pass in idle sorrow or impotent regret.
If you do, you will be hardened, and the worse for it,
and come nearer to that condition which the sorrow of
the world worketh, the awful death of the soul. Do
not wince from the knife before the roots of the
cancer are cut out. The pain is merciful. Better the
wound than the malignant growth. Yield yourselves
to the Spirit that would convince you of sin, and
listen to the voice that calls to you to forsake your
unrighteous ways and thoughts. But do not trust to
any tears, do not trust to any resolves, do not trust
to any reformation. Trust only to the Lord who died
on the Cross for you, whose death for you, whose
life in you, will be deliverance from your sin. Then
you will have a salvation which, in the striking
language of my text, 'is not to be repented of,' which
will leave no regrets in your hearts in the day when
all else shall have faded, and the sinful sweets of this
world shall have turned to ashes and bitterness on the
lips of the men that feed on them.

'The sorrow of the world works death.' There are
men and women listening to me now who are half
conscious of their sin, and are resisting the pleading
voice that comes to them, who at the last will open
their eyes upon the realities of their lives, and in a
wild passion of remorse, exclaim: 'I have played the
fool, and have erred exceedingly.' Better to make
thorough work of the sorrow, and by it to be led to

repentance toward God and faith in Christ, and so secure for our own that salvation for which no man will ever regret having given even the whole world, since he gains his own soul.

GIVING AND ASKING

'Moreover, brethren, we do you to wit of the grace of God bestowed on the churches of Macedonia; 2. How that in a great trial of affliction the abundance of their joy and their deep poverty abounded unto the riches of their liberality. 3. For to their power, I bear record, yea, and beyond their power they were willing of themselves; 4. Praying us with much entreaty that we would receive the gift, and take upon us the fellowship of the ministering to the saints. 5. And this they did, not as we hoped, but first gave their own selves to the Lord, and unto us by the will of God: 6. Insomuch that we desired Titus, that as he had begun, so he would also finish in you the same grace also. 7. Therefore, as ye abound in every thing, in faith, and utterance, and knowledge, and in all diligence, and in your love to us; see that ye abound in this grace also. 8. I speak not by commandment, but by occasion of the forwardness of others, and to prove the sincerity of your love. 9. For ye know the grace of our Lord Jesus Christ, that, though He was rich, yet for your sakes He became poor, that ye through His poverty might be rich. 10. And herein I give my advice: for this is expedient for you, who have begun before, not only to do, but also to be forward a year ago. 11. Now therefore perform the doing of it; that as there was a readiness to will, so there may be a performance also out of that which ye have. 12. For if there be first a willing mind, it is accepted according to that a man hath, and not according to that he hath not.'—2 COR. viii. 1-12.

A COLLECTION from Gentile churches for their poor brethren in Jerusalem occupied much of Paul's time and efforts before his last visit to that city. Many events, which have filled the world with noise and been written at length in histories, were less significant than that first outcome of the unifying spirit of common faith. It was a making visible of the grand thought, 'Ye are all one in Christ Jesus.' Practical help, prompted by a deep-lying sense of unity which overleaped gulfs of separation in race, language, a social conditions, was a unique novelty. It was t first pulsation of that spirit of Christian liberality wh has steadily grown in force and sweep ever si people gibe at some of its manifesta

Wiser ones regard its existence as not the least of the marks of the divine origin of Christianity.

This passage is a striking example of the inimitable delicacy of the Apostle. His words are full of what we should call tact, if it were not manifestly the spontaneous utterance of right feeling. They are a perfect model of the true way to appeal for money, and set forth also the true spirit in which such appeals should be made.

In verses 1 to 5, Paul seeks to stimulate the liberality of the Corinthians by recounting that of the Macedonian churches. His sketch draws in outline the picture of what all Christian money-giving should be. We note first the designation of the Macedonian Christians' beneficence as 'a grace' given by God to them. It is twice called so (vers. 1, 4), and the same name is applied in regard to the Corinthians' giving (vers. 6, 7). That is the right way to look at money contributions. The opportunity to give them, and the inclination to do so, are God's gifts. How many of us think that calls for service or money are troublesome obligations, to be got out of as easily as possible! A true Christian will be thankful, as for a love token from God, for every occasion of giving to Him. It would be a sharp test for many of us to ask ourselves whether we can , 'To me . . . is this grace given,' that I should part my money for Christ's sake.

te, further, the lovely picture of these Macedonian They were plunged in sorrows and troubles, did not dry their fount 'proof of their affliction,' meaning that it constituted a proof of their Christian character; that is, by the manner in which it was borne; and in it they had still 'abundance of joy,' for the paradox of the Christian life is that it admits of the co-existence of grief and gladness.

Again, Christian giving gives from scanty stores. 'Deep poverty' is no excuse for not giving, and will be no hindrance to a willing heart. 'I cannot afford it' is sometimes a genuine valid reason, but oftener an insincere plea. Why are subscriptions for religious purposes the first expenditure to be reduced in bad times?

Further, Christian giving gives up to the very edge of ability, and sometimes goes beyond the limits of so-called prudence. In all regions 'power to its last particle is duty,' and unless power is strained it is not fully exercised. It is in trying to do what we cannot do that we do best what we can do. He who keeps well within the limits of his supposed ability will probably not do half as much as he could. While there is a limit behind which generosity even for Christ may become dishonesty or disregard of other equally sacred claims, there is little danger of modern Christians transgressing that limit, and they need the stimulus to do a little more than they think they can do, rather than to listen to cold-blooded prudence.

Further, Christian giving does not wait to be ask but takes the opportunity to give as itself 'grace,' presses its benefactions. It is an unwonted experi for a collector of subscriptions to be besought take them 'with much entreaty,' but it would be so anomalous if Christian people understood pri

Further, Christian giving begins with the surrender of self to Christ, from which necessarily follows the glad offering of wealth. These Macedonians did more than Paul had hoped, and the explanation of the unexpected largeness of their contributions was their yielding of themselves to Jesus. That is the deepest source of all true liberality. If a man feels that he does not own himself, much less will he feel that his goods are his own. A slave's owner possesses the slave's bit of garden ground, his hut, and its furniture. If I belong to Christ, to whom does my money belong? But the consciousness that my goods are not mine, but Christ's, is not to remain a mere sentiment. It can receive practical embodiment by my giving them to Christ's representatives. The way for the Macedonians to show that they regarded their goods as Christ's, was to give them to Paul for Christ's poor saints. Jesus has His representatives still, and it is useless for people to talk or sing about belonging to Him, unless they verify their words by deeds.

Verse 6 tells the Corinthians that the success of the collection in Macedonia had induced Paul to send Titus to Corinth to promote it there. He had previously visited it on the same errand (chap. xii. 14), and now is coming to complete 'this grace.' The rest of the passage is Paul's appeal to the Corinthians for their help in the matter, and certainly never was such an appeal made in a more dignified, noble, and lofty tone. He has been dilating on the liberality of others, and thereby sanctioning the stimulating of Christian liberality, in the same way as other graces may legitimately be stimulated, by example. That is delicate ground to tread on, and needs caution if it is not to degenerate into an appeal to rivalry, as it too often does, but in itself is perfectly legitimate and wholesome. But, passing from that incitement, Paul rests his plea on deeper grounds.

First, Christian liberality is essential to the completeness of Christian character. Paul's praise in verse 7 is not mere flattery, nor meant to put the Corinthians into good humour. He will have enough to say hereafter about scandals and faults, but now he gives them credit for all the good he knew to be in them. Faith comes first, as always. It is the root of every Christian excellence. Then follow two graces, eminently characteristic of a Greek church, and apt to run to seed in it,—utterance and knowledge. Then two more, both of a more emotional character,—earnestness and love, especially to Paul as Christ's servant. But all these fair attributes lacked completeness without the crowning grace of liberality. It is the crowning grace, because it is the practical manifestation of the highest excellences. It is the result of sympathy, of unselfishness, of contact with Christ, of drinking in of His spirit. Love is best. Utterance and knowledge and earnestness are poor beside it. This grace is like the diamond which clasps a necklace of jewels.

Christian giving does not need to be commanded. 'I speak not by way of commandment.' That is poor virtue which only obeys a precept. Gifts given because it is duty to give them are not really gifts, but taxes. They leave no sweet savour on the hand that bestows, and bring none to that which receives. 'I call you not servants, but friends.' The region in which Christ's liberality moves is high above the realm of law and, correlative, obligation.

Further, Christian liberality springs spontaneous from conscious possession of Christ's riches. W

not here enter on the mysteries of Christ's emptying
Himself of His riches of glory. We can but touch the
stupendous fact, remembering that the place whereon
we stand is holy ground. Who can measure the nature
and depth of that self-denuding of the glory which He
had with the Father before the world was? But, thank
God, we do not need to measure it, in order to feel the
solemn, blessed force of the appeal which it makes to
us. Adoring wonder and gratitude, unfaltering trust
and absolute self-surrender to a love so self-sacrificing,
must ever follow the belief of that mystery of Divine
mercy, the incarnation and sacrifice of the eternal Son.

But Paul would have us remember that the same
mighty act of stooping love, which is the foundation of
all our hope, is to be the pattern for all our conduct.
Even in His divinest and most mysterious act, Christ is
our example. A dewdrop is rounded by the same laws
which shape the planetary spheres or the sun himself;
and Christians but half trust Christ if they do not
imitate Him. What selfishness in enjoyment of our
'own things' could live in us if we duly brought ourselves under the influence of that example? How
miserably poor and vulgar the appeals by which money
is sometimes drawn from grudging owners and tight-
uttoned pockets, sound beside that heart-searching
heart-moving one, 'Ye know the grace of our Lord
Christ!'

Christian liberality will not go off in good
and benevolent senti s.

to will, so there may be the completion also.' We all know where the road leads that is paved with good intentions.

Further, Christian liberality is accepted and rewarded according to willingness, if that is carried into act according to ability. While the mere wish to help is not enough, it is the vital element in the act which flows from it; and there may be more of it in the widow's mite than in the rich man's large donation — or there may be less. The conditions of acceptable offerings are twofold—first, readiness, glad willingness to give, as opposed to closed hearts or grudging bestowals; and, second, that willingness embodied in the largest gift possible. The absence of either vitiates all. The presence of both gives trifles a place in God's storehouse of precious things. A father is glad when his child brings him some utterly valueless present, not because he must, but because he loves; and many a parent has such laid away in sacred repositories. God knows how to take gifts from His children, not less well than we who are evil know how to do it.

But the gracious saying of our passage has a solemn side; for if only gifts 'according as a man hath' are accepted, what becomes of the many which fall far short of our ability, and are really given, not because we have the willing mind, but because we could not get out of the unwelcome necessity to part with a miserably inadequate percentage of our possessions. Is God likely to be satisfied with the small dividends which we offer as composition for our great debt?

RICH YET POOR

'For ye know the grace of our Lord Jesus Christ, that, though He was rich yet for your sakes He became poor, that ye through His poverty might be rich.'— 2 COR. viii. 9.

THE Apostle has been speaking about a matter which, to us, seems very small, but to him was very great, viz., a gathering of pecuniary help from the Gentile churches for the poor church in Jerusalem. Large issues, in his estimation, attended that exhibition of Christian unity, and, be it great or small, he applies the highest of all motives to this matter. 'For ye know the grace of the Lord Jesus Christ, that though He was rich yet for your sakes He became poor.' The trivial things of life are to be guided and shaped by reference to the highest of all things, the example of Jesus Christ; and that in the whole depth of His humiliation, and even in regard to His cross and passion. We have here set forth, as the pattern to which the Christian life is to be conformed, the deepest conception of what our Lord's career on earth was.

The whole Christian Church is about to celebrate the nativity of our Lord at this time. This text gives us the true point of view from which to regard it. We e here the work of Christ in its deepest motive, grace of our Lord Jesus.' We have it in its tran- t self-impoveris ent, 'Though He was ric r sakes He became poor.'

'Ye know the grace of our Lord Jesus Christ.'
Every word here is significant. It is very unusual in
the New Testament to find that expression 'grace'
applied to Jesus Christ. Except in the familiar benediction, I think there are only one or two instances of such
a collocation of words. It is 'the grace of God' which,
throughout the New Testament, is the prevailing expression. But here 'grace is attributed to Jesus';
that is to say, the love of the Divine heart is, without
qualification or hesitation, ascribed to Him. And what
de we mean by grace? We mean love in exercise to
inferiors. It is infinite condescension in Jesus to love.
His love stoops when it embraces us. Very significant,
therefore, is the employment here of the solemn full
title, 'the Lord Jesus Christ,' which enhances the condescension by making prominent the height from
which it bent. The 'grace' is all the more wonderful
because of the majesty and sovereignty, to say the
least of it, which are expressed in that title, the Lord.
The highest stoops and stands upon the level of the
lowest. 'Grace' is love that expresses itself to those
who deserve something else. And the deepest motive,
which is the very key to the whole phenomena of the
life of Jesus Christ, is that it is all the exhibition, as it
is the consequence, of a love that, stooping, forgives.
'Grace' is love that, stooping and forgiving, communi-
cates its whole self to unworthy and transgressing
recipients. And the key to the life of Jesus is that
we have set forth in its operation a love which
not content to speak only the ordinary language
human affection, or to do its ordinary deeds, but
self-impelled to impart what transcends all other
_____, and to give its very self
_____ ends, a love that _____

worthiness, is turned away by no sin, is unmoved to
any kind of anger, and never allows its cheek to flush
or its heart to beat faster, because of any provocation.
and a love that is content with nothing short of entire
surrender and self-impartation underlies all that
precious life from Bethlehem to Calvary.

But there is another word in our text that may well
be here taken into consideration. 'For your sakes,'
says the Apostle to that Corinthian church, made up
of people, not one of whom had ever seen or been seen
by Jesus. And yet the regard to them was part of the
motive that moved the Lord to His life, and His death.
That is to say, to generalise the thought, this grace,
thus stooping and forgiving and self-imparting, is a
love that gathers into its embrace and to its heart all
mankind; and is universal because it is individualising.
Just as each planet in the heavens, and each tiny
plant upon the earth, are embraced by, and separately
receive, the benediction of that all-encompassing arch
of the heaven, so that grace enfolds all, because it takes
account of each. Whilst it is love for a sinful world,
every soul of us may say: 'He loved me, and '—therefore—'gave Himself for me.' Unless we see beneath
the sweet story of the earthly life this deep-lying
source of it all, we fail to understand that life itself.
We may bring criticism to bear upon it; we may appre-
nd it in diverse affecting, elevating, educating
cts; but, oh! brethren, we miss the blazing centre
light, the warm heart of the fire, unless we see
throu all the individual f the li

So then, we have here set before us the work of Christ in its—

II. Most mysterious and unique self-impoverishment.

'He was . . . He became,' there is one strange contrast. 'He was *rich* . . . He became *poor*,' there is another. 'He was . . . He became.' What does that say? Well, it says that if you want to understand Bethlehem, you must go back to a time before Bethlehem. The meaning of Christ's birth is only understood when we turn to that Evangelist who does not narrate it. For the meaning of it is here; 'the Word became flesh, and dwelt among us.' The surface of the fact is the smallest part of the fact. They say that there is seven times as much of an iceberg under water as there is above the surface. And the deepest and most important fact about the nativity of our Lord is that it was not only the birth of an Infant, but the Incarnation of the Word. 'He was . . . He became.' We have to travel back and recognise that that life did not begin in the manger. We have to travel back and recognise the mystery of godliness, God manifest in the flesh.

And these two words 'He was . . . He became,' imply another thing, and that is, that Jesus Christ who died because He chose, was not passive in His being born, but as at the end of His earthly life, so at its beginning exercised His volition, and was born because He willed, and willed because of 'the grace of our Lord Jesus.'

Now in this connection it is very remarkable, and well worth our pondering, that throughout the who of the Gospels, when Jesus speaks of His coming in the world, He never uses the word 'born' but once, that was before the Roman governor, who would have understood or cared for anything furthe

whom He did say, 'To this end was I born.' But even
when speaking to him His consciousness that that word
did not express the whole truth was so strong that He
could not help adding—though He knew that the hard
Roman procurator would pay no attention to the
apparent tautology—the expression which more truly
corresponded to the fact, 'and for this cause came I
into the world.' The two phrases are not parallel.
They are by no means synonymous. One expresses the
outward fact; the other expresses that which underlay
it. 'To this end was I born.' Yes! 'And for this
cause came I.' He Himself put it still more definitely
when He said, 'I came forth from the Father, and am
come into the world. Again, I leave the world and go
unto the Father.' So the two extremities of the earthly
manifestation are neither of them ends; but before the
one, and behind the other, there stretches an identity
or oneness of Being and condition. The one as the
other, the birth and the death, may be regarded as, in
deepest reality, not only what He passively endured,
but what He actively did. He was born, and He died,
that in all points He might be 'like unto His brethren.'
He 'came' into the world, and He 'went' to the
Father. The end circled round to the beginning, and
in both He acted because He chose, and chose because
He loved.

So much, then, lies in the one of these two antitheses
y text; and the other is no less profound and
nt. 'He was rich; He became poor.' In this
tion 'rich' can only mean posses d of the
s and indepe ence: a ' ly

birth than in the birth of each of us, the words are grotesquely inappropriate to the facts of the case. For as between nothingness, which is the alternative, and the possession of conscious being, there is surely a contrast the very reverse of that expressed here. For us, to be born is to be endowed with capacities, with the wealth of intelligent, responsible, voluntary being; but to Jesus Christ, if we accept the New Testament teaching, to be born was a step, an infinite step, downwards, and He, alone of all men, might have been 'ashamed to call men brethren.' But this denudation of Himself, into the particulars of which I do not care to enter now, was the result of that stooping grace which 'counted it not a thing to be clutched hold of, to be equal with God; but He made Himself of no reputation, and was found in fashion as a man, and became obedient unto death, even the death of the Cross.'

And so, dear friends, we know the measure of the stooping love of Jesus only when we read the history by the light of this thought, that 'though He was rich' with all the fulness of that eternal Word which was 'in the beginning with God,' 'He became poor,' with the poverty, the infirmity, the liability to temptation, the weakness, that attach to humanity; 'and was found in all points like unto His brethren,' that He might be able to help and succour them all.

The last thing here is—

III. The work of Christ set forth in its highest issue.

'That we through His poverty might become rich.' Of course, the antithetical expressions must be taken to be used in the same sense, and with the same width of application, in both of the clauses. And if so, think reverently, wonderingly, thankfully, of the in

vista of glorious possibility that is open to us here.
Christ was rich in the possession of that Divine glory
which He had with the Father before the world was.
'He became poor,' in assuming the weakness of the
manhood that you and I carry, that we, in the human
poverty which is like His poverty, may become rich
with wealth that is like His riches, and that as He
stooped to earth veiling the Divine with the human,
we may rise to heaven, clothing the human with the
Divine.

For surely there is nothing more plainly taught in
Scripture, and I am bold to say nothing to which any
deep and vital Christian experience even here gives
more surely an anticipatory confirmation, than the
fact that Christ became like unto us, that each of us
may become like unto Him. The divine and the
human natures are similar, and the fact of the
Incarnation, on the one hand, and of man's glorifica-
tion by possession of the divine nature on the other,
equally rest upon that fundamental resemblance
between the divine nature and the human nature which
God has made in His own image. If that which in
each of us is unlike God is cleared away, as it can be
cleared away, through faith in that dear Lord, then the
likeness, as a matter of course, comes into force.

The law of all elevation is that whosoever desires to
lift must stoop ; and the end of all stooping is to lift
lowly to the place from which the love hath bent
And this is at once the law for the Incarnation
Christ, and for the elevation of the Christian. 'We
like Him for we shall see Him as is.' And

until all who have received it are 'changed from glory
to glory even into the image of the Lord.' We do not
understand Jesus, His cradle, or His Cross, unless on the
one hand we see in them His emptying Himself that He
might fill us, and, on the other hand, see, as the only
result which warrants them and satisfies Him, our
complete conformity to His image, and our participation in that glory which He has at the right hand of
God. That is the prospect for humanity, and it is
possible for each of us.

I do not dwell upon other aspects of this great self-
emptying of our Lord's, such as the revelation in it to
us of the very heart of God, and of the divinest thing
in the divine nature, which is love, or such as the sympathy which is made possible thereby to Him, and
which is not only the pity of a God, but the compassion
of a Brother. Nor do I touch upon many other aspects
which are full of strengthening and teaching. That
grand thought that Jesus has shared our human
poverty that we may share His divine riches is the very
apex of the New Testament teaching, and of the
Christian hope. We have within us, notwithstanding
all our transgressions, what the old divines used to
call a 'deiform nature,' capable of being lifted up into
the participation of divinity, capable of being cleansed
from all the spots and stains which make us so unlike
Him in whose likeness we were made.

Brethren, let us not forget that this stooping, and
pardoning, and self-imparting love, has for its main
instrument to appeal to our hearts, not the cradle but
the Cross. We are being told by many people to-day
that the centre of Christianity lies in the thought
an Incarnation. Yes. But our Lord Himself has t
us what that was for.

'The Son of Man came not to be ministered unto, but to minister, and to give His life a ransom for many.' It is only when we look to that Lord in His death, and see there the very lowest point to which He stooped, and the supreme manifestation of His grace, that we shall be drawn to yield our hearts and lives to Him in thankfulness, in trust, and in imitation: and shall set Him before us as the pattern for our conduct, as well as the Object of our trust.

Brethren, my text was spoken originally as presenting the motive and the example for a little piece of pecuniary liability. Do you take the cradle and the Cross as the law of your lives? For depend upon it, the same necessity which obliged Jesus to come down to our level, if He would lift us to His; to live our life and die our death, if He would make us partakers of His immortal life, and deliver us from death; makes it absolutely necessary that if we are to live for anything nobler than our own poor, transitory self-aggrandisement, we too must learn to stoop to forgive, to impart ourselves, and must die by self-surrender and sacrifice, if we are ever to communicate any life, or good of life, to others. He has loved us, and given Himself for us. He has set us therein an example which He commends to us by His own word when He tells us that 'if a corn of wheat' is to bring forth 'much fruit' it must die, else it 'abideth alone.' Unless we die, we never truly live; unless we die to ourselves for others, and like Jesus, we live alone in the solitude of a self-posed self-regard. So living, we are dead whilst we

WILLING AND NOT DOING

'Now therefore perform the doing of it; that as there was a readiness to will so there may be a performance also.'—2 COR. viii. 11.

THE Revised Version reads: 'But now complete the doing also; that as there was the readiness to will, so there may be the completion also out of your ability.' A collection of money for the almost pauper church at Jerusalem bulked very largely in the Apostle's mind at the date of the writing of the two letters to the Corinthian church. We learn that that church had been the first to agree to the project, and then had very distinctly hung back from implementing its promises and fulfilling its good intentions. So the Apostle, in the chapter from which my text is taken, with wonderful delicacy, dignity, and profundity, sets forth the true principle, not only of Christian giving, but of Christian asking. The text advises that the gushing sentiments of brotherly sympathy and liberality which had inspired the Corinthians a year ago should now bear some fruit in action. So Paul is going to send Titus, his right-hand man at the time, to hurry up and finish off the collection and have done with it. The text is in effect the message which Titus was to carry; but it has a far wider application than that. It is a needful advice for us all about a great many other things: 'As there was a readiness to will, so let there be a performance also.'

Resolutions, noble and good and Christlike, have strange knack of cheating the people who make So we all need the exhortation not to be befool that we have done, when we have only not do unless we will. But a wide gap, as our experience witnesses, between the two things. We all know what place it is to which, according to the old proverb, the road is paved with good intentions; and the only way to pull up that paving is to take Paul's advice here and always, and immediately to put into action the resolves of our hearts. Now I desire to say two or three very plain and simple things about this matter.

I. I would have you consider the necessity of this commandment.

Consider that the fault here warned against is a universal one. What different men we should be if our resolutions had fruited in conduct! In all regions of life that is true, but most emphatically is it true in regard to religion. The damning tragedy of many lives, and I dare say of those of some of my hearers, is that men have over and over again determined that they would be Christians, and they are not Christians yet; just because they have let 'the native hue of resolution be sicklied over' by some paleness or other, and so have resolved and resolved and resolved till every nerve of action is rotted away, and they will die unchristian. I dare say that there are men or women listening to me now, perhaps with grey hairs upon them, who can remember times, in the springtide of their youth, when they said, 'I will give my heart to Jesus Christ, and set my faith upon Him'; and they have not done it yet. Now, therefore, 'as there was a readiness to will, let there be also the performance.'

But it is not only in regard to that most important of all resolves that I wish to say a word. All Christians, I am sure, know what it is, over and over again, to have had stirrings in their hearts which they have been able to consolidate into determination, but have not been able to carry into act. 'The children have come to the birth, and there is not strength to bring them forth.' That is true about all of us, more or less, and it is very solemnly true of a great many of us professing Christians. We have tried to cure—we have determined that we will cure—manifest and flagrant defects or faults in our Christian life. We have resolved, and some nipping frost has come, and the blossoms have dropped on the grass before they have ever set into fruit. I know that is so about you, because I know that it is so about myself. And therefore, dear brethren, I appeal to you, and ask you whether the exhortation of my text has not a sharp point for every one of us—whether the universality of this defect does not demand that we all should gravely consider the exhortation here before us?

Then, again, let me remind you how this injunction is borne in upon us by the consideration of the strength of the opposition with which we have always to contend, in every honest attempt to bring to act our best resolutions. Did you ever try to cure some little habit, some mere trifle, a trick of manner or twist of the finger, or some attitude or tone that might be ugly and awkward, and that people told you that it would be better to get rid of? You know how hard it is. There is always a tremendous gulf between the ideal and its realisation in life. As long as we are moving *in vacuo* we move without any friction or difficulty; but as soon as we come out into a world where there are an atmosphere and opposing forces, then friction comes in, a speed diminishes; and we never become what we to be. We begin with grand purposes, and we with very poor results. We all start, in our days, with the notion that our lives are going t

radiant and beautiful, and all unlike what the limitations of power and the antagonisms that we have to
meet make of them at last.   The tree of our life's doings
has to grow, like those contorted pines on the slopes of
the Alps, in many storms, with heavy weights of snow
on its branches, and beaten about by tempests from
every quarter of the heavens; and so it gets gnarled
and knotted and very unlike the symmetrical beauty
that we dreamed would adorn it.   We begin with saying:
'Come!   Let us build a tower whose top shall reach to
heaven'; and we are contented at last, if we have put
up some little tumble-down shed where we can get
shelter for our heads from the blast.

And the difficulty in bringing into action our best
selves besets us in the matter of translating our resolutions into practice.   What are arrayed against it?   A
feeble will, enslaved too often by passions and flesh
and habits, and all about us lie obstacles to our
carrying into action our conscientious convictions, our
deepest resolutions; obstacles to our being true to our
true selves; to which obstacles, alas, far too many of
us habitually, and all of us occasionally, succumb.   That
being the case, do not we all need to ponder in our
deepest hearts, and to pray for grace to make the
motto of our lives, 'As there was a readiness to will,
let there be a performance'?

II. Consider the importance of this counsel.

That is borne in upon mind and conscience by look-
 at the disastrous effects of letting resolutions
 in sterile.   Consider how apt we are to deceive
 es with unfulfilled purposes.   The quick re-
 hich an easily-moved nature may make to

willing is almost as good as if we had done what we
half resolved on.   And there is a kind of glow of satisfaction that comes when such a man thinks, 'I have
done well in that I have determined.' The Devil will
let you resolve as much as you like—the more the
better; only the more easily you resolve, the more
certainly he will block the realisation. Let us take
care of that seducing temptation which is apt to lead
us all to plume ourselves on good resolutions, and to
fancy that they are almost equivalent to their own
fulfilment. Cheques are all very well if there be bullion
in the bank cellars to pay them with when they fall
due, but if that be not so, then the issuing of them is
crime and fraud. Our resolutions, made and forgotten
as so many of our good resolutions are, are very little
better.

Note, too, how rapidly the habit of substituting
lightly-made resolutions for seriously-endeavoured
acts grows.

And mark, further, how miserable and debilitating
it is to carry the dead weight of such unaccomplished
intentions.

Nothing so certainly weakens a man as a multitude
of resolves that he knows he has never fulfilled. They
weaken his will, burden his conscience, stand in the
way of his hopes, make him feel as if the entail of
evil was too firm and strong to be ever broken. 'O
wretched man that I am!' said one who had made
experience of what it was to will what was good, an
not to find how to perform, 'who shall deliver me fr
the body of this death?' It is an awful thing to h
to carry a corpse about on your back. And that
thought the man did who loaded his
abortive resolutions, that peri

the birth, and never grew up to maturity. Weak and miserable is always the man who is swift to resolve and slow to carry out his resolutions.

III. And now let me say a word before I close about how this universal and grave disease is to be coped with.

Well, I should say to begin with, let us take very soberly and continually into our consciousness the recognition of the fact that the disease is there. And then may I say, let us be rather slower to resolve than we often are. 'Better is it that thou shouldest not vow than that thou shouldest vow and not pay.' The man who has never had the determination to give up some criminal indulgence—say, drink—is possibly less criminal, and certainly less weak, than the man who, when his head aches, and the consequences of his self-indulgence are vividly realised by him, makes up his mind to be a teetotaller, and soon stumbles into the first dram-shop that is open, and then reels out a drunkard. Do not vow until you have made up your minds to pay. Remember that it is a solemn act to determine anything, especially anything bearing on moral and religious life; and that you had far better keep your will in suspense than spring to the resolution with thoughtless levity and leave it with the same.

Further, the habit of promptly carrying out our [res]olves is one that, like all other habits, can be culti[vat]ed. And we can cultivate it in little things, in the [least] trifles of daily life, which by their myriads [make u]p life itself, in order that it may be a fix[ed] [habit of] our minds wh[en] great make a great resolve about his religion, or about his conduct, will be most likely to carry it out. Get the magical influence of habit on your side, and you will have done much to conquer the evil of abortive resolutions.

But then there is something a great deal more than that to be said. The Apostle did not content himself, in the passage already referred to, with bewailing the wretchedness of the condition in which to will was present, but how to perform he found not. He asked, and he triumphantly answered, the question, 'Who shall deliver me?' with the great words, 'I thank God through Jesus Christ our Lord.' There is the secret; keep near Him, trust Him, open your hearts to the influences of that Divine Spirit who makes us free from the law of sin and death. And if thus, knowing our weakness, recognising our danger, humbly trying to cultivate the habit of prompt discharge of all discerned duty, we leave ourselves in Jesus Christ's hands, and wait, and ask, and believe that we possess, His cleansing Spirit, then we shall not ask and wait in vain. 'Work out your own salvation, . . . for it is God that worketh in you, both the willing and the doing.'

ALL GRACE ABOUNDING

'God is able to make all grace abound toward you; that ye, always having sufficiency in all things, may abound to every good work.'—2 COR. ix. 8.

IN addition to all his other qualities the Apostle was good man of business; and he had a field of that quality in the collection for which takes up so much of or so long a period so much

thoughts and efforts. It was for the sake of showing
by actual demonstration that would 'touch the hearts'
of the Jewish brethren, the absolute unity of the two
halves of the Church, the Gentile and the Jewish, that
the Apostle took so much trouble in this matter. The
words which I have read for my text come in the midst
of a very earnest appeal to the Corinthian Christians
for their pecuniary help. He is dwelling upon the same
thought which is expressed in the well-known words:
'What I gave I kept; what I kept I lost.'

But whilst the words of my text primarily applied
to money matters, you see that they are studiously
general, universal. The Apostle, after his fashion, is
lifting up a little 'secular' affair into a high spiritual
region; and he lays down in my text a broad general
law, which goes to the very depths of the Christian
life.

Now, notice, we have here in three clauses three
stages which we may venture to distinguish as the
fountain, the basin, the stream. 'God is able to make
all grace abound toward you';—there is the fountain.
'That ye always, having all-sufficiency in all things';
—there is the basin that receives the gush from the
fountain. 'May abound in every good work';—there
is the stream that comes from the basin. The fountain
pours into the basin, that the flow from the basin may
feed the stream.

Now this thought of Paul's goes to the heart of
life. So let us look at it.

Fountain.

'*all* grace . . . *all*-sufficiency for *all* things . . . *every* good work.' But even these expressions do not satisfy Paul, and he has to repeat the word 'abound,' in order to give some faint idea of his conception of the full tide which gushes from the fountain. It is 'all grace,' and it is abounding grace.

Now what does he mean by 'grace'? That word is a kind of shorthand for the whole sum of the unmerited blessings which come to men through Jesus Christ. Primarily, it describes what we, for want of a better expression, have to call a 'disposition' in the divine nature; and it means, then, if so looked at, the unconditioned, undeserved, spontaneous, eternal, stooping, pardoning love of God. That is grace, in the primary New Testament use of the phrase.

But there are no idle 'dispositions' in God. They are always energising, and so the word glides from meaning the disposition, to meaning the manifestation and activities of it, and the 'grace' of our Lord is that love in exercise. And then, since the divine energies are never fruitless, the word passes over, further, to mean all the blessed and beautiful things in a soul which are the consequences of the Promethean truth of God's loving hand, the outcome in life of the inward bestowment which has its cause, its sole cause, in God's ceaseless, unexhausted love, unmerited and free.

That, very superficially and inadequately set forth, is at least a glimpse into the fulness and greatness of meaning that lies in that profound New Testamer word, 'grace.' But the Apostle here puts emphasis the variety of forms which the one divine gift assun It is '*all* grace' which God is able to make abo to you. So then, you see this one transcen the divine heart, when it comes in human experience, is like a meteor when it passes into the atmosphere of earth, and catches fire and blazes, showering out a multitude of radiant points of light. The grace is many-sided—many-sided to us, but one in its source and in its character. For at bottom, that which God in His grace gives to us as His grace is what? Himself; or if you like to put it in another form, which comes to the same thing—new life through Jesus Christ. That is the encyclopædiacal gift, which contains within itself all grace. And just as the physical life in each of us, one in all its manifestations, produces many results, and shines in the eye, and blushes in the cheek, and gives strength to the arm, and flexibility and deftness to the fingers and swiftness to the foot: so also is that one grace which, being manifold in its manifestations, is one in its essence. There are many graces, there is one Grace.

But this grace is not only many-sided, but abounding. It is not congruous with God's wealth, nor with His love, that He should give scantily, or, as it were, should open but a finger of the hand that is full of His gifts, and let out a little at a time. There are no sluices on that great stream so as to regulate its flow, and to give sometimes a painful trickle and sometimes a full gush, but this fountain is always pouring itself out, and it abounds.'

But then we are pulled up short by another word in first clause: 'God is *able* to make.' Paul does not d will make.' He puts the whole weight of for that ability becoming o

And how do we do that? By desire, by expectance, by
petition, by faithful stewardship. If we have these
things, if we have tutored ourselves, and experience
has helped in the tuition, to make large our expect-
ancy, God will smile down upon us and 'do exceeding abundantly above all' that we 'think' as well as
above all that we 'ask.' Brethren, if our supplies are
scant, when the full fountain is gushing at our sides,
we are 'not straitened in God, we are straitened in
ourselves.' Christian possibilities are Christian obligations, and what we might have and do not have, is our
condemnation.

I turn, in the next place, to what I have, perhaps too
fancifully, called

II. The Basin.

'God is able to make all grace abound toward you,
that ye, having always all-sufficiency in all things,
may,' . . . etc.

The result of all this many-sided and exuberant outpouring of grace from the fountain is that the basin
may be full. Considering the infinite source and the
small receptacle, we might have expected something
more than 'sufficiency' to have resulted.

Divine grace is sufficient. Is it not more than sufficient? Yes, no doubt. But what Paul wishes us to
feel is this—to put it into very plain English—that the
good gifts of the divine grace will always be propor-
tioned to our work, and to our sufferings too. We
shall feel that we have enough, if we are as we ought
to be. Sufficiency is more than a man gets anywhere
else. 'Enough is as good as a feast.' And if we have
strength, which we may have, to do the day's tasks, and
strength to carry the day's crosses, and strength
accept the day's sorrows, and strength to master

day's temptations, that is as much as we need wish to
have, even out of the fulness of God. And we shall
get it, dear brethren, if we will only fulfil the conditions. If we exercise expectance, and desire and
petition and faithful stewardship, we shall get what
we need. 'Thy shoes shall be iron and brass,' if the
road is a steep and rocky one that would wear out
leather. 'As thy days so shall thy strength be.' God
does not hurl His soldiers in a blundering attack on
some impregnable mountain, where they are slain in
heaps at the base; but when He lays a commandment
on my shoulders, He infuses strength into me, and
according to the good homely old saying that has
brought comfort to many a sad and weighted heart,
makes the back to bear the burden. The heavy task or
the crushing sorrow is often the key that opens the
door of God's treasure-house. You have had very little
experience either of life or of Christian life, if you have
not learnt by this time that the harder your work, and
the darker your sorrows, the mightier have been God's
supports, and the more starry the lights that have
shone upon your path. 'That ye, always having all-
sufficiency in all things.'

One more word: this sufficiency *should be* more
uniform, *is* uniform in the divine intention, and in
so far as the flow of the fountain is concerned. Always
having had I may be sure that I always shall have. Of
course I know that, in so far as our physical nature
litions our spiritual experience, there will be ups
s, moments of e ncip ion and moments of
e will be ti es whe e wer opens,

than they have; that we could, if we would, have far more experimental knowledge of this 'always' of my text. God means that the basin should be always full right up to the top of the marble edge, and that the more is drawn off from it, the more should flow into it. But it is very often like the reservoirs in the hills for some great city in a drought, where great stretches of the bottom are exposed, and again, when the drought breaks, are full to the top of the retaining wall. That should not be. Our Christian life should run on the high levels. Why does it not? Possibilities are duties.

And now, lastly, we have here what, adhering to my metaphor, I call

III. The stream.

'That ye, always having all-sufficiency in all things, may abound to every good work.'

That is what God gives us His grace for; and that is a very important consideration. The end of God's dealings with us, poor, weak, sinful creatures, is character and conduct. Of course you can state the end in a great many other ways; but there have been terrible evils arising from the way in which Evangelical preachers have too often talked, as if the end of God's dealings with us was the vague thing which they call 'salvation,' and by which many of their hearers take them to mean neither more nor less than dodging Hell. But the New Testament, with all its mysticism, even when it soars highest, and speaks most about the perfection of humanity, and the end of God's dealings being that we may be 'filled with the fulness of God,' never loses its wholesome, sane hold of the common moralities of daily life, and proclaims that we recei all, in order that we may be able to 'maintain g

works for necessary uses.' And if we lay that to heart,
and remember that a correct creed, and a living faith,
and precious, select, inward emotions and experiences
are all intended to evolve into lives, filled and radiant
with common moralities and 'good works'—not meaning thereby the things which go by that name in
popular phraseology, but 'whatsoever things are lovely
. . . and of good report'—then we shall understand a
little better what we are here for and what Jesus
Christ died for, and what His Spirit is given and lives
in us for. So 'good works' is the end, in one very important aspect, of all that avalanche of grace which
has been from eternity rushing down upon us from
the heights of God.

There is one more thing to note, and that is that, in
our character and conduct, we should copy the 'giving
grace.' Look how eloquently and significantly, in the
first and last clauses of my text, the same words recur.
'God is able to make *all* grace abound, that ye may
abound in *all* good work.' Copy God in the many-
sidedness and in the copiousness of the good that flows
out from your life and conduct, because of your possession of that divine grace. And remember, 'to him
that hath shall be given.' We pray for more grace;
we need to pray for that, no doubt. Do we use the
grace that God has given us? If we do not, the
remainder of that great word which I have just quoted
will be fulfilled in you. God forbid that any of us
should receive the grace of God in vain, and there-
come under the stern and inevitable sentence,
him that hath not shall be taken away, even
!'

GOD'S UNSPEAKABLE GIFT

'Thanks be unto God for His unspeakable gift.'—2 COR. ix. 15.

IT seems strange that there should ever have been any doubt as to what gift it is which evokes this burst of thanksgiving. There is but one of God's many mercies which is worthy of being thus singled out. There is one blazing central sun which shines out amidst all the galaxy of lights which fill the heavens. There is one gift of God which, beyond all others, merits the designation of 'unspeakable.' The gift of Christ draws all other divine gifts after it. 'How should He not with Him also freely give us all things.'

The connection in which this abrupt jet of praise stands is very remarkable. The Apostle has been dwelling on the Christian obligation of giving bountifully and cheerfully, and on the great law that a glad giver is 'enriched' and not impoverished thereby, whilst the recipients, for their part, are blessed by having thankfulness evoked towards the givers. And that contemplation of the happy interchange of benefit and thanks between men leads the fervid Apostle to the thoughts which were always ready to spring to his lips—of God as the great pattern of giving and of the gratitude to Him which should fill all our souls. The expression here 'unspeakable' is what I wish chiefly to fix upon now. It means literally that which cannot be fully declared. Language fails because thought fails.

I. The gift comes from unspeakable love.

God *so* loved the world that He gave His only begotten Son. The love is the cause of the gift: the is the expression of the love. John's Gospel says the Son which is in the bosom of the Father has *declared* Him. Paul here uses a related word for *unspeakable* which might be rendered ' that which cannot be fully declared.' The declaration of the Father partly consists in this, that He is declared to be undeclarable, the proclamation of His name consists partly in this that it is proclaimed to be a name that cannot be proclaimed. Language fails when it is applied to the expression of human emotion; no tongue can ever fully serve the heart. Whether there be any thoughts too great for words or no, there are emotions too great. Language is ever ' weaker than our grief' and not seldom weaker than our love. It is but the surface water that can be run off through the narrow channel of speech : the central deep remains. If it be so with human affection, how much more must it be so with God's love? With lowly condescension He uses all sweet images drawn from earthly relationships, to help us in understanding His. Every dear name is pressed into the service—father, mother, husband, wife, brother, friend, and after all are exhausted, the love which clothed itself in them all in turn, and used them all to give some faint hint of its own perfection, remains unspoken. We know human love, its limitations, its changes, its extravagances, its shortcomings, and cannot but feel how unworthy it is to mirror for us that perfection in God which we venture to name by a name so soiled. The analogies between what we call love in man and love in God must be supplemented the differences between them, if we are ever to reach a worthy conception of the unspeakable love rlies the unspeakable gift.

treasures to its object and is then most blessed : divine love cannot come short of human in this most characteristic of its manifestations. Surely the copy is not to surpass the original, nor the mirror to flash more brightly than the sun which, at the brightest, it but reflects. In such a matter we can but stammer when we try to find words. As our text warns us, we are trying to utter the unutterable when we seek to speak of God's giving up for us ; but however such a thought may seem to be forbidden by other aspects of the divine nature, it seems to be involved in the great truth that 'God is love.' Since He is, His blessedness too, must be in imparting, and in parting with what He gives. A humble worshipper in Jewish times loved enough to say that he would not offer unto God an offering that cost him nothing, and that loving height of self-surrender was at the highest, but a lowly imitation of the love to which it looked up. When Paul in the Epistle to the Romans says, 'He that spared not His own Son but delivered Him up for us all,' he is obviously alluding to, and all but quoting, the divine words to Abraham, 'Seeing thou hast not withheld thy son, thine only son, from Me,' and the allusion permits us to parallel what God did when He sent His Son with what Abraham did when, with wrung heart, but with submission, he bound and laid Isaac on the altar and stretched forth his hand with the knife in it to slay him. Such a representation contradicts the vulgar conceptions of a passionless, self-sufficing, icy deity, but reflection on the facts of our own experience and on the blessed secrets of our own love, leads us to believe that some shadow of loss passed across the infinite and eternal completeness of the divine nature when 'God sent forth His Son made of a woman

And may we not go further and say that when Jesus
on the Cross cried from out of the darkness of eclipse,
'My God! My God! Why hast Thou forsaken me?'
there was something in the heavens corresponding to
the darkness that covered the earth and something in
the Father's heart that answered the Son's. But our
text warns us that such matters are not for our handling in speech, and are best dealt with, not as matters
of possibly erring speculation, but as materials for
lowly thanks unto God for His unspeakable gift.

But whatever may be true about the love of the
Father who sent, there can be no doubt about the love
of the Son who came. No man helps his fellows in
suffering but at the cost of his own suffering. Sympathy means *fellow-feeling*, and the one indispensable
condition of all rescue work of any sort is that the
rescuer must bear on his own shoulders the sins or
sorrows that he is able to bear away. Heartless help
is no help. It does not matter whether he who 'stands
and says, "Be ye clothed and fed,"' gives or does not
give 'the things necessary,' he will be but a 'miserable
comforter' if he has not in heart and feeling entered
into the sorrows and pains which he seeks to alleviate.
We need not dwell on the familiar truths concerning
Him who was a 'man of sorrows and acquainted with
grief.' All through His life He was in contact with
evil, and for Him the contact was like that of a naked
hand pressed upon hot iron. The sins and woes of the
world made His path through it like that of bare feet
on sharp flints. If He had never died it would still
have been true that 'He was wounded for our transgressions and bruised for our iniquities.' On the
Cross He completed the libation which had continued
throughout His life and 'poured out His soul unto

death' as He had been pouring it out all through His
life. We have no measure by which we can estimate
the inevitable sufferings in such a world as ours of
such a spirit as Christ's. We may know something of
the solitude of uncongenial society; of the pain of
seeing miseries that we cannot comfort, of the horrors
of dwelling amidst impurities that we cannot cleanse,
and of longings to escape from them all to some
nest in the wilderness, but all these are but the
feeblest shadows of the incarnate sorrows whose name
among men was Jesus. Nothing is more pathetic than
the way in which our Lord kept all these sorrows close
locked within His own heart, so that scarcely ever did
they come to light. Once He did permit a glimpse into
that hidden chamber when He said, 'O faithless generation, how long shall I be with you, how long shall I
suffer you?' But for the most part His sorrow was
unspoken because it was 'unspeakable.' Once beneath
the quivering olives in the moonlight of Gethsemane,
He made a pitiful appeal for the little help which three
drowsy men could give Him, when He cried, 'My soul
is exceeding sorrowful, even unto death. Tarry ye
here and watch with Me,' but for the most part the
silence at which His judges 'marvelled greatly,' and
raged as much as they marvelled, was unbroken, and
as 'a sheep before her shearers is dumb,' so 'He opened
not His mouth.' The sacrifice of His death was, for
the most part, silent like the sacrifice of His life.
Should it not call forth from us floods of praise a
thanks to God for His unspeakable gift?

III. The gift brings with it unspeakable results.

In Christ are hid 'all the treasures of wisdom
hen God gave us Him, He gave
ich are contained treasures o

which can never be fully comprehended, and which, even if comprehended, can never be exhausted. The mystery of the Divine Name revealed in Jesus, the mystery of His person, are themes on which the Christian world has been nourished ever since, and which are as full of food, not for the understanding only, but far more for the heart and the will, to-day as ever they were. The world may think that it has left the teaching of Jesus behind, but in reality the teaching is far ahead, and the world's practise is but slowly creeping towards its imperfect attainment. The Gospel is the guide of the race, and each generation gathers something more from it, and progresses in the measure in which it follows Christ; and as for the race, so for the individual. Each of Christ's scholars finds his own gift, and in the measure of his faithfulness to what he has found makes ever new discoveries in the unsearchable riches of Christ. After all have fed full there still remain abundant baskets full to be taken up.

He who has sounded the depths of Jesus most completely is ever the first to acknowledge that he has been but as a child 'gathering pebbles on the beach while the great ocean lies unsounded before him.' No single soul, and no multitude of souls, can exhaust Jesus; neither our individual experiences, nor the experiences of a believing world can fully realise the endless wealth laid up in Him. He is the Alpha and the Omega of all our speech, the first letter and the last of our alphabet, between which lie all the rest.

The gift is completed in consequences yet unspeakable. Even the first blessings which the humblest faith receives from the pierced hands have more in them than words can tell. Who has ever spoken adequately and in full correspondence with reality what it is to have

God's pardoning love flowing in upon the soul? Many
singers have sung sweet psalms and hymns and
spiritual songs on which generations of devout souls
have fed, but none of them has spoken the deepest
blessedness of a Christian life, or the calm raptures of
communion with God. It is easy to utter the words
'forgiveness, reconciliation, acceptance, fellowship,
eternal life'; the syllables can be spoken, but who
knows or can utter the depths of the meanings? After
all human words the half has not been told us, and as
every soul carries within itself unrevealable emotions,
and is a mystery after all revelation, so the things
which God's gift brings to a soul are after all speech
unspeakable, and the words 'cannot be uttered' which
they who are caught up into the third heavens hear.

Then we may extend our thoughts to the future
form of Christian experience. 'It doth not yet appear
what we should be.' All our conceptions of a future
existence must necessarily be inadequate. Nothing
but experience can reveal them to us, and our experience there will be capable of indefinite expansion, and
through eternity there will be endless growth in the
appropriation of the unspeakable gift.

For us the only recompense that we can make for the
unspeakable gift is to receive it with 'thanks unto
God' and the yielding up of our hearts to Him. God
pours this love upon us freely, without stint. It is
unspeakable in the depths of its source, in the manner
of its manifestation, in the glory of its issues. It i
like some great stream, rising in the trackless mou
t   s, b   ad and deep, and leading on to a su
o   We stand on the bank; let us trust ours
          bosom. It will bear us safe. And
              e not the g   of G in

A MILITANT MESSAGE

'Casting down imaginations, and every high thing that is exalted against the knowledge of God, and bringing every thought into captivity to the obedience of Christ; and being in readiness to avenge all disobedience, when your obedience shall be fulfilled.'—2 COR. x. 5 and 6 (R.V.).

NONE of Paul's letters are so full of personal feeling as this one is. It is written, for the most part, at a white heat; he had heard from his trusted Titus tidings which on one hand filled him with a thankfulness of which the first half of the letter is the expression; but there had also been tidings of a very different kind, and from this point onwards the letter is seething with the feelings which these had produced. There was in the Corinthian Church a party, probably Judaisers, which denied his authority and said bitter things about his character. They apparently had contrasted the force of his letters and the feebleness of his 'bodily presence' and speech. They insinuated that his 'bark was worse than his bite.' Their language put into plain English would be something like this, 'Ah! He is very bold at a distance, let him come and face us and we shall see a difference. Vapouring in his letters, he will be meek enough when he is here.'

These slanderers seem to have thought of Paul as if he 'warred according to flesh,' and it is this charge, that he was actuated in his opposition to the evils in Corinth by selfish considerations and worldly interests, which seems to have set the Apostle on fire. In answer ours out quick, indignant questionings, sharp irony, ment self-vindication, passionate remonstrances, of wrath, sudden jets of

crawling creatures who cannot believe in heroic self-
forgetfulness. He answers the taunt that he 'walked
according to the flesh' in the context by saying, 'Yes, .
I live in the flesh, my outward life is like that of other
men, but I do not go a-soldiering *according to* the flesh.
It is not for my own sinful self that I get the rules of
my life's battle, neither do I get my weapons from the
flesh. They could not do what they do if that were their
origin: they are of God and therefore mighty.' Then
the metaphor as it were catches fire, and in our text
he expands the figure of a warfare and sets before us
the destruction of fortresses, the capture of their
garrisons, and the leading of them away into another
land, the stern punishment of the rebels who still hold
out, and the merciful delay in administering it. It has
been suggested that there is an allusion in our text to
the extermination of the pirates in Paul's native Cilicia
which happened some fifty or sixty years before his
birth and ended in destroying their robber-holds and
taking some thousands of prisoners. Whether that be
so or no, the Apostle's kindled imagination sets forth
here great truths as to the effects which his message is
meant to produce and, thank God, has produced.

I. The opposing fortresses.

The Apostle conceives of himself and of his brother
preachers of Christ as going forth on a merciful warfare. He thinks of strong rock fortresses, with lofty
walls set on high, and frowning down on any assailants.
No doubt he is thinking first of the opposition which
he had to front in Corinth from the Judaisers to whom
we have referred, but the application of the metap
goes far beyond the petty strife in Corinth and car
the wholesome lesson that one main cause w
from Christ is a too high esti

themselves. Some of us are enclosed in the fortress of self-sufficiency: we will not humbly acknowledge our dependence on God, and have turned self-reliance into the law of our lives. There are many voices, some of them sweet and powerful, which to-day are preaching that gospel. It finds eager response in many hearts, and there is something in us all to which it appeals. We are often tempted to say defiantly, 'Who is Lord over us?' And the teaching that bids us rely on ourselves is so wholly in accord with the highest wisdom and the noblest life that what is good and what is evil in each of us contribute to reinforce it. Self-dependence is a great virtue, and the mother of much energy and nobleness, but it is also a great error and a great sin. To be so self-sufficing as not to need externals is good; to be so self-sufficing as not to need or to see God is ruin and death. The title which, as one of our great thinkers tells us, a humourist put on the back of a volume of heterodox tracts, 'Every man his own redeemer,' makes a claim for self-sufficiency which more or less unconsciously shuts out many men from the salvation of Christ.

There is the fortress of culture and the pride of it in which many of us are to-day entrenched against the Gospel. The attitude of mind into which persons of culture tend to fall is distinctly adverse to their reception of the Gospel, and that is not because the Gospel is adverse to culture, but because cultured people do care to be put on the same level with publicans arlots. They would be less disinclined to go into t if there were in it reserved s   r would be revealed to them too. Not knowledge but the superciliousness which is the result of the conceit of knowledge hinders from God, and is one of the strongest fortresses against which the weapons of our warfare have to be employed.

There is the fortress of ignorance. Most men who are kept from Christ are so because they know neither themselves nor God. The most widely prevailing characteristic of the superficial life of most men is their absolute unconsciousness of the fact of sin; they neither know it as universal nor as personal. They have never gone deeply enough down into the depths of their own hearts to have come up scared at the ugly things that lie sleeping there, nor have they ever reflected on their own conduct with sufficient gravity to discern its aberrations from the law of right, hence the average man is quite unconscious of sin, and is a complete stranger to himself. The cup has been drunk by and intoxicated the world, and the masses of men are quite unaware that it has intoxicated them.

They are ignorant of God as they are of themselves, and if at any time, by some flash of light, they see themselves as they are, they think of God as if He were altogether such an one as themselves, and fall back on a vague trust in the vaguer mercy of their half-believed-in God as their hope for a vague salvation. Men who thus walk in a vain show will never feel their need of Jesus, and the lazy ignorance of themselves and the as lazy trust in what they call their God, are a fortress against which it will task the power of God to make any weapons of warfare mighty to its pulling down.

II. The casting down of fortresses.

The first effect of any real contact with Christ and His Gospel is to reveal a man to himself, to shatter his delusive estimates of what he is, and to pull down about his ears the lofty fortress in which he has ensconced himself.   It seems strange work for what calls itself a Gospel to begin by forcing a man to cry out with sobs and tears, Oh, wretched man that I am! But no man will ever reach the heights to which Christ can lift him, who does not begin his upward course by descending to the depths into which Christ's Gospel begins its work by plunging him.   Unconsciousness of sin is sure to lead to indifference to a Saviour, and unless we know ourselves to be miserable and poor and blind and naked, the offer of gold refined by fire and white garments that we may clothe ourselves will make no appeal to us.   The fact of sin makes the need for a Saviour; our individual sense of sin makes us sensible of our need of a Saviour.

Paul believed that the weapons of his warfare were mighty enough to cast down the strongest of all strongholds in which men shut themselves up against the humbling Gospel of salvation by the mercy of God. The weapons to which he thus trusted were the same to which Jesus pointed His disciples when, about to leave them, He said, 'When the Comforter is come He will convict the world of sin because they believe not in Me.'   Jesus brought to the world the perfect revelation of the holiness of God, and set before us all a divine pattern of manhood to rebuke and condemn our stained and rebellious lives, and He turned us away from the superficial estimate of actions to the careful scrutiny of motives.   By all these and many other He presented Himself to the world a perfect man, ation of a holy God and th without a thrill, and they see in Him no 'beauty that they should desire Him,' and no healing to which they will trust.   Paul's way of kindling penitence in impenitent spirits was not to brandish over them the whips of law or to seek to shake souls with terror of any hell, still less was it to discourse with philosophic calm on the obligations of duty and the wisdom of virtuous living; his appeal to conscience was primarily the pressing on the heart of the love of God in Christ Jesus our Lord.   When the heart is melted, the conscience will not long continue indurated.   We cannot look lovingly and believingly at Jesus and then turn to look complacently on ourselves.   Not to believe on Him is the sin of sins, and to be taught that it is so is the first step in the work of Him who never merits the name of the Comforter more truly than when He convicts the world of sin.

For a Christianity that does not begin with the deep consciousness of sin has neither depth nor warmth and has scarcely vitality.   The Gospel is no Gospel, and we had almost said, 'The Christ is no Christ' to one who does not feel himself, if parted from Christ, 'dead in trespasses and sins.'   Our religion depends for all its force, our gratitude and love for all their devotion, upon our sense that 'the chastisement of our peace was laid upon Him, and that by His stripes we are healed.'   Since He gave Himself for us, it is meet that we give ourselves to Him, but there will be little fervour of devotion or self-surrender, unless there h been first the consciousness of the death of sin then the joyous consciousness of newness of life Christ Jesus.

The captives led away to another land.

ries on his metaphor one s

when he goes on to describe what followed the casting down of the fortresses. The enemy, driven from their strongholds, have nothing for it but to surrender and are led away in captivity to another land. The long strings of prisoners on Assyrian and Egyptian monuments show how familiar an experience this was. It may be noted that perhaps our text regards the obedience of Christ as being the far country into which 'every thought was to be brought.' At all events Paul's idea here is that the end of the whole struggle between 'the flesh' and the weapons of God is to make men willing captives of Jesus Christ. We are Christians in the measure in which we surrender our wills to Christ. That surrender rests upon, and is our only adequate answer to, His surrender for us. The 'obedience of Christ' is perfect freedom; His captives wear no chains and know nothing of forced service; His yoke is easy, not because it does not press hard upon the neck but because it is lined with love, and 'His burden is light' not because of its own weight but because it is laid on us by love and is carried by kindred love. He only commands himself who gladly lets Christ command him. Many a hard task becomes easy; crooked things are straightened out and rough places often made surprisingly plain for the captives of Christ, whom He leads into the liberty of obedience to Him.

IV. Fate of the disobedient.

l thinks that in Corinth there will be found some
opponents of whom he not hope t
ence shall be ful e

not'; that has been the brief summary of the experience of all God's messengers everywhere, and it is their experience to-day. No doubt when Paul speaks of 'being in readiness to avenge all disobedience,' he is alluding to the exercise of his apostolic authority against the obdurate antagonists whom he contemplates as still remaining obdurate, and it is beautiful to note the long-suffering patience with which he will hold his hand until all that can be won has been won. But we must not forget that Paul's demeanour is but a faint shadow of his Lord's, and that the weapons which were ready to avenge all disobedience were the weapons of God. If a man steels himself against the efforts of divine love, builds up round himself a fortress of self-righteousness and locks its gates against the merciful entrance of convictions of sin and the knowledge of a Saviour, and if he therefore lives, year in, year out, in disobedience, the weapons which he thinks himself to have resisted will one day make him feel their edge. We cannot set ourselves against the salvation of Jesus without bringing upon ourselves consequences which are wholly evil and harmful. Torpid consciences, hungry hearts, stormy wills, tyrannous desires, vain hopes and not vain fears come to be, by slow degrees, the tortures of the man who drops the portcullis and lifts the bridge against the entrance of Jesus. There are hells enough on earth if men's hearts were displayed.

But the love which is obliged to smite gives warning that it is ready to avenge, long before it lets the blow fall, and does so in order that it may never need to fall. As long as it is possible that the disobedient should become obedient to Christ, He holds back the ve~ ~ ~at is ready to fall and will one day fall 'o~

disobedience.' Not till all other means have been patiently tried will He let that terrible ending crash down. It hangs over the heads of many of us who are all unaware that we walk beneath the shadow of a rock that at any moment may be set in motion and bury us beneath its weight. It is 'in readiness,' but it is still at rest. Let us be wise in time and yield to the merciful weapons with which Jesus would make His way into our hearts. Or if the metaphor of our text presents Him in too warlike a guise, let us listen to His own gentle pleading, 'Behold, I stand at the door and knock; if any man hear My voice, and open the door, I will come in to him.'

SIMPLICITY TOWARDS CHRIST

'But I fear, lest by any means, as the serpent beguiled Eve through his subtilty, so your minds should be corrupted from the simplicity that is in Christ.—2 COR. xi. 3.

THE Revised Version, amongst other alterations, reads, 'the simplicity that is *towards* Christ.'

The inaccurate rendering of the Authorised Version is responsible for a mistake in the meaning of these words, which has done much harm. They have been supposed to describe a quality or characteristic belonging to Christ or the Gospel; and, so construed, they have sometimes been made the watchword of narrowness and of intellectual indolence. 'Give us the simple Gospel' has been the cry of people who have thought themselves to be evangelical when they were only lazy, e consequence has been that preach
to reite e co on

It is quite true that the Gospel is simple, but it is also true that it is deep, and they will best appreciate its simplicity who have most honestly endeavoured to fathom its depth. When we let our little sounding lines out, and find that they do not reach the bottom, we begin to wonder even more at the transparency of the clear abyss. It is not simplicity *in* Christ, but *towards* Christ of which the Apostle is speaking; not a quality in Him, but a quality in *us* towards Him. I wish, then, to turn to the two thoughts that these words suggest. First and chiefly, the attitude towards Christ which befits our relation to Him; and, secondly and briefly, the solicitude for its maintenance.

I. First, then, look at the attitude towards Christ which befits the Christian relation to Him.

The word 'simplicity' has had a touch of contempt associated with it. It is a somewhat doubtful compliment to say of a man that he is 'simple-minded.' All noble words which describe great qualities get oxidised by exposure to the atmosphere, and rust comes over them, as indeed all good things tend to become deteriorated in time and by use. But the notion of the word is really a very noble and lofty one. To be 'without a fold,' which is the meaning of the Greek word and of its equivalent 'simplicity,' is, in one aspect, to be transparently honest and true, and in another to be out and out of a piece. There is no underside of the cloth, doubled up beneath the upper which shows, and running in the opposite direction; but all tends in one w A man with no under-currents, no by-ends, who down to the very roots what he looks, and all wh g is knit together and hurled in one directi rvation or back-drawing, that is m the Apostle m s. Such

plicity is the truest wisdom ; such simplicity of devotion
to Jesus Christ is the only attitude of heart and mind
which corresponds to the facts of our relation to Him.
That relation is set forth in the context by a very
sweet and tender image, in the true line of scriptural
teaching, which in many a place speaks of the Bride
and Bridegroom, and which on its last page shows us
the Lamb's wife descending from Heaven to meet her
husband. The state of devout souls and of the community of such here on earth is that of betrothal.
Their state in heaven is that of marriage. Very beautiful it is to see how this fiery Paul, like the ascetic
John, who never knew the sacred joys of that state,
lays hold of the thought of the Bridegroom and the
Bride, and of his individual relation to both as indi-
cating the duties of the Church and the solicitude of
the Apostle. He says that he has been the inter-
mediary who, according to Oriental custom, arranged
the preliminaries of the marriage, and brought the
bride to the bridegroom, and, as the friend of the latter,
standing by rejoices greatly to hear the bridegroom's
voice, and is solicitous mainly that in the tremulous
heart of the betrothed there should be no admixture of
other loves, but a whole-hearted devotion, an exclusive
affection, and an absolute obedience. 'I have espoused
you,' says he, 'to one husband that I may present you
as a chaste virgin to Christ. But I fear lest . . . your
mind should be corrupted from the simplicity that is
ards Him.'

that metaphor carries in its implication all that
say about the exclusiv ess, th
pervasiven

by other Scripture metaphors, the *slave* and the *soldier* of Christ. But all that is repellent or harsh in these is softened and glorified when we contemplate it in the light of the metaphor of my text.

So I might leave it to do its own work, but I may perhaps be allowed to follow out the thought in one or two directions.

The attitude, then, which corresponds to our relation to Jesus Christ is that, first, of a faith which looks to Him exclusively as the source of salvation and of light. The specific danger which was alarming Paul, in reference to that little community of Christians in Corinth, was one which, in its particular form, is long since dead and buried. But the principles which underlay it, the tendencies to which it appealed, and the perils which alarmed Paul for the Corinthian Church, are perennial. He feared that these Judaising teachers, who dogged his heels all his life long, and whose one aim seemed to be to build upon his foundation and to overthrow his building, should find their way into this church and wreck it. The keenness of the polemic, in this and in the contextual chapters, shows how real and imminent the danger was. Now what they did was to tell people that Jesus Christ had a partner in His saving work. They said that obedience to the Jewish law, ceremonial and other, was a condition of salvation, along with trust in Jesus Christ as the Messiah. And because they thus shared out the work of salvation between Jesus Christ and something else, Paul thundered and lightened at them all his life, and, as he tells us in this context, regarded them as preaching another Jesus, another spirit, and another gospel. That particular error is long dead and buried.

nothing else that has come into its

Has this old foe not got a new face, and does not it live amongst us as really as it lived then? I think it does; whether in the form of the grosser kind of sacramentarianism and ecclesiasticism which sticks sacraments and a church in front of the Cross, or in the form of the definite denial that Jesus Christ's death on the Cross is the one means of salvation, or simply in the form of the coarse, common wish to have a finger in the pie and a share in the work of saving oneself, as a drowning man will sometimes half drown his rescuer by trying to use his own limbs. These tendencies that Paul fought, and which he feared would corrupt the Corinthians from their simple and exclusive reliance on Christ, and Christ alone, as the ground and author of their salvation, are perennial in human nature, and we have to be on our guard for ever and for ever against them. Whether they come in organised, systematic, doctrinal form, or whether they are simply the rising in our own hearts of the old Adam of pride and self-trust, they equally destroy the whole work of Christ, because they infringe upon its solitariness and uniqueness. It is not Christ and anything else. Men are not saved by a syndicate. It is Jesus Christ alone, and 'beside Him there is no Saviour.' You go into a Turkish mosque and see the roof held up by a forest of slim pillars. You go into a cathedral chapterhouse and see one strong support in the centre that the whole roof. The one is an emblem of the s multiplicity of vain supports, the other

And in like manner He is the sole light and teacher of men as to God, themselves, their duty, their destinies and prospects. He, and He alone, brings these things to light. His word, whether it comes from His lips or from the deeds which are part of His revelation, or from the voice of the Spirit which takes of His and speaks to the ages through His apostles, should be 'the end of all strife.' What He says, and all that He says, and nothing else than what He says, is the creed of the Christian. He, and He only, is 'the light which lighteth every man that cometh into the world.' In this day of babblements and confusions, let us listen for the voice of Christ and accept all which comes from Him, and let the language of our deepest hearts be, 'Lord, to whom shall we go? Thou only hast the words of eternal life.'

Again, our relation to Jesus Christ demands exclusive love to Him. 'Demands' is an ugly word to bracket with love. We might say, and perhaps more truly, permits or privileges. It is the joy of the betrothed that her duty is to love, and to keep her heart clear from all competing affections. But it is none the less her duty because it is her joy. What Christ is to you, if you are a Christian, and what He longs to be to us all, whether we are Christians or not, is of such a character as that the only fitting attitude of our hearts to Him in response is that of exclusive affection. I do not mean that we are to love nothing but Him, but I mean that we are to love all things else in Him, and that, if any creature so delays or deflects our love that either it does not pass, by means of the creatu into the presence of the Christ, or is turned away f the Christ by the creature, then we have fallen ber th level of our lofty privilege, and have wo ourselves the misery due to distracted and idolatrous hearts. Love to one who has done what He has done for us is in its very nature exclusive, and its exclusiveness is all-pervasive exclusiveness. The centre diamond makes the little stones set round it all the more lustrous. We must love Jesus Christ all in all or not at all. Divided love incurs the condemnation that falls heavily upon the head of the faithless bride.

Dear friends, the conception of the essence of religion as being love is no relaxation, but an increase, of its stringent requirements. The more we think of that sweet bond as being the true union of the soul with God, who is its only rest and home, the more reasonable and imperative will appear the old commandment, 'Thou shalt love Him with all thy heart, and soul, and strength, and mind.'

But, further, our relation to Jesus Christ is such as that nothing short of absolute obedience to His commandment corresponds to it. There must be the simplicity, the single-mindedness that thus obeys, obeys swiftly, cheerfully, constantly. In all matters His command is my law, and, as surely as I make His command my law, will He make my desire His motive. For He Himself has said, in words that bring together our obedience to His will and His compliance with our wishes, in a fashion that we should not have ventured upon unless He had set us an example, 'If ye love Me, keep My commandments. If ye ask anything y name I will do it.' The exclusive love the binds son of our faith in Him alone, to

draw out what the words of my text imply. But such
as they are, let us remember that they do set forth the
only proper response of the saved man to the saving
Christ. 'Ye cannot serve God and Mammon.' Anything short of a faith that rests on Him alone, of a love
that knits itself to His single, all-sufficient heart, and
of an obedience that bows the whole being to the sweet
yoke of His commandment is an unworthy answer to
the Love that died, and that lives for us all.

II. And now I have only time to glance at the solicitude for the maintenance of this exclusive single-
mindedness towards Christ.

Think of what threatens it. I say nothing about the
ferment of opinion in this day, for for one man that
is swept away from a thorough whole-hearted faith by
intellectual considerations, there are a dozen from
whom it is filched without their knowing it, by their
own weaknesses and the world's noises. And so it is
more profitable that we should think of the whole
crowd of external duties, enjoyments, sweetnesses,
bitternesses, that solicit us, and would seek to draw us
away. Who can hear the low voice that speaks peace
and wisdom when Niagara is roaring past his ears?
'The world is too much with us, late and soon. Buying
and selling we lay waste our powers,' and break ourselves away from our simple devotion to that dear
Lord. But it is possible that we may so carry into all
the whirl the central peace, as that we shall not be
disturbed by it; and possible that 'whether we eat or
drink, or whatsoever we do, we may do all to His glory,'
so that we can, even in the midst of our daily pre
avocations and cares be keeping our hearts in t
heavens, and our souls in touch with our Lord.

But it is not only things without that draw us a

Our own weaknesses and waywardnesses, our strong
senses, our passions, our desires, our necessities, all
these have a counteracting force, which needs continual
watchfulness in order to be neutralised. No man can
grasp a stay, which alone keeps him from being im-
mersed in the waves, with uniform tenacity, unless
every now and then he tightens his muscles. And no
man can keep himself firmly grasping Jesus Christ
without conscious effort directed to bettering his hold.

If there be dangers around us, and dangers within
us, the discipline which we have to pursue in order to
secure this uniform, single-hearted devotion is plain
enough. Let us be vividly conscious of the peril—which
is what some of us are not. Let us take stock of ourselves lest creeping evil may be encroaching upon us,
while we are all unaware—which is what some of us
never do. Let us clearly contemplate the possibility of
an indefinite increase in the closeness and thoroughness of our surrender to Him—a conviction which has
faded away from the minds of many professing Christians. Above all, let us find time or make time for the
patient, habitual contemplation of the great facts
which kindle our devotion. For if you never think of
Jesus Christ and His love to you, how can you love
Him back again? And if you are so busy carrying
out your own secular affairs, or pursuing your own
ambitions, or attending to your own duties, as they
may seem to be, that you have no time to think of
Christ, His death, His life, His Spirit, His yearning
heart over His bride, how can it be expected that you
will have any depth of love to Him? Let us, too, wait
with prayerful patience for that Divine Spirit who will
knit us more closely to our Lord.

Unless we do so, we shall get no happiness out of our

religion, and it will bring no praise to Christ or profit
to ourselves. I do not know a more miserable man
than a half-and-half Christian, after the pattern of, I
was going to say, the ordinary average of professing
Christians of this generation. He has religion enough
to prick and sting him, and not enough to impel him
to forsake the evil which yet he cannot comfortably
do. He has religion enough to 'inflame his conscience,'
not enough to subdue his will and heart. How many
of my hearers are in that condition it is for them to
settle. If we are to be Christian men at all, let us be it
out and out. Half-and-half religion is no religion.

> 'One foot in sea, and one on shore;
> To one thing constant never!'

That is the type of thousands of professing Christians.
'I fear lest by any means your minds be corrupted
from the simplicity that is towards Christ.'

STRENGTH IN WEAKNESS

'For this thing I besought the Lord thrice, that it might depart from me. And
He said unto me, My grace is sufficient for thee; for My strength is made perfect
in weakness. Most gladly therefore will I rather glory in my infirmities, that
the power of Christ may rest upon me.'—2 COR. xii. 8, 9.;

THIS very remarkable page in the autobiography of
the Apostle shows us that he, too, belonged to the
great army of martyrs who, with hearts bleeding and
pierced through and through with a dart, yet did th
work for God. It is of little consequence what
thorn in the flesh may have been. The original w
suggests very much heavier sorrow than the meta
of   horn' might imply. It really seems to
            it of thorn that might lie

the finger tip, but one of those hideous stakes on which
the cruel punishment of impalement used to be inflicted.
And Paul's thought is, not that he·has a little, trivial
trouble to bear, but that he is, as it were, forced quivering upon that tremendous torture

Unquestionably, what he means is some bodily ailment
or other. The hypothesis that the 'thorn in the flesh'
was the sting of the animal nature inciting him to evil
is altogether untenable, because such a thorn could
never have been left when the prayer for its removal
was earnestly presented; nor could it ever have been,
when left, an occasion for glorifying. Manifestly it
was no weakness removable by his own effort, no
incapacity for service which in any manner approxi-
mated to being a fault, but purely and simply some
infliction from God's hand (though likewise capable of
being regarded as a 'messenger of Satan') which
hindered him in his work, and took down any proud
flesh and danger of spiritual exaltation in consequence
of the largeness of his religious privileges.

Our text sets before us three most instructive windings, as it were, of the stream of thoughts that passed
through the Apostle's mind, in reference to this burden
that he had to carry, and may afford wholesome contemplation for us to-day. There is, first, the instinctive
shrinking which took refuge in prayer. Then there is
the insight won by prayer into the sustaining strength
and the purposes of, the thorn that was not to be
out. And then, finally, there is the

There is a wonderful, a beautiful, and, I suppose, an intentional parallel between the prayers of the servant and of the Master. Paul's petitions are the echo of Gethsemane. There, under the quivering olives, in the broken light of the Paschal moon, Jesus 'thrice' prayed that the cup might pass from Him. And here the servant, emboldened and instructed by the example of the Master, 'thrice' reiterates his human and natural desire for the removal of the pain, whatever it was, which seemed to him so to hinder the efficiency and the fulness, as it certainly did the joy, of his service.

But He who prayed in Gethsemane was He to whom Paul addressed his prayer. For, as is almost always the case in the New Testament, 'the Lord' here evidently means Christ, as is obvious from the connection of the answer to the petition with the Apostle's final confidence and acquiescence. For the answer was, 'My strength is made perfect in weakness'; and the Apostle's conclusion is, 'Most gladly will I glory in infirmity,' that the strength or 'power *of Christ* may rest upon me.' Therefore the prayer with which we have to deal here is a prayer offered to Jesus, who prayed in Gethsemane, and to whom we can bring our petitions and our desires.

Notice how this thought of prayer directed to the Master Himself helps to lead us deep into the sacredest and most blessed characteristics of prayer. It is only telling Christ what is in our hearts. Oh, if we lived in the true understanding of what prayer really is—th emptying out of our inmost desire and thoughts befo our Brother, who is likewise our Lord—questions as it was permissible to pray for, and what it w to pray for, would be irrelevant, themselves. If we had a less f notion of prayer, and realised more thoroughly what it was—the speech of a confiding heart to a sympathising Lord—then everything that fills our hearts would be seen to be a fitting object of prayer. If anything is large enough to interest me, it is not too small to be spoken about to Him.

So the question, which is often settled upon very abstract and deep grounds that have little to do with the matter—the question as to whether prayer for outward blessings is permissible—falls away of itself. If I am to talk to Jesus Christ about everything that concerns me, am I to keep my thumb upon all that great department and be silent about it? One reason why our prayers are often so unreal is, because they do not fit our real wants, nor correspond to the thoughts that are busy in our minds at the moment of praying. Our hearts are full of some small matter of daily interest, and when we kneel down not a word about it comes to our lips. Can that be right?

The difference between the different objects of prayer is not to be found in the rejection of all temporal and external, but in remembering that there are two sets of things to be prayed about, and over one set must ever be written 'If it be Thy will,' and over the other it need not be written, because we are sure that the granting of our wishes *is* His will. We know about the one that 'if we ask anything according to His will, heareth us.' That may seem to be a very poor and nken kind of hope to give a man, that if his prayer nformity with the previous

set we can only say, 'Not my will, but Thine be done.'
With that sentence, not as a formula upon our lips but
deep in our hearts, let us take everything into His
presence—thorns and stakes, pinpricks and wounds out
of which the life-blood is ebbing—let us take them all
to Him, and be sure that we shall take none of them in
vain.

So then we have the Person to whom the prayer is
addressed, the subjects with which it is occupied, and
the purpose to which it is directed. 'Take away the
burden' was the Apostle's petition; but it was a mistaken petition and, therefore, unanswered.

II. That brings me to the second of the windings, as
I have ventured to call them, of this stream—viz. the
insight into the source of strength for, and the purpose
of, the thorn that could not be taken away. The Lord
said unto me, 'My grace is sufficient for thee. For My
strength' (where the word 'My' is a supplement, but a
necessary one) 'is made perfect in weakness.'

The answer is, in form and in substance, a gentle
refusal of the form of the petition, but it is a more than
granting of its essence. For the best answer to such
a prayer, and the answer which a true man means
when he asks, 'Take away the burden,' need not be the
external removal of the pressure of the sorrow, but the
infusing of power to sustain it. There are two ways
of lightening a burden, one is diminishing its actual
weight, the other is increasing the strength of the
shoulder that bears it. And the latter is God's way, is
Christ's way, of dealing with us.

Now mark that the answer which this faithful prayer
receives is no communication of anything fresh, but it
is the opening of the man's eyes to see that already b
at he needs. The reply is not, 'I *will*

thee grace sufficient,' but 'My grace' (which thou hast now) '*is* sufficient for thee.' That grace is given and possessed by the sorrowing heart at the moment when it prays. Open your eyes to see what you have, and you will not ask for the load to be taken away. Is not that always true? Many a heart is carrying some heavy weight; perhaps some have an incurable sorrow, some are stricken by disease that they know can never be healed, some are aware that the shipwreck has been total, and that the sorrow that they carry to-day will lie down with them in the dust. Be it so! 'My grace (not shall be, but) *is* sufficient for thee.' And what thou hast already in thy possession is enough for all that comes storming against thee of disease, disappointment, loss, and misery. Set on the one side all possible as well as all actual weaknesses, burdens, pains, and set on the other these two words—'My grace,' and all these dwindle into nothingness and disappear. If troubled Christian men would learn what they have, and would use what they already possess, they would less often beseech Him with vain petitions to take away their blessings which are in the thorns in the flesh. 'My grace is sufficient.'

How modestly the Master speaks about what He gives! 'Sufficient'? Is not there a margin? Is there not more than is wanted? The overplus is 'exceeding abundant,' not only 'above what we ask or think, but more than our need. 'Two hundr increases; the gift grows as it is employed. 'Unto him that hath shall be given.' And the 'sufficiency' is not a bare adequacy, just covering the extent of the need, with no overlapping margin, but is large beyond expectation, desire, or necessity; so leading onwards to high hopes and a wider opening of the open mouths of our need that the blessing may pour in.

The other part of this great answer, that the Christ from Heaven spoke in or to the praying spirit of this not disappointed, though refused, Apostle, unveiled the purpose of the sorrow, even as the former part had disclosed the strength to bear it. For, says He, laying down therein the great law of His kingdom in all departments and in all ways, 'My strength is made perfect'—that is, of course, perfect in its manifestation or operations, for it is perfect in itself already. 'My strength is made perfect in weakness.' It works in and through man's weakness.

God works with broken reeds. If a man conceits himself to be an iron pillar, God can do nothing with or by him. All the self-conceit and confidence have to be taken out of him first. He has to be brought low before the Father can use him for His purposes. The lowlands hold the water, and, if only the sluice is open, the gravitation of His grace does all the rest and carries the flood into the depths of the lowly heart.

His strength loves to work in weakness, only the weakness must be conscious, and the conscious weakness must have passed into conscious dependence. There, then, you get the law for the Church, for the works of Christianity on the widest scale, and in individual lives. Strength that conceits itself to be weakness; weakness that knows itself to The only true source of Power, for Christian work and in all other respects, is God Himself; and our strength is ours but by derivation from Him. And the only way to secure that derivation is through humble dependence, which we call faith in Jesus Christ. And the only way by which that faith in Jesus Christ can ever be kindled in a man's soul is through the sense of his need and emptiness. So when we know ourselves weak, we have taken the first step to strength; just as, when we know ourselves sinners, we have taken the first step to righteousness; just as in all regions the recognition of the doleful fact of our human necessity is the beginning of the joyful confidence in the glad, triumphant fact of the divine fulness. All our hollownesses, if I may so say, are met with His fulness that fits into them. It only needs that a man be aware of that which he is, and then turn himself to Him who is all that he is not, and then into his empty being will flow rejoicing the whole fulness of God. ' My strength is made perfect in weakness.'

III. Lastly, mark the calm final acquiescence in the loving necessity of continued sorrow. 'Most gladly, therefore, will I rather glory in my infirmity that the power of Christ may rest upon me.' The will is entirely harmonised with Christ's. The Apostle begins with instinctive shrinking, he passes onwards to a perception of the purpose of his trial and of the sustaining ꞏe; and he comes now to acquiescence which is not ꞏvity, but glad triumph. He is more than sub-ꞏ, he gladly glories in his infirmity in order that ꞏr of Christ may 'spread a tab

to cling, and, clinging, I am strong, and conquer evil.'
Far better is it that the sting of our sorrow should be
taken away, by our having learned what it is for,
and having bowed to it, than that it should be taken
away by the external removal which we sometimes
long for. A grief, a trial, an incapacity, a limitation, a
weakness, which we use as a means of deepening our
sense of dependence upon Him, is a blessing, and not a
sorrow. And if we would only go out into the world
trying to interpret its events in the spirit of this great
text, we should less frequently wonder and weep over
what sometimes seem to us the insoluble mysteries of
the sorrows of ourselves and of other men. They are
all intended to make it more easy for us to realise our
utter hanging upon Him, and so to open our hearts to
receive more fully the quickening influences of His
omnipotent and self-sufficing grace.

Here, then, is a lesson for those who have to carry
some cross and know they must carry it throughout
life. It will be wreathed with flowers if you accept it.
Here is a lesson for all Christian workers. Ministers
of the Gospel especially should banish all thoughts
of their own cleverness, intellectual ability, culture,
sufficiency for their work, and learn that only when
they are emptied can they be filled, and only when
they know themselves to be nothing are they ready
for God to work through them. And here is a lesson
for all who stand apart from the grace and power
of Jesus Christ as if they needed it not. Wheth
you know it or not, you are a broken reed; and
only way of your ever being bound up and m
strong is that you shall recognise your sinful
y cessity, your abject poverty, your utter e
me to Him who is righteousness,

fulness, and say, 'Because I am weak, be Thou my strength.' The secret of all noble, heroic, useful, happy life lies in the paradox, 'When I am weak, then am I strong,' and the secret of all failures, miseries, hopeless losses, lies in its converse, 'When I am strong, then am I weak.'

NOT YOURS BUT YOU

'I seek not yours, but you.'—2 COR. xii. 14.

MEN are usually quick to suspect others of the vices to which they themselves are prone. It is very hard for one who never does anything but with an eye to what he can make out of it, to believe that there are other people actuated by higher motives. So Paul had, over and over again, to meet the hateful charge of making money out of his apostleship. It was one of the favourite stones that his opponents in the Corinthian Church, of whom there were very many, very bitter ones, flung at him. In this letter he more than once refers to the charge. He does so with great dignity, and with a very characteristic and delicate mixture of indignation and tenderness, almost playfulness. Thus, in the context, he tells these Corinthian grumblers that he must beg their pardon for not having taken thing of them, and so honoured them. Then he ms them that he is coming again to see them for time, and th at y will which feels obliged, and yet reluctant, to stoop to say that it *is* love, and that it *is* disinterested. Where did Paul learn this passionate desire to possess these people, and this entire suppression of self in the desire? It was a spark from a sacred fire, a drop from an infinite ocean, an echo of a divine voice. The words of my text would never have been Paul's if the spirit of them had not first been Christ's. I venture to take them in that aspect, as setting forth Christ's claims upon us, and bearing very directly on the question of Christian service and of Christian liberality.

I. So, then, first of all, I remark, Christ desires personal surrender.

'I seek not yours, but *you*,' is the very mother-tongue of love; but upon our lips, even when our love is purest, there is a tinge of selfishness blending with it, and very often the desire for another's love is as purely selfish as the desire for any material good. But in so far as human love is pure in its desire to possess another, we have the right to believe the deep and wonderful thought that there is something corresponding to it in the heart of Christ, which is a revelation for us of the heart of God; and that, however little we may be able to construe the whole meaning of the fact, He does stretch out an arm of desire towards us; and for His own sake, as for ours, would fain draw us near to Himself, and is 'satisfied,' as He is not without it, when men's hearts yield themselves up to Him, and let Him love them and lavish Himself upon them. I d not venture into these depths, but I would lay up our hearts that the very inmost meaning of all th s Christ has said, and is saying, to each of us s of His life, by the pathos of His death is Resurrection, by the glory of

Ascension, by the power of His granted Spirit, is, 'I
seek you.'

And, brethren, our self-surrender is the essence of our
Christianity.   Our religion lies neither in our heads
nor in our acts; the deepest notion of it is that it is
the entire yielding up of ourselves to Jesus Christ our
Lord.   There is plenty of religion which is a religion
of the head and of creeds.   There is plenty of religion
which is the religion of the hand and of the tongue,
and of forms and ceremonies and sacraments; external
worship.   There is plenty of religion which surrenders
to Him some of the more superficial parts of our
personality, whilst the ancient Anarch, Self, sits undisturbed on his dark throne, in the depths of our
being.   But none of these are the religion that either
Christ requires or that we need.   The only true notion
of a Christian is a man who can truly say, 'I live, yet
not I, but Christ liveth in me.'

And that is the only kind of life that is blessed; our
only true nobleness and beauty and power and sweetness are measured by, and accurately correspond with,
the completeness of our surrender of ourselves to Jesus
Christ.   As long as the earth was thought to be the
centre of the planetary system there was nothing but
confusion in the heavens.   Shift the centre to the sun
and all becomes order and beauty.   The root of sin,
and the mother of death, is making myself my own
law and Lord; the germ of righteousness, and the first
pulsations of life, lie in yielding ourselves to God in
Christ, because He has yielded Himself unto us.

I need not remind you, I suppose, that this self-
surrender is a great deal more than a vivid metaphor:
that it implies a very hard fact; implies at least two
things, that we have yielded ourselves to Jesus Christ,

by the love of our hearts, and by the unreluctant submission of our wills, whether He commands or whether
He sends sufferings or joys.

And, oh, brethren, be sure of this, that no such giving
of myself away, in the sweet reciprocities of a higher
than human affection, is possible, in the general, and
on the large scale, if you evacuate from the Gospel the
great truth, 'He loved me, and gave Himself for me.'
I believe—and therefore I am bound to preach it—that
the only power which can utterly annihilate and cast
out the dominion of self from a human soul is the
power that is lodged in the sacrifice of Jesus Christ on
the Cross for sinful men.

And whilst I would fully recognise all that is noble,
and all that is effective, in systems either of religion,
or of irreligious morality, which have no place within
their bounds for that great motive, I am sure of this,
that the evil self within us is too strong to be exorcised
by anything short of the old message, 'Jesus Christ
has given His life for thee, wilt thou not give thyself
unto Him?'

II. Christ seeks personal service.

'I seek . . . you'; not only for My love, but for My
tools; for My instruments in carrying out the purposes
for which I died, and establishing My dominion in the
world. Now I want to say two or three very plain
things about this matter, which lies very near my
heart, as to some degree responsible for the amount of
Christian activity and service in this my congregatio
Brethren, the surrender of ourselves to Jesus Chris
acts of direct Christian activity and service, will be
outcome of a real surrender of ourselves to Hi
bedience.

ot imagine a man who, in any deep sen

realised his obligations to that Saviour, and in any
real sense has made the great act of self-renunciation,
and crowned Christ as his Lord, living for the rest of
his life, as so many professing Christians do, dumb and
idle, in so far as work for the Master is concerned. It
seems to me that, among the many wants of this
generation of professing Christians, there is none that
is more needed than that a wave of new consecration
should pass over the Church. If men who call themselves Christians lived more in habitual contact with
the facts of their redeeming Saviour's sacrifice for
them, there would be no need to lament the fewness of
the labourers, as measured against the overwhelming
multitude of the fields that are white to harvest. If
once that flood of a new sense of Christ's gift, and a
consequent new completeness of our returned gifts to
Him, flowed over the churches, then all the little empty
ravines would be filled with a flashing tide. Not a
shuttle moves, not a spindle revolves, until the strong
impulse born of fire rushes in; and then, all is activity.
It is no use to flog, flog, flog, at idle Christians, and try
to make them work. There is only one thing that will
set them to work, and that is that they shall live nearer
their Master, and find out more of what they owe to
Him; and so render themselves up to be His instruments for any purpose for which He may choose to use
them.

   This surrender of ourselves for direct Christian service
is the only solution of the problem of how to win the
world for Jesus Christ. Professionals cannot do it.
Men of my class cannot do it. We are clogged very
largely by the fact that, being necessarily dependent
on our congregations for a living, we cannot, with as
clear an emphasis as you can, go to people and say,

'We seek not yours, but you.' I have nothing to
say about the present ecclesiastical arrangements of
modern Christian communities. That would take me
altogether from my present purposes, but I want to
lay this upon your consciences, dear brethren, that
you who have other means of living than proclaiming Christ's name have an advantage, which it is
at your peril that you fling away. As long as the
Christian Church thought that an ordained priest was
a man who could do things that laymen could not do,
the limitation of Christian service to the priesthood was
logical. But when the Christian Church, especially as
represented by us Nonconformists, came to believe that
a minister was only a man who preached the Gospel,
which every Christian man is bound to do, the limitations of Christian service to the official class became an
illogical survival, utterly incongruous with the fundamental principles of our conception of the Christian
Church. And yet here it is, devastating our churches
to-day, and making hundreds of good people perfectly
comfortable, in an unscriptural and unchristian indolence, because, forsooth, it is the minister's business
to preach the Gospel. I know that there is not nearly
as much of that indolence as there used to be. Thank
God for that. There are far more among our congregations than in former times who have realised the
fact that it is *every* Christian man's task, somehow or
other, to set forth the great name of Jesus Christ. But
still, alas, in a church with, say, 400 members, you may
knock off the last cypher, and you will get a probably
not too low statement of the number of people in it
w   ve realised and fulfilled this obligation. Wh
          er 360 'dumb dogs, that will not ba
          360 there will probably be several m

who can make speeches on political platforms, and in scientific lecture-halls, and about social and economical questions, only they cannot, for the life of them, open their mouths and say a word to a soul about Him whom they say they serve, and to whom they say they belong.

Brethren, this direct service cannot be escaped from, or commuted by a money payment. In the old days a man used to escape serving in the militia if he found a substitute, and paid for him. There are a great many good Christian people who seem to think that Christ's army is recruited on that principle. But it is a mistake. 'I seek you, not yours.'

III. Lastly, and only a word. Christ seeks us, *and* ours.

Not you *without* yours, still less yours without you. This is no place, nor is the fag end of a sermon the time, to talk about so wide a subject as the ethics of Christian dealing with money. But two things I will say—consecration of self is extremely imperfect which does not include the consecration of possessions, and, conversely, consecration of possessions which does not flow from, and is not accompanied by, the consecration of self, is nought.

If, then, the great law of self-surrender is to run through the whole Christian life, that law, as applied to our dealing with what we own, prescribes three things. The first is *stewardship*, not ownership; and that all round the circumference of our possessions. Depend upon it, the angry things that we hear to-day about the unequal distribution of wealth will get angrier and angrier, and will be largely justified in becoming so by the fact that so many of us, *Christians included*, have firmly grasped the notion of posses-

sion, and utterly forgotten the obligation of stewardship.

Again, the law of self-surrender, in its application to
all that we have, involves our continual reference to
Jesus Christ in our disposition of these our possessions.
I draw no line of distinction, in this respect, between
what a man spends upon himself, and what he spends
upon 'charity,' and what he spends upon religious
objects. *One* principle is to govern, getting, hoarding,
giving, enjoying, and that is, that in it all Christ shall
be Master.

Again, the law of self-surrender, in its application to
our possessions, implies that there shall be an element
of sacrifice in our use of these; whether they be
possessions of intellect, of acquirement, of influence, of
position, or of material wealth. The law of help is
sacrifice, and the law for a Christian man is that he
shall not offer unto the Lord his God that which costs
him nothing.

So, dear friends, let us all get near to that great
central fire till it melts our hearts. Let the love which
is our hope be our pattern. Remember that though
only faintly, and from afar, can the issues of Christ's
great sacrifice be reproduced in any actions of ours,
the spirit which brought Him to die is the spirit
which must instruct and inspire us to live. Unless we
can say, 'He loved me, and gave Himself for me; I
yield myself to Him'; and unless our lives confirm the
utterance, we have little right to call ourselves His
disciples.

GALATIANS

FROM CENTRE TO CIRCUMFERENCE

'The life which I now live in the flesh I live by the faith of the Son of God, who loved me, and gave Himself for me.'—GAL. ii. 20.

WE have a bundle of paradoxes in this verse. First, 'I am crucified with Christ, nevertheless I live.' The Christian life is a dying life. If we are in any real sense joined to Christ, the power of His death makes us dead to self and sin and the world. In that region, as in the physical, death is the gate of life; and, inasmuch as what we die to in Christ is itself only a living death, we live because we die, and in proportion as we die.

The next paradox is, 'Yet not I, but Christ liveth in me.' The Christian life is a life in which an indwelling Christ casts out, and therefore quickens, self. We gain ourselves when we lose ourselves. His abiding in us does not destroy but heightens our individuality. We then most truly live when we can say, 'Not I, but Christ liveth in me'; the soul of my soul and the self of myself.

And the last paradox is that of my text, 'The life which I live in the flesh, I live in' (not 'by') 'the faith of the Son of God.' The true Christian life moves in two spheres at once. Externally and superficially it is 'in the flesh,' really it is 'in faith.' It belongs not to the material nor is dependent upon the physical body in which we are housed. We are strangers here, and the true region and atmosphere of the Christian life is that invisible sphere of faith.

So, then, we have in these words of my text a Christian man's frank avowal of the secret of his own life. It is like a geological cutting, it goes down from the surface, where the grass and the flowers are, through the various strata, but it goes deeper than these, to the fiery heart, the flaming nucleus and centre of all things. Therefore it may do us all good to make a section of our hearts and see whether the *strata* there are conformable to those that are here.

I. Let us begin with the centre, and work to the surface. We have, first, the great central fact named last, but round which all the Christian life is gathered.

'The Son of God, who loved me, and gave Himself for me.' These two words, the 'loving' and the 'giving,' both point backwards to some one definite historical fact, and the only fact which they can have in view is the great one of the death of Jesus Christ. That is His giving up of Himself. That is the signal and highest manifestation and proof of His love.

Notice (though I can but touch in the briefest possible manner upon the great thoughts that gather round these words) the three aspects of that transcendent fact, the centre and nucleus of the whole Christian life, which come into prominence in these words before us. Christ's death is a great act of self-surrender, of which the one motive is His own pure and perfect love. No doubt in other places of Scripture we have set forth the death of Christ as being the result of the Father's purpose, and we read that in that wondrous surrender there were two givings up. The Father 'freely gave Him up to the death for us

all.' That divine surrender, the Apostle ventures, in
another passage, to find dimly suggested from afar, in
the silent but submissive and unreluctant surrender
with which Abraham yielded his only begotten son on
the mountain top. But besides that ineffable giving
up by the Father of the Son, Jesus Christ Himself,
moved only by His love, willingly yields Himself. The
whole doctrine of the sacrifice of Jesus Christ has been
marred by one-sided insisting on the truth that God
sent the Son, to the forgetting of the fact that the Son
'came'; and that He was bound to the Cross neither
by cords of man's weaving nor by the will of the
Father, but that He Himself bound Himself to that
Cross with the 'cords of love and the bands of a man,'
and died from no natural necessity nor from any
imposition of the divine will upon Him unwilling, but
because He would, and that He would because He
loved. 'He loved me, and gave Himself for me.'

Then note, further, that here, most distinctly, that
great act of self-surrendering love which culminates
on the Cross is regarded as being for man in a special
and peculiar sense. I know, of course, that from the
mere wording of my text we cannot argue the atoning
and substitutionary character of the death of Christ,
for the preposition here does not necessarily mean
'instead of,' but 'for the behoof of.' But admitting
that, I have another question. If Christ's death is for
'the behoof of' men, in what conceivable sense does it
benefit them, unless it is in the place of men? The
death 'for me' is only for me when I understand that
it is 'instead of' me. And practically you will find
that wherever the full-orbed faith in Christ Jesus as
the death for all the sins of the whole world, bearing
the penalty and bearing it away, has begun to falter

and grow pale, men do not know what to do with
Christ's death at all, and stop talking about it to a
very large extent.

Unless He died as a sacrifice, I, for one, fail to see in
what other than a mere sentimental sense the death of
Christ is a death for men.

And lastly, about this matter, observe how here we
have brought into vivid prominence the great thought
that Jesus Christ in His death has regard to single
souls. We preach that He died for all. If we believe
in that august title which is laid here as the vindica-
tion of our faith on the one hand, and as the ground
of the possibility of the benefits of His death being
world-wide on the other—viz. the Son of God—then
we shall not stumble at the thought that He died for
all, because He died for each. I know that if you only
regard Jesus Christ as human I am talking utter
nonsense; but I know, too, that if we believe in the
divinity of our Lord, there need be nothing to stumble
us, but the contrary, in the thought that it was not an
abstraction that He died for, that it was not a vague
mass of unknown beings, clustered together, but so
far away that He could not see any of their faces,
for whom He gave His life on the Cross. That is the
way in which, and in which alone, *we* can embrace
the whole mass of humanity—by losing sight of the
individuals. We generalise, precisely because we do
not see the individual units; but that is not God's
way, and that is not Christ's way, who is divine.
For Him the *all* is broken up into its parts, and when
we say that the divine love loves all, we mean that
the divine love loves each. I believe (and I commend
the thought to you) that we do not fathom the depth
of Christ's sufferings unless we recognise that the sins

of each man were consciously adding pressure to the load beneath which He sank; nor picture the wonders of His love until we believe that on the Cross it distinguished and embraced each, and, therefore, comprehended all. Every man may say, 'He loved me, and gave Himself for me.'

II. So much, then, for the first central fact that is here. Now let me say a word, in the second place, about the faith which makes that fact the foundation of my own personal life.

'I live by the faith of the Son of God, who loved me, and gave Himself for me.' I am not going to plunge into any unnecessary dissertations about the nature of faith; but may I say that, like all other familiar conceptions, it has got worn so smooth that it glides over our mental palate without roughening any of the *papillæ* or giving any sense or savour at all? And I do believe that dozens of people like you, who have come to church and chapel all your lives, and fancy yourselves to be fully *au fait* at all the Christian truth that you will ever hear from my lips, do not grasp with any clearness of apprehension the meaning of that fundamental word 'faith.'

It is a thousand pities that it is confined by the accidents of language to our attitude in reference to Jesus Christ. So some of you think that it is some kind of theological juggle which has nothing to do with, and never can be seen in operation in, common life. Suppose, instead of the threadbare, technical 'faith' we took to a new translation for a minute, and said '*trust*,' do you think that would freshen up the thought to you at all? It is the very same thing which makes the sweetness of your relations to wife and husband and friend and parent, which, transferred to Jesus Christ and glorified in the process, becomes the seed of immortal life and the opener of the gate of Heaven. Trust Jesus Christ. That is the living centre of the Christian life; that is the process by which we draw the general blessing of the Gospel into our own hearts, and make the world-wide truth, our truth.

I need not insist either, I suppose, on the necessity, if our Christian life is to be modelled upon the Apostolic lines, of our faith embracing the Christ in all these aspects in which I have been speaking about His work. God forbid that I should seem to despise rudimentary and incomplete feelings after Him in any heart which may be unable to say 'Amen' to Paul's statement here. I want to insist very earnestly, and with special reference to the young, that the true Christian faith is not merely the grasp of the person, but it is the grasp of the Person who is 'declared to be the Son of God,' and whose death is the voluntary self-surrender motived by His love, for the carrying away of the sins of every single soul in the whole universe. That is the Christ, the full Christ, cleaving to whom our faith finds somewhat to grasp worthy of grasping. And I beseech you, be not contented with a partial grasp of a partial Saviour; neither shut your eyes to the divinity of His nature, nor to the efficacy of His death, but remember that the true Gospel preaches Christ and Him crucified; and that for us, saving faith is the faith that grasps the Son of God 'Who loved me and gave Himself for me.'

Note, further, that true faith is personal faith, which appropriates, and, as it were, fences in as my very own, the purpose and benefit of Christ's giving self. It is always difficult for lazy people (us are lazy) to transfer into their own pers lives, and to bring into actual contact with themselves and their own experience, wide, general truths. To assent to them, when we keep them in their generality, is very easy and very profitless. It does no man any good to say 'All men are mortal'; but how different it is when the blunt end of that generalisation is shaped into a point, and I say 'I have to die!' It penetrates then, and it sticks. It is easy to say 'All men are sinners.' That never yet forced anybody down on his knees. But when we shut out on either side the lateral view and look straight on, on the narrow line of our own lives, up to the Throne where the Lawgiver sits, and feel 'I am a sinful man,' that sends us to our prayers for pardon and purity. And in like manner nobody was ever wholesomely terrified by the thought of a general judgment. But when you translate it into 'I must stand there,' the terror of the Lord persuades men.

In like manner that great truth which we all of us say we believe, that Christ has died for the world, is utterly useless and profitless to us until we have translated it into Paul's world, 'loved *me* and gave Himself for *me*.' I do not say that the essence of faith is the conversion of the general statement into the particular application, but I do say that there is no faith which does not realise one's personal possession of the benefits of the death of Christ, and that until you turn the wide word into a message for yourself alone, you have not yet got within sight of the blessedness of the Christian life. The whole river may flow past me, but only so much of it as I can bring into my own garden by my own sluices, and lift in my own bucket, and put to my own lips, is of any use to me. The death of Christ for the world is a commonplace of superficial Christianity, which is no Christianity; the death of Christ for myself, as if He and I were the only beings in the universe, that is the death on which faith fastens and feeds.

And, dear brother, you have the right to exercise it. The Christ loves each, and therefore He loves all; that is the process in the divine mind. The converse is the process in the revelation of that mind; the Bible says to us, Christ loves all, and therefore we have the right to draw the inference that He loves each. You have as much right to take every 'whosoever' of the New Testament as your very own, as if on the page of your Bible that 'whosoever' was struck out, and your name, John, Thomas, Mary, Elizabeth, or whatever it is, were put in there. 'He loved *me*.' Can *you* say that? Have you ever passed from the region of universality, which is vague and profitless, into the region of personal appropriation of the person of Jesus Christ and His death?

III. And now, lastly, notice the life which is built upon this faith.

The true Christian life is dual. It is a life in the flesh, and it is also a life in faith. These two, as I have said, are like two spheres, in either of which a man's course is passed, or, rather, the one is surface and the other is central. Here is a great trailing spray of seaweed floating golden on the unquiet water, and rising and falling on each wave or ripple. Aye! but its root is away deep, deep, deep below the storms, below where there is motion, anchored upon a hidden rock that can never move. And so my life, if it be a Christian life at all, has its surface amidst the shifting mutabilities of earth, but its root in the silent eternities of the centre of all things, which is

Christ in God. I live in the flesh on the outside, but if I am a Christian at all, I live in the faith in regard of my true and proper being.

This faith, which grasps the Divine Christ as the person whose love-moved death is my life, and who by my faith becomes Himself the indwelling Guest in my heart; this faith, if it be worth anything, will mould and influence my whole being. It will give me motive, pattern, power for all noble service and all holy living. The one thing that stirs men to true obedience is that their hearts be touched with the firm assurance that Christ loved them and died for them.

We sometimes used to see men starting an engine by manual force; and what toil it was to get the great cranks to turn, and the pistons to rise! So we set ourselves to try and move our lives into holiness and beauty and nobleness, and it is dispiriting work. There is a far better, surer way than that: let the steam in, and that will do it. That is to say—let the Christ in His dying power and the living energy of His indwelling Spirit occupy the heart, and activity becomes blessedness, and work is rest, and service is freedom and dominion.

The life that I live in the flesh is poor, limited, tured with anxiety, weighed upon by sore distress, mes dark and gray and dreary often as we travel er the end, and is always full of miseries and of

But if within that life in the flesh there be a h, which is the life of Christ Hi t

ou h, that lif

what it grasps and what it does. If it grasps a whole Christ, in all the glory of His nature and the blessedness of His work, it is genuine; and it proves its genuineness if, and only if, it works in you by love; animating all your action, bringing you ever into the conscious presence of that dear Lord, and making Him pattern, law, motive, goal, companion and reward. 'To me to live is Christ.'

If so, then we live indeed; but to live in the flesh is to die; and the death that we die when we live in Christ is the gate and the beginning of the only real life of the soul.

THE EVIL EYE AND THE CHARM

'Who hath bewitched you, that ye should not obey the truth, before whose eyes Jesus Christ hath been evidently set forth, crucified among you?'—GAL. iii. 1.

THE Revised Version gives a shorter, and probably correct, form of this vehement question. It omits the two clauses 'that ye should not obey the truth' and 'among you.' The omission increases the sharpness of the thrust of the interrogation, whilst it loses nothing of the meaning.

Now, a very striking metaphor runs through the whole of this question, which may easily be lost sight of by ordinary readers. You know the old superstition as to the Evil Eye, almost universal at the date of this letter and even now in the East, and lingering still amongst ourselves. Certain persons were supposed to have the power, by a look, to work mischief, and by fixing the gaze of their victims, to suck the very life out of them. So Paul asks who the malign sorcerer is who has thus fascinated the fickle Galatians, and is draining their Christian life out of their eyes.

Very appropriately, therefore, if there is this reference, which the word translated 'bewitched' carries with it, he goes on to speak about Jesus Christ as having been displayed before their eyes. They had seen Him. How did they come to be able to turn away to look at anything else?

But there is another observation to be made by way of introduction, and that is as to the full force of the expression 'evidently set forth.' The word employed, as commentators tell us, is that which is used for the display of official proclamations, or public notices, in some conspicuous place, as the Forum or the market, that the citizens might read. So, keeping up the metaphor, the word might be rendered, as has been suggested by some eminent scholars, 'placarded'—'Before whose eyes Jesus Christ has been placarded.' The expression has acquired somewhat ignoble associations from modern advertising, but that is no reason why we should lose sight of its force. So, then, Paul says, 'In my preaching, Christ was conspicuously set forth. It is like some inexplicable enchantment that, having seen Him, you should turn away to gaze on others.' It is insanity which evokes wonder, as well as sin which deserves rebuke; and the fiery question of my text conveys both.

I. Keeping to the metaphor, I note first the placard which Paul had displayed.

'Jesus Christ crucified has been conspicuously set before you,' he says to these Galatians. Now, he referring, of course, to his own work of preaching to them at the beginning. And the vivid clamation. The one virtue of a proclamation is that it should be brief and plain. It must be authoritative, it must be urgent, it must be 'writ large,' it must be easily intelligible. And he that makes it public has nothing to do except to fasten it up, and make sure that it is legible. If I might venture into modern phraseology, what Paul means is that he was neither more nor less than a bill-sticker, that he went out with the placards and fastened them up.

Ah! if we ministers universally acted up to the implications of this metaphor, do you not think the pulpit would be more frequently a centre of power than it is to-day? And if, instead of presenting our own ingenuities and speculations, we were to realise the fact that we have to hide ourselves behind the broad sheet that we fasten up, there would be a new breath over many a moribund church, and we should hear less of the often warrantable sarcasms about the inefficiency of the modern pulpit.

But I turn from Paul's conception of the office to his statement of his theme. '*Jesus* was displayed amongst you.' If I might vary the metaphor a little, the placard that Paul fastened up was like those that modern advertising ingenuity displays upon all our walls. It was a picture-placard, and on it was portrayed one sole figure —Jesus, the Person. Christianity is Christ, and Christ is Christianity; and wherever there is a pulpit or book which deals rather with doctrines than with H who is the Fountain and Quarry of all doctrine, the is divergence from the primitive form of the Gospel.

I know, of course, that doctrines—which are o formal and orderly statements of principles invo facts—must flow from the proclamation of , Christ. I am not such a fool as to run a against theology, as some people in this day do. But what I wish to insist upon is that the first form of Christianity is not a theory, but a history, and that the revelation of God is the biography of a man. We must begin with the person, Christ, and preach Him. Would that all our preachers and all professing Christians, in their own personal religious life, had grasped this—that, since Christianity is not first a philosophy but a history, and its centre not an ordered sequence of doctrines but a living person, the act that makes a man possessor of Christianity is not the intellectual process of assimilating certain truths, and accepting them, but the moral process of clinging, with trust and love, to the person, Jesus.

But, further, if any of you consult the original, you will see that the order of the sentence is such as to throw a great weight of emphasis on that last word 'crucified.' It is not merely a person that is portrayed on the placard, but it is that person *upon the Cross.* Ah! brethren, Paul himself puts his finger, in the words of my text, on what, in his conception, was the throbbing heart of all his message, the vital point from which all its power, and all the gleam of its benediction, poured out upon humanity—'Christ crucified.' If the placard is a picture of Christ in other attitudes and in other aspects, without the picture of Him crucified, it is imperfect representation of the Gospel that Paul ̣hed and that Christ was.

̣ow, think, secondly, of the fascinators that drew ̣he eyes.

̣ ̣tion is not one of ignorance, but it is a

polemic worked in fire, and not in frost, as some argumentation is, against a very well-marked class of teachers—viz. those emissaries of Judaism who had crept into the Church, and took it as their special function to dog Paul's steps amongst the heathen communities that he had gathered together through faith in Christ, and used every means to upset his work.

I cannot but pause for a moment upon this original reference of my text, because it is very relevant to the present condition of things amongst us. These men whom Paul is fighting as if he were in a sawpit with them, in this letter, what was their teaching? This: they did not deny that Jesus was the Christ; they did not deny that faith knit a man to Him, but what they said was that the observance of the external rites of Judaism was necessary in order to entrance into the Church and to salvation. They did not in their own estimation detract from Christ, but they added to Him. And Paul says that to add is to detract, to say that anything is necessary except faith in Jesus Christ's finished work is to deny that that finished work, and faith in it, are the means of salvation; and the whole evangelical system crumbles into nothingness if once you admit that.

Now, is there anybody to-day who is saying the same things, with variations consequent upon change of external conditions? Are there no people within the limits of the Christian Church who are reiterating the old Jewish notion that external ceremonies—baptism and the Lord's Supper—are necessary to salvation and union with the Christian Church? And it was then, that though they did not represent these external

as to detract, from the sole necessity of faith in the perfected work of Jesus Christ? The centre is shifted from
personal union with a personal Saviour by a personal
faith to participation in external ordinances. And I
venture to think that the lava stream which, in this
Epistle to the Galatians, Paul pours on the Judaisers
of his day needs but a little deflection to pour its hot
current over, and to consume, the sacramentarian
theories of this day. 'O foolish Galatians, who hath
bewitched you?' Is it not like some malignant sorcery,
that after the Evangelical revival of the last century
and the earlier part of this, there should spring up
again this old, old error, and darken the simplicity of
the Gospel teaching, that Christ's work, apprehended
by faith, without anything else, is the means, and the
only means, of salvation?

But I need not spend time upon that original application. Let us rather come more closely to our own
individual lives and their weaknesses. It is a strange
thing, so strange that if one did not know it by one's
own self, one would be scarcely disposed to believe it
possible, that a man who has 'tasted the good word
of God and the powers of the world to come,' and has
known Jesus Christ as Saviour and Friend, should
decline from Him, and turn to anything besides. And
yet, strange and sad, and like some enchantment as it
it is the experience at times and in a measure, of us
and, alas! it is the experience, in a very tragical
ee, of many who have walked for a little while
the Master, and then have turned away
no with Him.

and the wandering of our own affections. We often court the coming of the evil influence, and are willing to be fascinated and to turn our backs upon Jesus. Mysterious it is, for why should men cast away diamonds for paste? Mysterious it is, for we do not usually drop the substance to get the shadow. Mysterious it is, for a man does not ordinarily empty his pockets of gold in order to fill them with gravel. Mysterious it is, for a thirsty man will not usually turn away from the full, bubbling, living fountain, to see if he can find any drops still remaining, green with scum, stagnant and odorous, at the bottom of some broken cistern. But all these follies are sanity as compared with the folly of which we are guilty, times without number, when, having known the sweetness of Jesus Christ, we turn away to the fascinations of the world. Custom, the familiarity that we have with Him, the attrition of daily cares—like the minute grains of sand that are cemented on to paper, and make a piece of sandpaper that is strong enough to file an inscription off iron— the seductions of worldly delights, the pressure of our daily cares—all these are as a ring of sorcerers that stand round about us, before whom we are as powerless as a bird in the presence of a serpent, and they bewitch us and draw us away.

The sad fact has been verified over and over again on a large scale in the history of the Church. After every outburst of renewed life and elevated spirituality there is sure to come a period of reaction when torpor and formality again assert themselves. What followed the Reformation in Germany? A century of death. What followed Puritanism in England? An outburst of and godlessness.

ys been, and so it is with us individuall

as we too well know. Ah, brethren! the seductions are omnipresent, and our poor eyes are very weak, and we turn away from the Lord to look on these misshapen monsters that are seeking by their gaze to draw us into destruction. I wonder how many professing Christians are in this audience who once saw Jesus Christ a great deal more clearly, and contemplated Him a great deal more fixedly, and turned their hearts to Him far more lovingly, than they do to-day? Some of the great mountain peaks of Africa are only seen for an hour or two in the morning, and then the clouds gather around them, and hide them for the rest of the day. It is like the experience of many professing Christians, who see Him in the morning of their Christian life far more vividly than they ever do after. 'Who hath bewitched you?' The world; but the arch-sorcerer sits safe in our own hearts.

III. Lastly, keeping to the metaphor, let me suggest, although my text does not touch upon it, the Amulet.

One has seen fond mothers in Egypt and Palestine who hang on their babies' necks charms, to shield them from the influence of the Evil Eye; and there is a charm that we may wear if we will, which will keep us safe. There is no fascination in the Evil Eye if you do not look at it.

The one object that the sorcerer has is to withdraw gaze from Christ; it is not illogical to say that way to defeat the object is to keep our . If you do not look at the it will nor by seeing the fair forms, of the sirens on their island. To look fixedly at Jesus Christ, and with the resolve never to turn away from Him, is the only safety against these tempting delights around us.

But, brethren, it is the crucified Christ, looking to whom, we are safe amidst all seductions and snares. I doubt whether a Christ who did not die for men has power enough over men's hearts and minds to draw them to Himself. The cords which bind us to Him are the assurance of His dying love which has conquered us. If only we will, day by day, and moment by moment, as we pass through the duties and distractions, the temptations and the trials, of this present life, by an act of will and thought turn ourselves to Him, then all the glamour of false attractiveness will disappear from the temptations around us, and we shall see that the sirens, for all their fair forms, end in loathly fishes' tails and sit amidst dead men's bones.

Brethren, 'looking *off* unto Jesus' is the secret of triumph over the fascinations of the world. And if we will habitually so look, then the sweetness that we shall experience will destroy all the seducing power of lesser and earthly sweetness, and the blessed light of the sun will dim and all but extinguish the deceitful gleams that tempt us into the swamps where we shall be drowned. Turn away, then, from these things; cleave to Jesus Christ; and though in ourselves we may be as weak as a humming-bird before a snake, or a rabbit before a tiger, He will give us strength, and the light of His face shining down upon us will f
ou   and make us insensible to the fascinatio
o   orcerers. So we shall not need to dread t
          hath bewitched you?' but oursel
                  mig   t of the fascination

the triumphant question, 'Who shall separate us from the love of Christ?'

Help us, O Lord! we beseech Thee, to live near Thee. Turn away our eyes from beholding vanity, and enable us to set the Lord always before us that we be not moved.

LESSONS OF EXPERIENCE

'Have ye suffered so many things in vain?'—GAL. iii. 4.

THIS vehement question is usually taken to be a reminder to the fickle Galatians that their Christian faith had brought upon them much suffering from the hands of their unbelieving brethren, and to imply an exhortation to faithfulness to the Gospel lest they should stultify their past brave endurance. Yielding to the Judaising teachers, and thereby escaping the 'offence of the Cross,' they would make their past sufferings vain. But it may be suggested that the word 'suffered' here is rather used in what is its known sense elsewhere, namely, with the general idea of *feeling*, the nature of the feeling being undefined. It is a touching proof of the preponderance of pain and sorrow that by degrees the significance of the word has become inextricably intertwined with the ght of sadness; still, it is possible to take it in the s meaning *experienced* or *felt*, and to r rd the as referring to the whole of the and as foundin

Taking the words in this more general sense they become a question which it is well for us to ask ourselves at such a time as this, when the calendar naturally invites us to look backwards and ask ourselves what we have made of all our experiences in the past, or rather what, by the help of them all, we have made of ourselves.

I. The duty of retrospect.

For almost any reason it is good for us to be delivered from our prevailing absorption in the present. Whatever counterpoises the overwhelming weight of the present is, so far, a blessing and a good, and whatever softens the heart and keeps up even the lingering remembrance of early, dewy freshness and of the high aspirations which, even for a brief space, elevated our past selves is gain amidst the dusty commonplaces of to-day. We see things better and more clearly when we get a little away from them, as a face is more distinctly visible at armslength than when held close.

But our retrospects are too often almost as trivial and degrading as is our absorption in the present, and to prevent memory from becoming a minister of frivolity if not of sin, it is needful that such a question as that of our text be urgently asked by each of us. Memory must be in closest union with conscience, as all our faculties must be, or she is of little use. There is a mere sentimental luxury of memory which finds a pensive pleasure in the mere passing out from the hard present into the soft light, not without illusion in i[t] be[a]ms, of the 'days that are no more.' Merely to li[ve] o[ver again i]n our sorrows and joys without any clear [ ] the[ir eff]ects on our moral cha[racter] [ ] [no]t the retrospect that bec[omes us].

however it might suit an animal. We have to look back as a man might do escaping from the ocean on to some frail sand-bank which ever breaks off and crumbles away at his very heels. To remember the past mainly as it affected our joy or our sorrow is as unworthy as to regard the present from the same point of view, and robs both of their highest worth. To remember is only then blessed and productive of its highest possible good in us, when the question of our text insists on being faced, and the object of retrospect is not to try to rekindle the cold coals of past emotions, but to ascertain what effect on our present characters our past experiences have had. We have not to turn back and try to gather some lingering flowers, but to look for the fruit which has followed the fallen blossoms.

II. The true test for the past.

The question of our text implies, as we have already suggested, that our whole lives, with all their various and often opposite experiences, are yet an ordered whole, having a definite end. There is some purpose beyond the moment to be served. Our joys and our sorrows, our gains and our losses, the bright hours and the dark hours, and the hours that are neither eminently bright nor supremely dark, our failures and our successes, our hopes disappointed or fulfilled, and all the infinite variety of condition and environment through which our varying days and years have led o-operate for one end. It is life that makes men; nt is a bundle of possibilities, and as the years one possible avenue of

But all this variety of impulses and complicated experiences need the co-operation of the man himself if they are to reach their highest results in him. If he is simply recipient of these external forces acting upon him, they will shape him indeed, but he will be a poor creature. Life does not make men unless men take the command of life, and he who lets circumstances and externals guide him, as the long water weeds in a river are directed by its current, will, from the highest point of view, have experienced the variations of a lifetime in vain.

No doubt each of our experiences has its own immediate and lower purpose to serve, and these purposes are generally accomplished, but beyond these each has a further aim which is not reached without diligent carefulness and persistent effort on our parts. If we would be sure of what it is to suffer life's experiences in vain, we have but to ask ourselves what life is given us for, and we all know that well enough to be able to judge how far we have used life to attain the highest ends of living. We may put these ends in various ways in our investigation of the results of our manifold experiences. Let us begin with the lowest— we received life that we might learn truth, then if our experience has not taught us wisdom it has been in vain. It is deplorable to have to look round and see how little the multitude of men are capable of forming anything like an independent and intelligent opinion, and how they are swayed by gusts of passion, by blind prejudice, by pretenders and quacks of all sorts. It is no less sad for us to turn our eyes within and discover, perhaps not without surprise and shame, how few of us are self-complacent enough to call our own convictions.

If we ever are honest enough with ourselves to catch a glimpse of our own unwisdom, the question of our text will press heavily upon us, and may help to make us wiser by teaching us how foolish we are. An infinite source of wisdom is open to us, and all the rich variety of our lives' experiences has been lavished on us to help us, and what have we made of it all?

But we may rise a step higher and remember that we are made moral creatures. Therefore, whatever has not developed infant potentialities in us, and made them moral qualities, has been experienced in vain. 'Not enjoyment and not sorrow is our destined end and way.' Life is meant to make us love and do the good, and unless it has produced that effect on us, it has failed. If this be true, the world is full of failures, like the marred statues in a bad sculptor's studio, and we ourselves have earnestly to confess that the discipline of life has too often been wasted upon us, and that of us the divine complaint from of old has been true: 'In vain have I smitten thy children, they have received no correction.'

There is no sadder waste than the waste of sorrow, and alas! we all know how impotent our afflictions have been to make us better. But not afflictions only have failed in their appeal to us, our joys have as often been in vain as our sorrows, and memory, when it turns its lamp on the long past, sees so few points at which life has taught us to love goodness, and be good, that she may well quench her light and let the dead bury its dead.

We must rise still higher, and think of men as

this chief end is in fullest harmony with the lower ends
to which we have just referred, and they will never be
realised in their fullest completeness unless that completeness is sought in this the chief end. From of old
meditative souls have known that the beginning of
wisdom is the fear of the Lord, and that that fear is as
certainly the beginning of goodness. It was not an
irrelevant rebuke to the question, 'What good thing
shall I do?' when Jesus set the eager young soul who
asked it, to justify to himself his courteous and superficial application to Him of the abused and vulgarised
title of ' Good,' and pointed him to God as the only Being
to whom that title, in its perfectness, could be given.
If 'there is none good but one, that is God,' man's goodness must be drawn from Him, and morality without
religion will in theory be incomplete, and in practice
a delusion. If, then, men are made to need God, and
capable of possessing Him, and of being possessed by
Him, then the great question for all of us is, has life,
with all its rapid whirl of changing circumstance and
varying fortunes, drawn us closer to God, and made us
more fit to receive more of Him? So supreme is this
chief end that a life which has not attained it can only
be regarded as 'in vain' whatever other successes it
may have attained. So unspeakably more important
and necessary is it, that compared with it all else sinks
into nothingness; hence many lives which are dazzling
successes in the eyes of men are ghastly failures in
reality.

Now, if we take these plain principles with us in our
retrospect of the past year we shall be launched on
ous inquiry, and brought face to face with
r. Some of us may have had
the tears may be scarcely dry upon

cheeks : some of us may have had great gladnesses,
and our hearts may still be throbbing with the thrill :
some of us may have had great successes, and some of
us heavy losses, but the question for us to ask is not of
the quality of our past experiences, but as to their
effects upon us.   Has life been so used by us as to help
us to become wiser, better, more devout ?   And the
answer to that question, if we are honest in our
scrutiny of ourselves, and if memory has not been a
mere sentimental luxury, must be that we have too
often been but unfaithful recipients alike of God's
mercies and God's chastisements, and have received
much of the discipline of life, and remained undis-
ciplined.   The question of our text, if asked by me,
would be impertinent, but it is asked of each of us
by the stern voice of conscience, and for some of us
by the lips of dear ones whose loss has been among
our chiefest sufferings.   God asks us this question, and
it is hard to make-believe to Him.

III. The best issue of the retrospect.

The world says, 'What I have written I have written,'
and there is a very solemn and terrible reality in the
thought of the irrevocable past.   Whether life has
achieved the ends for which it was given or no, it
has achieved some ends.   It may have made us into
characters the very opposite of God's intention for us,
but it has made us into certain characters which, so
as the world sees, can never be unmade or re-made.
world harshly preaches the indelibility of c-

that anything will obliterate the marks of 'what once hath been,' is in violent contradiction to the large hope brought into the world by Jesus Christ. What we have written we *have* written, and we have no power to erase the lines and make the sheet clean again, but Jesus Christ has taken away the hand-writing 'that was against us,' nailing it to His cross. Instead of our old sin-worn and sin-marked selves, He proffers to each of us a new self, not the outcome of what we have been, but the image of what He is and the prophecy of what we shall be. By the great gift of holiness for the future by the impartation of His own life and spirit, Jesus makes all things new. The Gospel recognises to the full how bad some who have received it were, but it can willingly admit their past foulness, because it contrasts with all that former filth their present cleanness, and to the most inveterately depraved who have trusted in Christ rejoices to say, 'Ye were washed, ye were sanctified, ye were justified in the name of the Lord Jesus Christ.'

THE UNIVERSAL PRISON

'But the Scripture hath concluded all under sin, that the promise by faith of Jesus Christ might be given to them that believe.'—GAL. iii. 22.

THE Apostle uses here a striking and solemn figure, which is much veiled for the English reader by the ambiguity attaching to the word 'concluded.' It literally means 'shut up,' and is to be taken in its literal sense of confining, and not in its second sense of inferring. So, then, we are to conceive of a prison in which mankind is confined.

then, very characteristically, the Apostle passes at once to another metaphor when he goes on to say 'under sin.' What a moment before had presented itself to his vivid imagination as a great dungeon is now represented as a heavy weight, pressing down upon those beneath; if, indeed, we are not, perhaps, rather to think of the low roof of the dark dungeon as weighing on the captives.

Further, he says that Scripture has driven men into this captivity. That, of course, cannot mean that revelation makes us sinners, but it does mean that it makes us more guilty, and that it declares the fact of human sinfulness as no other voice has ever done. And then the grimness of the picture is all relieved and explained, and the office ascribed to God's revelation harmonised with God's love, by the strong, steady beam of light that falls from the last words, which tell us that the prisoners have not been bound in chains for despair or death, but in order that, gathered together in a common doleful destiny, they may become recipients of a common blessed salvation, and emerge into liberty and light through faith in Jesus Christ.

So here are three things—the prison-house, its guardian, and its breaker. 'The Scripture hath shut up all under sin, in order that the promise by faith of Jesus Christ might be given unto all them that believe.'

I. First, then, note the universal prison-house.

Now the Apostle says two things—and we may put away the figure and look at the facts that underlie it. The one is that all sin is imprisonment, the other is that all men are in that dungeon, unless they have come out of it through faith in Jesus Christ.

All sin is imprisonment. That is the direct contrary

of the notion that many people have. They say to
themselves, 'Why should I be fettered and confined
by these antiquated restrictions of a conventional
morality? Why should I not break the bonds, and do
as I like?' And they laugh at Christian people who
recognise the limitations under which God's law has
put them; and tell us that we are 'cold-blooded folks
who live by rule,' and contrast their own broad 'emanci-
pation from narrow prejudice.' But the reality is the
other way. The man who does wrong is a slave in the
measure in which he does it. If you want to find out
—and mark this, you young people, who may be
deceived by the false contrasts between the restraints
of duty and the freedom of living a dissolute life—if
you want to find out how utterly ' he that committeth
sin is the slave of sin,' try to break it off, and you will
find it out fast enough. We all know, alas! the impotence of the will when it comes to hand grips with
some evil to which we have become habituated; and
how we determine and determine, and try, and fail,
and determine again, with no better result. We are
the slaves of our own passions; and no man is free who
is hindered by his lower self from doing that which his
better self tells him he ought to do. The tempter
comes to you, and says, 'Come and do this thing, just
for once. You can leave off when you like, you know.
There is no need to do it a second time.' And when
you have done it, he changes his note, and says, 'Ah!
you are in, and you cannot get out. You have done it
once; and in my vocabulary once means twice, and
once and twice mean *always*.'

Some people are sometimes tempted into a house
 by being made to believe that it is a g
 they are just going to pay a

visit, and can come away when they like. But once inside the walls, they never get past the lodge gates any more. The foolish birds do not know that there is lime on the twigs, and their little feet get fastened to the branch, and their wings flutter in vain. 'He that committeth sin is the slave of sin—shut up,' dungeoned, 'under sin.'

But do not forget, either, the other metaphor in our text, in which the Apostle, with characteristic rapidity, and to the horror of rhetorical propriety, passes at once from the thought of a dungeon to the thought of an impending weight, and says, 'Shut up *under* sin.'

What does that mean? It means that we are guilty when we have done wrong; and it means that we are under penalties which are sure to follow. No deed that we do, howsoever it may fade from the tablets of our memory, but writes in visible characters, in proportion to its magnitude, upon our characters and lives. All human acts have perpetual consequences. The kick of the rifle against the shoulder of the man that fires it is as certain as the flight of the bullet from its muzzle. The chalk cliffs that rise above the Channel entomb and perpetuate the relics of myriads of evanescent lives; and our fleeting deeds are similarly preserved in our present selves. Everything that a man wills, whether it passes into external act or not, leaves, in its measure, ineffaceable impressions on himself. And so we are not only dungeoned in, but weighed upon by, and lie under, the evil that we do.

Nor, dear friends, dare I pass in silence what is too often passed in silence in the modern pulpit, the plain fact that there is a future waiting for each of us beyond the grave, of which the most certain character-

istic, certified by our own forebodings, required by the
reasonableness of creation, and made plain by the
revelation of Scripture, is that it is a future of retribution, where we shall have to carry our works; and
as we have brewed so shall we drink; and the beds
that we have made we shall have to lie upon. 'God
shut up all under sin.'

Note, again, the universality of the imprisonment.

Now I am not going to exaggerate, I hope. I want
to keep well within the limits of fact, and to say
nothing that is not endorsed by your own consciences,
if you will be honest with yourselves. And I say that
the Bible does not charge men universally with gross
transgressions. It does not talk about the virtues that
grow in the open as if they were splendid vices; but it
does say, and I ask you if our own hearts do not tell
us that it says truly, that no man is, or has been, does,
or has done, that which his own conscience tells him
he should have been and done. We are all ready to
admit faults, in a general way, and to confess that we
have come short of what our own consciousness tells
us we ought to be. But I want you to take the other
step, and to remember that since we each stand in a
personal relation to God, therefore all imperfections,
faults, negligences, shortcomings, and, still more,
transgressions of morality, or of the higher aspirations
of our lives, are sins. Because sin—to use fine words
—is the correlative of God. Or, to put it into plainer
language, the deeds which in regard to law may be
crimes, or those which in regard to morality may be
vices, or in regard to our own convictions of duty may
be shortcomings, seeing they all have some referenc
assume a very much graver character,

Oh, brethren, if we realise how intimately and inseparably we are knit to God, and how everything that we do, and do not do, but should have done, has an aspect in reference to Him, I think we should be less unwilling to admit, and less tinged with levity and carelessness in admitting, that all our faults are transgressions of His law, and we should find ourselves more frequently on our knees before Him, with the penitent words on our lips and in our hearts, 'Against Thee, Thee only have I sinned, and done this evil in Thy sight.'

That was the prayer of a man who had done a foul evil in other people's sight; who had managed to accumulate about as many offences to as many people in one deed as was possible. For, as a king he had sinned against his nation, as a friend he had sinned against his companion, as a captain he had sinned against his brave subordinate, as a husband he had sinned against his wife, and he had sinned against Bathsheba. And yet, with all that tangle of offences against all these people, he says, 'Against Thee, Thee only.' Yes! Because, accurately speaking, the *sin* had reference to God, and to God alone. And I wish for myself and for you to cultivate the habit of connecting, thus, all our actions, and especially our imperfections and our faults, with the thought of God, that may learn how universal is the enclosure of man is dreadful prison-house.

And so, I come, in the second place, to look at the of the prison.

the same expression in the Epistle to the Romans, where Paul directly traces the 'concluding all in disobedience' to God Himself.

There may be other subtle thoughts connected with that expression which I do not need to enter upon now. But one that I would dwell upon, for a moment, is this, that one great purpose of Scripture is to convince us that we are sinful in God's sight. I do not need to remind you, I suppose, how that was, one might almost say, the dominant intention of the whole of the ceremonial and moral law of Israel, and explains its many else inexplicable and apparently petty commandments and prohibitions. They were all meant to emphasise the difference between right and wrong, obedience and disobedience, and so to drive home to men's hearts the consciousness that they had broken the commandments of the living God. And although the Gospel comes with a very different guise from that ancient order, and is primarily gift and not law, a Gospel of forgiveness, and not the promulgation of duty or the threatening of condemnation, yet it, too, has for one of its main purposes, which must be accomplished in us before it can reach its highest aim in us, the kindling in men's hearts of the same consciousness that they are sinful men in God's sight.

Ah, brethren, we all need it. There is nothing that we need more than to have driven deep into us the penetrating point of that conviction. There must be some external standard by which men may be convinced of their sinfulness, for they carry no such standard within them. Your conscience is only *you* ... on moral questions, and, of course, as y... ...change too. A man's whole state d... ... with which conscience shall spea...

him, and so the worse he is, and the more he needs it, the less he has it. The rebels cut the telegraph wires. The waves break the bell that hangs on the reef, and so the black rocks get many a wreck to gnaw with their sharp teeth. A man makes his conscience dumb by the very sins that require a conscience trumpet-tongued to reprehend them. And therefore it needs that God should speak from Heaven, and say to us, ' *Thou* art the man,' or else we pass by all these grave things that I am trying to urge upon you now, and fall back upon our complacency and our levity and our unwillingness to take stock of ourselves, and front the facts of our condition. And so we build up a barrier between ourselves and God, and God's grace, which nothing short of that grace and an omnipotent love and an all-powerful Redeemer can ever pull down.

I wish to urge in a few words, yet with much earnestness, this thought, that until we have laid to heart God's message about our own personal sinfulness we have not got to the place where we can in the least understand the true meaning of His Gospel, or the true work of His Son. May I say that I, for one, am old-fashioned enough to look with great apprehension on certain tendencies of present-day presentations of Christianity which, whilst they dwell much upon the social blessings which it brings, do seem to me to be in great peril of obscuring the central characteristic of the Gospel, that it is addressed to sinful men, and that the only way by which individuals can come to the possession of any of its blessings is by coming as penitent ers, and casting themselves on the mercy of God in Christ? The beginning of all lies here, where Paul 'the Scripture hath herded all men,' in drove, n, that it might have mercy upon all.

Dear friend, as the old proverb has it, deceit lurks in generalities. I have no doubt you are perfectly willing to admit that all are sinful. Come a little closer to the truth, I beseech you, and say each is sinful, and I am one of the captives.

III. And so, lastly, the breaker of the prison-house.

I need not spend your time in commenting on the final words of this text. Suffice it to gather their general purport and scope. The apparently stern treatment which God by revelation applies to the whole mass of mankind is really the tenderest beneficence. He has shut them up in the prison-house in order that, thus shut up, they may the more eagerly apprehend and welcome the advent of the Deliverer. He tells us each our state, in order that we may the more long for, and the more closely grasp, the great mercy which reverses the state. And so how shallow and how unfair it is to talk about evangelical Christianity as being gloomy, stern, or misanthropical! You do not call a doctor unkind because he tells an unsuspecting patient that his disease is far advanced, and that if it is not cured it will be fatal. No more should a man turn away from Christianity, or think it harsh and sour, because it speaks plain truths. The question is, are they true? not, are they unpleasant?

If you and I, and all our fellows, are shut up in this prison-house of sin, then it is quite clear that none of us can do anything to get ourselves out. And so the way is prepared for that great message with which Jesus opened His ministry, and which, whilst it has a far wider application, and reference to social as well as to individual evils, begins with the proclamation of o the captives, and the opening of the prison th t re bound.

There was once a Roman emperor who wished that all his enemies had one neck, that he might slay them all at one blow. The wish is a fact in regard to Christ and His work, for by it all our tyrants have been smitten to death by one stroke; and the death of Jesus Christ has been the death of sin and death and hell— of sin in its power, in its guilt, and in its penalty. He has come into the prison-house, and torn the bars away, and opened the fetters, and every man may, if he will, come out into the blessed sunshine and expatiate there.

And if, brethren, it is true that the universal prison - house is opened by the death of Jesus Christ, who is the Propitiation for the sins of the whole world, and the power by which the most polluted may become clean, then there follows, as plainly, that the only thing which we have to do is, recognising and feeling our bound impotence, to stretch out chained hands and take the gift that He brings. Since all is done for each of us, and since none of us can do sufficient for himself to break the bond, then what we should do is to trust to Him who has broken every chain and let the oppressed go free.

Oh, dear friend, if you want to get to the heart of the sweetness and the blessedness and power of the gospel, you must begin here, with the clear and content consciousness that you are a sinful man in his sight, and can do nothing to cleanse, help, or yourself. Is Jesus Christ the breaker of the ? Do you learn from Him wh do, oh, then a great light will shine in the prison-house, and your chains will drop from your wrists, and the iron door will open of its own accord, and you will come out into the morning sunshine of a new day, because you have confessed and abhorred the bondage into which you have cast yourselves, and accepted the liberty wherewith Christ hath made you free.

THE SON SENT

'When the fulness of the time came, God sent forth His Son, born of a woman, born under the law, that He might redeem them which were under the law, that we might receive the adoption of sons.'—GAL. iv. 4, 5 (R.V.).

IT is generally supposed that by the 'fulness of time' Paul means to indicate that Christ came at the moment when the world was especially prepared to receive Him, and no doubt that is a true thought. The Jews had been trained by law to the conviction of sin: heathenism had tried its utmost, had reached the full height of its possible development, and was decaying. Rome had politically prepared the way for the spread of the Gospel. Vague expectations of coming change found utterance even from the lips of Roman courtier poets, and a feeling of unrest and anticipation pervaded society; but while no doubt all this is true and becomes more certain the more we know of the state of things into which Christ came, it is to be noted that Paul is not thinking of the fulness of time primarily in reference to the world which received Him, but to the Father who sent Him. Our text immediately follows words in which the air is described as being 'under guardians and stewards' until the time appointed of His Father, and the fulness of time is therefore the moment which God had ordained from the beginning for His coming

He, from of old, had willed that at that moment this
Son should be born, and it is to the punctual accomplishment of His eternal purpose that Paul here directs
our thoughts. No doubt the world's preparedness is
part of the reason for the divine determination of the
time, but it is that divine determination rather than
the world's preparedness to which the first words of
our text must be taken to refer.

The remaining portion of our text is so full of meaning that one shrinks from attempting to deal with it
in our narrow space, but though it opens up depths
beyond our fathoming, and gathers into one concentrated brightness lights on which our dim eyes can
hardly look, we may venture to attempt some imperfect consideration even of these great words. Following their course of thought we may deal with

I. The mystery of love that sent.

The most frequent form under which the great fact
of the incarnation is represented in Scripture is that
of our text—'God sent His Son.' It is familiar on the
lips of Jesus, but He also says that 'God gave His Son.'
One can feel a shade of difference in the two modes of
expression. The former bringing rather to our thoughts
the representative character of the Son as Messenger,
and the latter going still deeper into the mystery of
Godhead and bringing into view the love of the
ther who spared not His Son but freely bestowed
 on men. Yet another word is used by Jesus Him-
 hen He says, 'I came forth from God,' and that
 n brings into iew the perf t wil
 th Son accepted the   ssion

flash into different colours, and all must be held fast if we would understand the unspeakable gift of God. Jesus was sent; Jesus was given; Jesus came. The mission from the Father, the love of the Father, the glad obedience of the Son, must ever be recognised as interpenetrating, and all present in that supreme act.

There have been many men specially sent forth from God, whose personal existence began with their birth, and so far as the words are concerned, Jesus might have been one of these. There was a man sent from God whose name was John, and all through the ages he has had many companions in his mission, but there has been only one who 'came' as well as 'was sent,' and He is the true light which lighteth every man. To speak in theological language of the pre-existence of the Son is cold, and may obscure the truth which it formulates in so abstract a fashion, and may rob it of power to awe and impress. But there can be no question that in our text, as is shown by the juxtaposition of 'sent' and 'born,' and in all the New Testament references to the subject, the birth of Jesus is not regarded as the beginning of the being of the Son. The one lies far back in the depths of eternity and the mystery of the divine nature, the other is a historical fact occurring in a definite place and at a dated moment. Before time was the Son was, delighting in the Father, and 'in the beginning was the word and the word was with God,' and He who in respect of His expression of the Father's mind and will was the Word, was the Son in respect of the love that bound the Father and Him in one. Into the mysteries of that love and union no eyes can penetrate, but unless our fathers hold of it, we know not the God whom Je... ...d to us. The mysteries of that divine unio...

and communion lie beyond our reach, but well within
the grasp of our faith and the work of the Son in the
world, ever since there was a world, is not obscurely
declared to all who have eyes to see and hearts to
understand. For He has through all ages been the
active energy of the divine power, or as the Old Testament words it, 'The Arm of the Lord,' the Agent of
creation, the Revealer of God, the Light of the world
and the Director of Providence. 'He was in the world
and the world was made by Him, and the world knew
Him not.'

Now all this teaching that the Son was long before
Jesus was born is no mere mysterious dogma without
bearing on daily needs, but stands in the closest connection with Christ's work and our faith in it. It is the
guarantee of His representative character; on it depends the reliableness of His revelation of God. Unless
He is the Son in a unique sense, how could God have
spoken unto us in Him, and how could we rely on His
words? Unless He was 'the effulgence of His glory and
the express image of His person': how could we be
sure that the light of His countenance was light from
God and that in His person God was so presented as
that he who had seen Him had seen the Father? The
completeness and veracity of His revelation, the authoritative fulness of His law, the efficacy of His sacrifice
and the prevalence of His intercession all depend on
the fact of His divine life with God long before His
human life with men. It is a plain historical fact that
Christianity which has no place for a pre-existent
the bosom of the Father has only a maimed
ce to the needs of

Nor is this truth less needful in its bearing on modern theories which will have nothing to say to the supernatural, and in a fatalistic fashion regard history as all the result of an orderly evolution in which the importance of personal agents is minimised. To it Jesus, like all other great men, is a product of His age, and the immediate result of the conditions under which He appeared. But when we look far beyond the manger of Bethlehem into the depths of Eternity and see God so loving the world as to give His Son, we cannot but recognise that He has intervened in the course of human history and that the mightiest force in the development of man is the eternal Son whom He sent to save the world.

II. The miracle of lowliness that came.

The Apostle goes on from describing the great fact which took place in heaven to set forth the great fact which completed it on earth. The sending of the Son took effect in the birth of Jesus, and the Apostle puts it under two forms, both of which are plainly designed to present Christ's manhood as His full identification of Himself with us. The Son of God became the son of a woman; from His mother He drew a true and complete humanity in body and soul. The humanity which He received was sufficiently kindred with the divinity which received it to make it possible that the one should dwell in the other and be one person. As born of a woman the Son of God took upon Himself all human experiences, became capable of sharing our pure emotions, wept our tears, partook in our joys, ho__d and feared as we do, was subject to our changes __ grow, and in everything but sin, was a m__ __.

__could not be as the sons of

Him the Father heard always. Even when He came down from Heaven and became the Son of Man, He continued to be 'The Son of Man which is in Heaven.' Amid all the distractions and limitations of His earthly life, the continuity and depth of His communion with the Father were unbroken and the completeness of His obedience undiminished. He was a Man, but He was also the Man, the one realised ideal of humanity that has ever walked the earth, to whom all others, even the most complete, are fragments, the fairest foul, the most gracious harsh. In Him and in Him only has been 'given the world assurance of a man.'

The other condition which is here introduced is 'born under the law,' by which it may be noted that the Apostle does not mean the Jewish law, inasmuch as he does not use the definite article with the word. No doubt our Lord was born as a Jew and subject to the Jewish law, but the thought here and in the subsequent clause is extended to the general notion of law. The very heart of our Lord's human identification is that He too had duties imperative upon Him, and the language of one of the Messianic psalms was the voice of His filial will during all His earthly life; 'Lo! I come, in the volume of the Book it is written of Me, I delight to do Thy will and Thy law is within My heart.' The very secret of His human life was discovered by the heathen centurion, at whose faith He marvelled, who said, 'I *also* am a man under authority'; so was Jesus. The Son had ever been obedient in the sweet communion of Heaven, but the obedience of Jesus was not less perfect, continual and unstained. It was the man Jesus who summed up His earthly life in 'I do always the things that please Him'; it was the man Jesus who, under the olives in Gethsemane, made the

great surrender and yielded up His own will to the
will of the Father who sent Him.

He was under law in that the will of God dominated
His life, but He was not so under it as we are on whom
its precepts often press as an unwelcome obligation,
and who know the weight of guilt and condemnation.
If there is any one characteristic of Jesus more conspicuous than another it is the absence in Him of any
consciousness of deficiency in His obedience to law, and
yet that absence does not in the smallest degree infringe on His claim to be 'meek and lowly in heart.'
'Which of you convinceth Me of sin?' would have been
from any other man a defiance that would have provoked a crushing answer if it had not been taken as a
proof of hopeless ignorance of self, but when Christ asks
the question, the world is silent. The silence has been
all but unbroken for nineteen hundred years, and of
all the busy and often unfriendly eyes that have been
occupied with Him and the hostile pens that have been
eager to say something new about Him, none have
discovered a flaw, or dared to 'hint a fault.' That
character has stamped its own impression of perfectness
on all eyes even the most unfriendly or indifferent.
In Him there is seen the perfect union and balance of
opposite characteristics; the rest of us, at the best,
are but broken arcs; Jesus is the completed round.
He is under law as fully, continuously and joyfully
obedient; but for Him it had no accusing voice, and it
laid on Him no burden of broken commandments. He
was born of a woman, born under law, but he lived
separate from sinners though identified with them.

III. The marvel of exaltation that results.

Our Lord's lowliness is described in the two clauses
that have just been considering. They are

His identification with us from a double point of view, and that double point of view is continued in the final clauses of our text which state the double purpose of God in sending His Son. He became one with us that we might become one with Him. The two elements of this double purpose are stated in the reverse order to the two elements of Christ's lowliness. The redemption of them that were under law is presented as the reason for His being born under law, and our reception of the 'adoption of sons' is the purpose of the Son's being sent and born of a woman. The order in which Paul here deals with the two parts of the divine purpose is not to be put down to mere rhetorical ornament, but corresponds to the order in which these two elements are realised by men. For there must be redemption from law before there is the adoption of sons.

We have already had occasion to point out that 'law' here must be taken in the wide sense and not restricted to the Jewish law. It is a world-wide redemption which the Father's love had in view in sending His Son, but that all-comprehending, fatherly love could not reach its aim by the mere forth-putting of its own energy. A process was needed if the divine heart was to accomplish its desire, and the majestic stages in that process are set forth here by Paul. The world under law in a very sad fashion, and though Jesus came to redeem them that are under law, the weight of commandments flouted and d
done

Jesus Christ has become one of us, and in His sinless life has 'magnified the law and made it honourable,' and in His sinless death He endures the consequences of sin, not as due to Himself, but because they are man's. But we must carefully keep in view, that as we have already pointed out, we are to think of Christ's mission as His coming as well as the Father's sending, and that therefore we do not grasp the full idea of our Lord's enduring the consequences of sin unless we take it as meaning His voluntary identification of Himself in love with us sinful men. His obedience was perfect all His life long, and His last and highest act of obedience was when He became obedient unto death, even the death of the Cross.

This is the only means by which the burden of law in any of its forms can be taken away from us. For a law which is not loved will be heavy and hard however holy and just and good it may be, and a law which we have broken will become sooner or later its own avenger. Faithful in *Pilgrim's Progress* tells how 'So soon as a man overtook me he was but a word and a blow, for down he knocked me and laid me for dead. . . . He struck me another deadly blow on the breast and beat me down backward, so I lay at his foot as dead as before, so when I came to myself again I cried him "Mercy," but he said, "I know not how to show mercy," and with that knocked me down again; he had doubtless made an end of me but that one came by and bid him forbear. . . . I did not know him first, but as he went by I perceived the holes in hands and in his sides.' He was born under law He might redeem them that were under law.

The slaves bought into freedom are received int family. The Son has become flesh that the

dwell in the flesh may rise to be sons, but the Son
stands alone even in the midst of His identification
with us, and of the great results which follow for us
from it. He is the Son by nature; we are sons by
adoption. He became man that we might share in the
possession of God. When the burden of law is lifted off
it is possible to bestow the further blessing of sonship,
but that blessing is only possible through Him in whom,
and from whom, we derive a life which is divine life.
There is a profound truth in the prophetic sentence,
'Behold I and the children which God hath given me!'
for, in one aspect, believers are the children of Christ,
and in another, they are sons of God.

We have been speaking of the Son's identification
with us in His mission, and our identification with
Him, but that identification depends on ourselves and
is only an accomplished fact through our faith. When
we trust in Him it is true that all His—His righteousness, His Sonship, His union with the Father—is ours,
and that all ours—our sins, our guilt, our alienation
from God and our dwelling in the far-off land of rags
and vice—is His. In His voluntary identification with
us, He has borne our griefs and carried our sorrows.
It is for us to determine whether we will lay on Him
our iniquities, as the Father has already laid the
iniquities of us all. Are we by faith in Him who was
n of a woman, born under law, making our very
the redemption from the law which He has wrought
adoption of sons which He b s?

WHAT MAKES A CHRISTIAN: CIRCUMCISION OR FAITH?

'In Jesus Christ neither circumcision availeth any thing, nor uncircumcision, but faith which worketh by love.'—GAL. v. 6.

IT is a very singular instance of imaginative misreading of plain facts that the primitive Church should be held up as a pattern Church. The early communities had apostolic teaching; but beyond that, they seem to have been in no respect above, and in many respects below, the level of subsequent ages. If we may judge of their morality by the exhortations and dehortations which they received from the Apostle, Corinth and Thessalonica were but beginners in holiness. If we may judge of their intelligence by the errors into which they were in danger of falling, these first congregations had indeed need that one should teach them which were the first principles of the oracles of God. It could not be otherwise. They were but just rescued from heathenism, and we need not wonder if their spirits long bore the scars of their former bondage. If we wish to know what the apostolic churches were like, we have but to look at the communities gathered by modern missionaries. The same infantile simplicity, the same partial apprehensions of the truth, the same danger of being led astray by the low morality of their heathen kindred, the same openness to strange heres, the same danger of blending the old with the new, opinion and in practice, beset both.

The history of the first theological difference in the early churches is a striking confutation of the d were perfect, and a striking illustation the dangers to which they were exposed from the attempt, so natural to us all, to put new wine into old bottles. The Jewish and the Gentile elements did not coalesce. The point round which the strife was waged was not whether Gentiles might come into the Church. That was conceded by the fiercest Judaisers. But it was whether they could come in as Gentiles, without first being incorporated into the Jewish nation by circumcision, and whether they could remain in as Gentiles, without conforming to Jewish ceremonial and law.

Those who said 'No' *were* members of the Christian communities, and, being so, they still insisted that Judaism was to be eternal. They demanded that the patched and stiff leathern bottle, which had no elasticity or pliability, should still contain the quick fermenting new wine of the kingdom. And certainly, if ever man had excuse for clinging to what was old and formal, these Judaising Christians held it. They held by a law written with God's own finger, by ordinances awful by reason of divine appointment, venerable by reason of the generations to which they had been of absolute authority, commended by the very example of Christ Himself. Every motive which can bind heart and conscience to the reverence and the practice of the traditions of the Fathers, bound them to the Law and the ordinances which had been Israel's treasure from Abraham to Jesus.

se who said 'Yes' were mostly Gentiles, headed spired by a Hebrew of the Hebrews. They Ju m was preparatory, and th its compel all Gentile converts to enter Christ's kingdom through the gate of circumcision.

The fight was stubborn and bitter. I suppose it is harder to abolish forms than to change opinions. Ceremonies stand long after the thought which they express has fled, as a dead king may sit on his throne stiff and stark in his golden mantle, and no one come near enough to see that the light is gone out of his eyes, and the will departed from the hand that still clutches the sceptre. All through Paul's life he was dogged and tormented by this controversy. There was a deep gulf between the churches he planted and this reactionary section of the Christian community. Its emissaries were continually following in his footsteps. As he bitterly reproaches them, they entered upon another man's line of things made ready to their hand, not caring to plant churches of circumcised Gentiles themselves, but starting up behind him as soon as his back was turned, and spoiling his work.

This Epistle is the memorial of that foot-to-foot feud. It is of perennial use, as the tendencies against which it is directed are constant in human nature. Men are ever apt to confound form and substance, to crave material embodiments of spiritual realities, to elevate outward means into the place of the inward and real, to which all the outward is but subsidiary. In every period of strife between the two great opponents, this letter has been the stronghold of those who fight for the spiritual conception of religion. With it Luther waged his warfare, and in this day, too, its words are precious.

My text contains Paul's condensed statement of his whole position in the controversy. It tells what he fought for, and why he fought, against attempt to suspend union to Christ on an outward rite.

I. The first grand principle contained in these words is that faith working by love makes a Christian.

The antithesis of our text appears in somewhat varied forms in two other places in the Apostle's writings. To the Corinthians he says, 'Circumcision is nothing, and uncircumcision is nothing, but the keeping of the commandments of God. His last word to the Galatians—the gathering up into one strong sentence of his whole letter—is, 'In Christ Jesus, neither circumcision availeth anything, nor uncircumcision, but a new creature.'

Now, all these assertions embody substantially the same opposition between the conception of Christianity as depending upon a ceremonial rite, and as being a spiritual change. And the variations in the second member of the contrast throw light on each other. In one, the essential thing is regarded from the divine side as being not a rite performed on the body, but a new nature, the result of a supernatural regeneration. In another, the essential thing is set forth as being not an outward act, but an inward principle, which produces appropriate effects on the whole being. In yet another the essential thing is conceived as being not a mere ceremonial, but practical obedience, the consequence of the active principle of faith, and the sign of the new life. There is an evident sequence in the three sayings. They begin with the deepest, the divine act a new creation—and end with the outermost, the result and object of both the others—deeds of mity to God's law.

in its triple aspects Paul, con-

there between it, in any of its parts, and a carnal
ordinance? They belong to wholly different categories,
and it is the most preposterous confusion to try to mix
them up together. Are we to tack on to the solemn
powers and qualities, which unite the soul to Christ,
this beggarly addition that the Judaisers desire, and to
say, the essentials of Christianity are a new creature,
faith, obedience—and circumcision? That is, indeed,
sewing old cloth on a new garment, and huddling
together in grotesque chaos things which are utterly
diverse. It is as absurd bathos as to say the essentials
of a judge are integrity, learning, patience—and an
ermine robe!

There would be less danger of being entangled in
false notions of the sort which devastated Galatia and
have afflicted the Church ever since, if people would
put a little more distinctly before their own minds
what they mean by 'religion'; what sort of man they
intend when they talk about 'a Christian.' A clear
notion of the thing to be produced would thin away a
wonderful deal of mist as to the way of producing it.
So then, beginning at the surface, in order to work
inward, my first remark is that religion is the harmony
of the soul with God, and the conformity of the life to
His law.

The loftiest purpose of God, in all His dealings, is to
make us like Himself; and the end of all religion is the
complete accomplishment of that purpose. There is
no religion without these elements—consciousness of
kindred with God, recognition of Him as the sum of
all excellence and beauty, and of His will as uncond
tion y binding upon us, aspiration and effort after
ord of heart and soul with Him and with
nd humble confidence that that sovereign bea

will be ours. 'Be ye imitators of God as dear children'
is the pure and comprehensive dictate which expresses
the aim of all devout men. 'To keep His commandments' goes deeper than the mere external deeds.
Were it not so, Paul's grand words would shrink to a
very poor conception of religion, which would then
have its shrine and sphere removed from the sacred
recesses of the inmost spirit to the dusty Babel of the
market-place and the streets.   But with that due and
necessary extension of the words which results from
the very nature of the case, that obedience must be
the obedience of a man, and not of his deeds only,
and must include the submission of the will and the
prostration of the whole nature before Him; they teach
a truth which, fully received and carried out, clears
away whole mountains of theoretical confusion and
practical error. Religion is no dry morality; no slavish,
punctilious conforming of actions to a hard law. Religion is not right thinking alone, nor right emotion
alone, nor right action alone. Religion is still less the
semblance of these in formal profession, or simulated
feeling, or apparent rectitude. Religion is not nominal
connection with the Christian community, nor participation in its ordinances and its worship. But to be
godly is to be godlike. The full accord of all the soul
with His character, in whom, as their native home,
dwell 'whatsoever things are pure, whatsoever things
are lovely,' and the full glad conformity of the will to
His sovereign will, who is the life of our lives—this,
and nothing shallower, nothing narrower, is religion
in its perfection; and the measure in which we have
ned to this harmony with God, is the measure in
Christians. As two stringed instrume
ote   you st

one, a faint ethereal echo is heard from the other, which blends undistinguishably with its parent sound; so, drawing near to God, and brought into unison with His mind and will, our responsive spirits vibrate in accord with His, and give forth tones, low and thin indeed, but still repeating the mighty music of heaven. 'Circumcision is nothing, and uncircumcision is nothing, but the keeping of the commandments of God.'

But our text tells us, further, that if we look backwards from character and deed to motive, this harmony with God results from love becoming the ruling power of our lives. The imitation of the object of worship has always been felt to be the highest form of worship. Many an ancient teacher, besides the Stoic philosopher, has said, 'He who copies the gods worships them adequately.' One of the prophets lays it down as a standing rule, 'The people will walk every one in the name of his God.' But it is only in the Christian attitude towards God that the motive power is found which makes such imitation more than an impossible duty, even as it is only in the revealed character of God that a pattern is found, to imitate which is to be perfect. Everywhere besides, harmony with the gods meant discord with conscience and flagrant outrages of the commonest moralities. Everywhere else, the task of copying them was one lightened by no clear confidence in their love, and by no happy consciousness of our own. But for us, the love revealed is the perfect law, and the love evoked is the fulfilling of the law.

And this is the might and nobleness of the Christian love to God; that it is no idle emotion or lazy rapture no vague sentiment, but the root of all practical goo wheels of life and to bear precious freightage on its bosom; not to flow away in profitless foam. Love is the fruitful mother of bright children, as our great moralist-poet learned when he painted her in the House of Holiness:

> ' A multitude of babes about her hung,
>   Playing their sport that joyed her to behold.'

Her sons are Strength and Justice, and Self-control and Firmness, and Courage and Patience, and many more besides; and her daughters are Pity with her sad eyes, and Gentleness with her silvery voice, and Mercy whose sweet face makes sunshine in the shade of death, and Humility all unconscious of her loveliness; and linked hand in hand with these, all the radiant band of sisters that men call Virtues and Graces. These will dwell in our hearts, if Love their mighty mother be there. If we are without her, we shall be without them.

There is discord between man and God which can only be removed by the sweet commerce of love, established between earth and heaven. God's love has come to us. When ours springs responsive to Him, then the schism is ended, and the wandering child forgets his rebellion, as he lays his aching head on the father's bosom, and feels the beating of the father's heart. Our souls by reason of sin are 'like sweet bells jangled, out of tune and harsh.' Love's master hand laid upon m restores to them their part in 'the fair music all creatures make to their great Lord,' and brings o such accord with God that religion **is** concord with God, and the power which makes that concord is love to God.

But this text leads to a still further consideration, namely, the dominion of love to God in our hearts arises from faith.

We thus reach the last link, or rather the staple, of the chain from which all hangs. Religion is harmony with God; that harmony is produced by love; and that love is produced by faith. Therefore the fundamental of all Christianity in the soul is faith. Would this sound any fresher and more obvious if we varied the language, and said that to be religious we must be like God, that to be like Him we must love Him, and that to love Him we must be sure that He loves us? Surely that is too plain to need enlarging on.

And is it not true that faith must precede our love to God, and affords the only possible basis on which that can be built? How can we love Him so long as we are in doubt of His heart, or misconceive His character, as if it were only power and wisdom, or awful severity? Men cannot love an unseen person at all, without some very special token of his personal affection for them. The history of all religions shows that where the gods have been thought of as unloving, the worshippers have been heartless too. It is only when we know and believe the love that God hath to us, that we come to cherish any corresponding emotion to Him. Our love is secondary, His is primary; ours is reflection, His the original beam; ours is echo, His the mother-tone. Heaven must bend to earth before earth can rise to heaven. The skies must open an drop down love, ere love can spring in the fruitf fi lds. And it is only when we look with true trust t at unveiling of the heart of God which

Jesus Christ, only when we can say, 'Herein is love—
that He gave His Son to be the propitiation for our
sins,' that our hearts are melted, and all their snows
are dissolved into sweet waters, which, freed from
their icy chains, can flow with music in their ripple
and fruitfulness along their course, through our otherwise silent and barren lives.   Faith in Christ is the
only possible basis for active love to God.

And this thought presents the point of contact between the teaching of Paul and John.   The one dwells
on faith, the other on love, but he who insists most on
the former declares that it produces its effects on
character by the latter; and he who insists most on
the latter is forward to proclaim that it owes its very
existence to the former.

It presents also the point of contact between Paul
and James.   The one speaks of the essential of
Christianity as faith, the other as works.   They are
only striking the stream at different points, one at the
fountain-head, one far down its course among the
haunts of men.   They both preach that faith must be
'faith that worketh,' not a barren assent to a dogma,
but a living trust that brings forth fruits in the life.
Paul believes as much as James that faith without
works is dead, and demands the keeping of the commandments as indispensable to all true Christianity.
James believes as much as Paul that works without
faith are of none effect.   So all three of these great
teachers of the Church are represented in this text, to
which each of them might seem to have contributed a
rd embodying his characteristic type of doctrine.
threefold rays into which the prism parts the
blend again here, where faith, love, and
comp s

Jesus Christ neither circumcision availeth anything, nor uncircumcision, but faith which worketh by love.'

The sum of the whole matter is this—He who is one in will and heart with God is a Christian. He who loves God is one in will and heart with Him. He who trusts Christ loves God. That is Christianity in its ultimate purpose and result. That is Christianity in its means and working forces. That is Christianity in its starting-point and foundation.

II. But we have to consider also the negative side of the Apostle's words. They affirm that in comparison with the essential—faith, all externals are infinitely unimportant.

Paul's habit was always to settle questions by the widest principles he could bring to bear upon them—which one may notice in passing is the very opposite to the method that has been in favour with many Church teachers and guides since, who have preferred to live from hand to mouth, and to dispose of difficulties by the narrowest considerations that would avail to quiet them. In our text the question in hand is settled on a ground which covers a great deal more than the existing dispute. Circumcision is regarded as one of a whole class—namely, the class of outward rites and observances; and the contrast drawn between it and faith extends to all the class to which it belongs. It is not said to be powerless because it is an Old Testament rite, but because it is a rite. Its impotence lies in the very nature which it has in common with all extern institutions, whether they be of the Old Testament of the New, whether they be enjoined of God or in vented by men. To them all the same characteris compared with faith they are of no a e absolutely useless. They have

place, but '*in Christ Jesus*' they are nothing. Union
to Him depends on quite another order of facts, which
may or may not exist along with circumcision, or with
baptism, or with the Lord's Supper. However important these may be, they have no place among the
things which bind a soul to its Saviour. They may be
helps to these things, but nothing more. The rite does
not ensure the faith, else the antithesis of our text
were unmeaning. The rite does not stand in the place
of faith, or the contrast implied were absurd. But the
two belong to totally different orders of things, which
may co-exist indeed, but may also be found separately;
the one is the indispensable spiritual experience which
makes us Christians, the other belongs to a class of
material institutions which are much as helps to, but
nothing as substitutes or equivalents for, faith.

Keep firm hold of the positive principle with which
we have been dealing in the former part of this sermon,
and all forms and externals fall as a matter of course
into their proper place. If religion be the loving
devotion of the soul to God, resting upon reasonable
faith, then all besides is, at the most, a means which
may further it. If loving trust which apprehends the
truth, and cleaves to the Person, revealed to us in the
Gospel, be the link which binds men to God, then the
only way by which these externals can be 'means of
grace' is by their aiding us to understand better and
to feel more the truth as it is in Jesus, and to cleave
closer to Him who is the truth. Do they enlighten
_nderstanding? Do they engrave deeper the loved
_en on the tablets of memory, which the
lly _es is ever_ _ing, and

that the cleansing stream may flow through them? Do they, through the senses, minister to the soul its own proper food of clear thought, vivid impressions, loving affections, trustful obedience? Do they bring Christ to us, and us to Him, in the only way in which approach is possible—through the occupation of mind and heart and will with His great perfectness? Then they are means of grace, precious and helpful, the gifts of His love, the tokens of His wise knowledge of our weakness, the signs of His condescension, in that He stoops to trust some portion of our remembrance of Him to the ministry of sense. But in comparison with that faith which they cannot plant, though they may strengthen it, they are nothing; and in the matter of uniting the soul to God and making men 'religious,' they are of no avail at all.

And such thoughts as these have a very wide sweep, as well as a very deep influence. Religion is the devotion of the soul to God. Then *everything* besides is not religion, but at most a means to it. That is true about all Christian ordinances. Baptism is spoken about by Paul in terms which plainly show that he regarded it as 'nothing' in the same sense, and under the same limitations, as he thought that circumcision was nothing. 'I baptized some of you,' says he to the Corinthians; 'I scarcely remember whom, or how many. I have far more important work to do—to preach the Gospel.' It is true about all acts and forms of Christian worship. These are not religion, but means to it. Their only value and their only test is— Do they help men to know and feel Christ and His truth? It is true about laws of life, and many points of conventional morality. Remember the grand free dom with which the same Apostle dealt with questio about meats offered to idols, and the observance of days and seasons. The same principle guided him there too, and he relegated the whole question back to its proper place with, 'Meat commendeth us not to God; for neither if we eat are we the better, neither if we eat not are we the worse.' 'He that regardeth the day, regardeth it unto the Lord; and he that regardeth not the day, to the Lord he doth not regard it.' It is true, though less obviously and simply, about subordinate doctrines. It is true about the mere intellectual grasp of the fundamental truths of God's revelation. These, and the belief of these, are not Christianity, they are helps towards it.

The separation is broad and deep. On one side are all externals, rites, ceremonies, politics, Church arrangements, forms of worship, modes of life, practices of morality, doctrines, and creeds—all which are externals to the soul: on the other is faith working through love, the inmost attitude and deepest emotion of the soul. The great heap is fuel. The flame is loving faith. The only worth of the fuel is to feed the flame. Otherwise it is of no avail, but lies dead and cold, a mass of blackness. We are joined to God by faith. Whatever strengthens that faith is precious as a help, but is worthless as a substitute.

III. There is a constant tendency to exalt these unimportant externals into the place of faith.

The whole purpose of the Gospel may be described deliverance from the dominion of

symbols for realities, bank-notes for wealth. The eye
will be tempted to stay on the rich colours of the glowing
glass, instead of passing through them to heaven's light
beyond. To make the senses a ladder for the soul to
climb to heaven by, will be perilously likely to end in
the soul-going down the ladder instead of up. Forms
are sure to encroach, to overlay the truth that lies at
their root, to become dimly intelligible, or quite unmeaning, and to constitute at last the end instead of the
means. Is it not then wise to minimise these potent
and dangerous allies? Is it not needful to use them
with the remembrance that a minute quantity may
strengthen, but an overdose will kill—ay, and that the
minute quantity may kill too? Christ instituted two
outward rites. There could not have been fewer if
there was to be an outward community at all, and they
could not have been simpler; but look at the porten-
tous outgrowth of superstition, and the unnumbered
evils, religious, moral, social, and even political, which
have come from the invincible tendency of human
nature to corrupt forms, even when the forms are the
sweet and simple ones of Christ's own appointment.
What a lesson the history of the Lord's Supper, and its
gradual change from the domestic memorial of the
dying love of our Lord to the 'tremendous sacrifice,'
reads us as to the dangerous ally which spiritual religion—and there is no other religion than spiritual—
enlists when it seeks the help of external rites!

But remember that this danger of converting religio
into outward actions has its root in us all, and is n
annihilated by our rejection of an elaborate ceremon
T   e is much significance in the double negation
        ther circumcision nor uncircumcision
            ere tempted to insist on the f

as indispensable, their antagonists were as much
tempted to insist on the latter. The one were saying,
'A man cannot be a Christian unless he be circumcised.'
The other would be in danger of replying, 'He cannot
be a Christian if he is.' There may be as much
formalism in protesting against forms as in using
them. Extremes meet; and an unspiritual Quaker,
for instance, is at bottom of the same way of thinking
as an unspiritual Roman Catholic. They agree in their
belief that certain outward acts are essential to worship, and even to religion. They only differ as to what
these acts are. The Judaiser who says, 'You must be
circumcised,' and his antagonist who says, 'You must
be uncircumcised,' are really in the same boat.

And this is especially needful to be kept in mind by
those who, like the most of us, hold fast by the free
and spiritual conception of Christianity. That freedom
we may turn into a bondage, and that spirituality into
a form, if we confound it with the essentials of Christianity, and deny the possibility of the life being
developed except in conjunction with it. My text has
a double edge. Let us use it against all this Judaising
which is going on round about us, and against all the
tendency to it in our own hearts. The one edge smites
the former, the other edge the latter. Circumcision is
nothing, as most of us are forward to proclaim. But,
also, remember, when we are tempted to trust in our
freedom, and to fancy that in itself it is good, *uncircumcision is nothing.* You are no more a Christian for
your rejection of forms than another man is for his
 them. Your negation no more unites you to
 does his affirmation.

in outward acts and ceremonies, and by tempting others of us to place it in rejecting the forms which our brethren abuse.

IV. When an indifferent thing is made into an essential, it ceases to be indifferent, and must be fought against.

Paul proclaimed that circumcision and uncircum- cision were alike unavailing. A man might be a good Christian either way. They were not unimportant in all respects, but in regard to being united to Christ, it did not matter which side one took. And, in accord- ance with this noble freedom, he for himself practised Jewish rites; and, when he thought it might conciliate prejudice without betraying principle, had Timothy circumcised. But when it came to be maintained as a principle that Gentiles *must* be circumcised, the time for conciliation was past. The other side had made further concession impossible. The Apostle had no objection to circumcision. What he objected to was its being forced upon all as a necessary preliminary to entering the Church. And as soon as the opposite party took that ground, then there was nothing for it but to fight against them to the last. They had turned an indifferent thing into an essential, and he could no longer treat it as indifferent.

So whenever parties or Churches insist on external rites as essential, or elevate any of the subordinate means of grace into the place of the one bond which fastens our souls to Jesus, and is the channel of grace as well as the bond of union, then it is time to arm f t ce of the spirituality of Christ's kingdom, a e attempt to bind on free shoulders en and parties do as they li t turn their forms into e

In broad freedom of speech and spirit, which holds by the one central principle too firmly to be much troubled about subordinate matters—in tolerance of diversities, which does not spring from indifference, but from the very clearness of our perception of, and from the very fervour of our adherence to, the one essential of the Christian life—let us take for our guide the large, calm, lofty thoughts which this text sets forth before us. Let us thankfully believe that men may love Jesus, and be fed from His fulness, whether they be on one side of this undying controversy or on the other. Let us watch jealously the tendencies in our own hearts to trust in our forms or in our freedom. And whensoever or wheresoever these subordinates are made into things essential, and the ordinances of Christ's Church are elevated into the place which belongs to loving trust in Christ's love, then let *our* voices at least be heard on the side of that mighty truth that 'in Jesus Christ neither circumcision availeth anything, nor uncircumcision, but faith which worketh by love.'

'WALK IN THE SPIRIT'

'Walk in the Spirit, and ye shall not fulfil the lust of the flesh.'—GAL. v. 16.

WE are not to suppose that the Apostle here uses the familiar contrast of spirit and flesh to express simply different elements of human nature. Without entering here on questions for which a sermon is scarcely a ___ble vehicle of discussion, it may be sufficient for ___resent purpose to say that, as usually, when ___g this antithesis the Apostle means by Spirit

other member of the contrast, 'flesh,' is similarly not
to be taken as equivalent to body, but rather as meaning the whole human nature considered as apart
from God and kindred with earth and earthly things.
The flesh, in its narrower sense, is no doubt a predominant part of this whole, but there is much in
it besides the material organisation. The, ethics of
Christianity suffered much harm and were degraded
into a false and slavish asceticism for long centuries, by
monastic misunderstandings of what Paul meant by
the flesh, but he himself was too clear-sighted and too
high-toned to give his adhesion to the superficial
notion that the body is the seat and source of sin. We
need look no further than the catalogue of the 'works
of the flesh' which immediately follows our text, for,
although it begins with gross sins of a purely fleshly
kind, it passes on to such as hatred, emulations, wrath,
envyings and suchlike. Many of these works of the
flesh are such as an angel with an evil heart could do,
whether he had a body or not. It seems therefore
right to say that the one member of the contrast is the
divine Spirit of holiness, and the other is man as he is,
without the life-giving influence of the Spirit of God.
In Paul's thought the idea of the flesh always included
the idea of sin, and the desires of the flesh were to him
not merely rebellious, sensuous passion, but the sinful
desires of godless human nature, however refined, and
as some would say, 'spiritual' these might be. We do
not need to inquire more minutely as to the meaning
of the Apostle's terms, but may safely take them as, on
the one hand, referring to the divine Spirit which
imparts life and holiness, and on the other hand,
b   ture severed from God, and distracted by
          use wrenched away from Him.

The text is Paul's battle-cry, which he opposed to the Judaising disturbers in Galatia. They said 'Do this and that; labour at a round of observances; live by rule.' Paul said, 'No! That is of no use; you will make nothing of such an attempt nor will ever conquer evil so. Live by the spirit and you will not need a hard outward law, nor will you be in bondage to the works of the flesh.' That feud in the Galatian churches was the earliest battle which Christianity had to fight between two eternal tendencies of thought—the conception of religion as consisting in outward obedience to a law, and consequently as made up of a series of painful efforts to keep it, and the conception of religion as being first the implanting of a new, divine life, and needing only to be nourished and cared for in order to drive forth evils from the heart, and so to show itself living. The difference goes very far and very deep, and these two views of what religion is have each their adherents to-day. The Apostle throws the whole weight of his authority into the one scale, and emphatically declares this as the one secret of victory, 'Walk in the Spirit, and ye shall not fulfil the lusts of the flesh.'

I. What it is to walk in the Spirit.

The thought which is but touched upon here is set forth more largely, and if we may so say, profoundly, in the Epistle to the Romans (chap. viii.). There, to walk after the flesh, is substantially the same as to be lly minded, and that 'mind of th   ' is re-pressure is taken off, some ebullient liquid will bubble. They that are after the flesh of course will 'mind the things of the flesh.' The vehement desires which we cherish when we are separated from God and which we call sins, are graver as a symptom than even they are in themselves, for they show which way the wind blows, and are tell-tales that betray the true direction of our nature. If we were not after the flesh we should not mind the things of the flesh. The one expression points to the deep-seated nature, the other to the superficial actions to which it gives rise.

And the same duality belongs to the life of those who are 'after the Spirit.' 'To walk,' of course, means to carry on the practical life, and the Spirit is here thought of not so much perhaps as the path on which we are to travel, but rather as the norm and direction by which we are to travel on life's common way. Just as the desires of the flesh were certain to be done by those who in their deepest selves belonged to the flesh, so every soul which has received the unspeakable gift of newness of life through the Spirit of God will have the impulses to mind and do the things of the Spirit. If we live in the Spirit we shall also—and let us also— walk in the Spirit.

But let us make no mistakes, or think that our text in its great commandment and radiant hope has any word of cheer to those who have not received into their hearts, in however feeble a manner and minute a measure, the Spirit of the Son. The first question for us all is, have we received the Holy Ghost?—and th answer to that question is the answer to the oth ha we accepted Christ? It is through Him a th in Him that that supreme gift of a li d. And only when our spirit

witness with that Spirit that we are the children of
God, have we a right to look upon the text as pointing
our duty and stimulating our hope. If our practical
life is to be directed by the Spirit of God, He must
enter into our spirits, and we shall not be in Him but
in the measure that He is in us. Nor will our spirits
be life because of righteousness unless He dwells in us
and casts forth the works of the flesh. There will be
no practical direction of our lives by the Spirit of God
unless we make conscience of cultivating the reception
of His life-giving and cleansing influences, and unless
we have inward communion with our inward guide,
intimate and frank, prolonged and submissive. If we
are for ever allowing the light of our inward godliness
to be blown about by gusts, or to show in our inmost
hearts but a faint and flickering spark, how can we
expect that it will shine safe direction on our outward
path?

II. Such walking in the Spirit conquers the flesh.

We all know it as a familiar experience that the
surest way to conquer any strong desire or emotion is
to bring some other into operation. To concentrate
attention on any overmastering thought or purpose,
even if our object is to destroy it, is but too apt to
strengthen it. And so to fix our minds on our own
desires of the flesh, even though we may be honestly
wishing to suppress them, is a sure way to invest them
with new force; therefore the wise counsels of sages
moralists are, for the most part, destined to lead
who listen to them astray. Many a man has, in
set himself to c   quer   evil

way, which he has proved to his own experience, and now, with full confidence and triumph, presses upon his hearers. He would have them give up the monotonous and hopeless fight against the flesh and bring another ally into the field. His chief exhortation is a positive, not a negative one. It is vain to try to tie up men with restrictions and prohibitions, which when their desires are stirred will be burst like Samson's bonds. But if once the positive exhortation here is obeyed, then it will surely make short work of the desires and passions which otherwise men, for the most part, do not wish to get rid of, and never do throw off by any other method.

We have pointed out that in our text to walk in the Spirit means to regulate the practical life by the Spirit of God, and that the 'desires of the flesh' mean the desires of the whole human nature apart from God. But even if we take the contrasted terms in their lower and commonly adopted sense, the text is true and useful. A cultivated mind habituated to lofty ideas, and quick to feel the nobility of 'spiritual' pursuits and possessions, will have no taste for the gross delights of sense, and will recoil with disgust from the indulgences in which more animal natures wallow. But while this is true, it by no means exhausts the great principle laid down here. We must take the contrasted terms in their fullest meaning if we would arrive at it. The spiritual life derived from Jesus Christ and lodged in the human spirit has to be guarded, cherished and made dominant, and then it will drive out the old. If the Spirit which is life because of righteousness is allowed free course in a human spirit, it will send forth it powers into the body which is 'dead because of w te its desires, and if needful will supp them. And it is wiser and more blessed to rely on this overflowing influence than to attempt the hopeless task of coercing these desires by our own efforts.

If we walk in the Spirit, we shall thereby acquire new tastes and desires of a higher kind which will destroy the lower. They to whom manna is sweet as angel's food find that they have lost their relish for the strong-smelling and rank-flavoured Egyptian leeks and garlic. A guest at a king's table will not care to enter a smoky hovel and will not be hungry for the food to be found there. If we are still dependent on the desires of the flesh we are still but children, and if we are walking in the Spirit we have outgrown our childish toys. The enjoyment of the gifts which the Spirit gives deadens temptation and robs many things that were very precious of their lustre.

We may also illustrate the great principle of our text by considering that when we have found our supreme object there is no inducement to wander further in the search after delights. Desires are confessions of discontent, and though the absolute satisfaction of all our nature is not granted to us here, there is so much of blessedness given and so many of our most clamant desires fully met in the gift of life in Christ, that we may well be free from the prickings of desires which sting men into earnest seeking after often unreal good. 'The fruit of the Spirit is love, joy, peace,' and surely if we have these we may well leave the world its troubled delights and felicities. Christ's joy remains in us and our joy is full. The world desires it does not possess. When a deeper well is a lower one

Further, we may note, that this walking in the Spirit brings into our lives the mightiest motives of holy living and so puts a bridle on the necks and a bit in the mouths of our untamed desires. Holding fellowship with the divine Indweller and giving the reins into His strong hand, we receive from Him the spirit of adoption and learn that if we are children then are we heirs. Is there any motive that will so surely still the desires of the flesh and of the mind as the blessed thought that God is ours and we His? Surely their feet should never stumble or stray, who are aware of the Spirit of the Son bearing witness with their spirit that they are the children of God. Surely the measure in which we realise this will be the measure in which the desires of the flesh will be whipped back to their kennels, and cease to disturb us with their barks.

The whole question here as between Paul and his opponents just comes to this; if a field is covered with filth, whether is it better to set to work on it with wheelbarrows and shovels, or to turn a river on it which will bear away all the foulness? The true way to change the fauna and flora of a country is to change the level, and as the height increases they change themselves. If we desire to have the noxious creatures expelled from ourselves, we must not so much labour at their expulsion as see to the elevation of our own personal being and then we shall succeed. That is what Paul says, 'Walk in the Spirit, and ye shall not fulfil the lusts of the flesh.'

III. Such a life is not freed from the necessity of struggle.

The highest condition, of course, would be that we to grow, not to fight. It will come some drop away, and that to walk in

Spirit will need no effort, but that time has not come yet. So in addition to all that we have been saying in this sermon, we must further say that Paul's exhortation has always to be coupled with the other to fight the good fight. The highest word for our earthly lives is not 'victory' but 'contest.' We shall not walk in the Spirit without many a struggle to keep ourselves within that charmed atmosphere. The promise of our text is not that we shall not feel, but that we shall not fulfil, the desires of the flesh.

Now this is very commonplace and threadbare teaching, but it is none the less important, and is especially needful to be strongly emphasised when we have been speaking as we have just been doing. It is a historical fact, illustrated over and over again since Paul wrote, and not without illustration to-day, that there is constant danger of lax morality infecting Christian life under pretence of lofty spirituality. So it must ever be insisted upon that the test of a true walking in the Spirit is that we are thereby fitted to fight against the desires of the flesh. When we have the life of the Spirit within us, it will show itself as Paul has said in another place by the righteousness of the law being fulfilled in us, and by our 'mortifying the deeds of the body.' The gift of the Spirit does not take us out of the ranks of the combatants, but teaches us to fight, and arms us with its ․․n sword for the conflict. There will be abundant ․․tunities of courage in attacking the sin that doth ․․ us ․․․ n r․․ing ․․tations which with the help of an unseen ally in heaven and fighting with a Spirit within us who helpeth our infirmities and Himself makes us able to contend, and sure, if we keep true to Him, to be more than conquerers through Him that loveth us.

Such a conflict is a gift and a joy. It is hard but it is blessed, because it is an expression of our truest love; it comes from our deepest will; it is full of hope and of assured victory. How different is the painful, often defeated and monotonous attempt to suppress our nature by main force, and to tread a mill-horse round! The joyous freedom and buoyant hope taught us in the gospel way of salvation have been cramped and confined and all their glories veiled as by a mass of cobwebs spun beneath a golden roof, but our text sweeps away the foul obstruction. Let us learn the one condition of victorious conflict, the one means of subduing our natural humanity and its distracting desires, and let nothing rob us of the conviction that this is God's way of making men like angels. 'Walk in the Spirit, and ye shall not fulfil the lusts of the flesh.'

THE FRUIT OF THE SPIRIT

'But the fruit of the Spirit is love, joy, peace, long-suffering, gentleness, goodness, faith. 23. Meekness, temperance '—GAL. v. 22, 23.

'THE fruit of the Spirit,' says Paul, not the fruits, as we might more naturally have expected, and as the phrase is most often quoted; all this rich variety of graces, of conduct and character, is thought of as one. The individual members are not isolated graces, but all connected, springing from one root and constituting an organic whole. There is further to be noted th

the Apostle designates the results of the Spirit as
fruit, in strong and intentional contrast with the
results of the flesh, the grim catalogue of which
precedes the radiant list in our text. The works of
the flesh have no such unity, and are not worthy of
being called fruit. They are not what a man ought to
bring forth, and when the great Husbandman comes,
He finds no fruit there, however full of activity the
life has been. We have then here an ideal of the
noblest Christian character, and a distinct and profound teaching as to how to attain it. I venture to
take the whole of this list for my text, because the
very beauty of each element in it depends on its being
but part of a whole, and because there are important
lessons to be gathered from the grouping.

I. The threefold elements of character here.

It is perhaps not too artificial to point out that we
have here three triads of which the first describes the
life of the Spirit in its deepest secret; the second, the
same life in its manifestations to men; and the third,
that life in relation to the difficulties of the world, and
of ourselves.

The first of these three triads includes love, joy, and
peace, and it is not putting too great a strain on the
words to point out that the source of all three lies in
the Christian relation to God. They regard nothing
but God and our relation to Him; they would be all
the same if there were no other men in the world, or
there were no world. We cannot call them duties
...es; they are simply the results of communion
...—the certain manifestations of the better

in the heart by the Holy Spirit. It is the life sap which rises through the tree and gives form to all the clusters. The remaining two members of this triad are plainly consequences of the first. Joy is not so much an act or a grace of character as an emotion poured into men's lives, because in their hearts abides love to God. Jesus Christ pledged Himself to impart His joy to remain in us, with the issue that our joy should be full. There is only one source of permanent joy which takes possession of and fills all the corners and crannies of the heart, and that is a love towards God equally abiding and all-pervasive. We have all known joys so perturbed, fragmentary and fleeting, that it is hard to distinguish them from sorrows, but there is no need that joys should be like green fruit, hard and savourless and ready to drop from the tree. If God is 'the gladness of our joy,' and all our delights come from communion with Him, our joy will never pass and will fill the whole round of our spirits as the sea laves every shore.

Peace will be built upon love and joy, if our hearts are ever turning to God and ever blessed with the inter-communion of love between Him and us. What can be strong enough to disturb the tranquillity that fills the soul independent of all externals? However long and close may be the siege, the well in the castle courtyard will be full. True peace comes not from the absence of trouble but from the presence of God, and will be deep and passing all understanding in the exact measure in which we live in, and partake of the love of God.

The second triad is long-suffering, kindness, goodness. These three obviously refer to the spiritual relations of men. The first of the long-suffering—describes the attitude of patient endurance towards inflictors of injury or enemies, if we come forth from the blessed fellowship with God, where love, joy, and peace reign unbroken, and are met with a cold gust of indifference or with an icy wind of hate. The reality of our happy communion and the depth of our love will be tested by the patience of our long-suffering. Love suffereth long, is not easily provoked, is not soon angry. He has little reason to suppose that the love of God is shed abroad in his heart, or that the Spirit of God is bringing forth fruit in him, who has not got beyond the stage of repaying hate with hate, and scorn with scorn. Any fool can answer a fool according to his folly, but it takes a wise and a good man to overcome evil with good, and to love them that hate; and yet how certainly the fires of mutual antagonism would go out if there were only one to pile on the fuel! It takes two to make a quarrel, and no man living under the influence of the Spirit of God can be one of such a pair.

The second and third members of this triad—kindness, goodness, slide very naturally into one another. They do not only require the negative virtue of not retaliating, but express the Christian attitude towards all of meeting them, whatever their attitude, with good. It is possible that kindness here expresses the ard disposition and goodness, the habitual actions ich that disposition shows itself. If for the spiritual enjoyments of fellowship with God. The true field of religion is in moving amongst men, and the true basis of all service of men is love and fellowship with God.

The third triad—faithfulness, meekness, temperance— seems to point to the world in which the Christian life is to be lived as a scene of difficulties and oppositions. The rendering of the Revised Version is to be preferred to that of the Authorised in the first of the three, for it is not faith in its theological sense to which the Apostle is here referring. Possibly, however, the meaning may be trustfulness just as in 1 Corinthians xiii. it is given as a characteristic of love that it 'believeth all things.' More probably, however, the meaning is faithfulness, and Paul's thought is that the Christian life is to manifest itself in the faithful discharge of all duties and the honest handling of all things committed to it. Meekness even more distinctly contemplates a con- dition of things which is contrary to the Christian life, and points to a submissiveness of spirit which does not lift itself up against oppositions, but bends like a reed before the storm. Paul preached meekness and practised it, but Paul could flash into strong opposition and with a resonant ring in his voice could say 'To whom we gave place by subjection, No! not for an hour. The last member of the triad—temperance— points to the difficulties which the spiritual life is apt to meet with in the natural passions and desires, an insists upon the fact that conflict and rigid an habitual self-control are sure to be marks of th life.

II. The unity of the fruit.

...ve already pointed out the Apostle s rem ... the word 'fruit' here, by which he indi

that all the results of the life of the Spirit in the human
spirit are to be regarded as a whole that has a natural
growth. The foundation of all is of course that love
which is the fulfilling of the law. It scarcely needs to
be pointed out how love brings forth both the other
elements of the first triad, but it is no less important to
note that it and its two companions naturally lead on
to the relations to men which make up the second
triad. It is, however, worth while to dwell on that
fact because there are many temptations for Christian
people to separate between them. The two tables of
the law are not seldom written so far apart that their
unity ceases to be noted. There are many good people
whose notions of religious duties are shut up in
churches or chapels and limited to singing and praying,
reading the Bible and listening to sermons, and who,
even while they are doing good service in common life,
do not feel that it is as much a religious duty to
suppress the wish to retaliate as it is to sit in the
sunshine of God's love and to feel Christ's joy and
peace filling the heart. On the other hand many loud
voices, some of them with great force of words and
influence on the popular mind, are never wearied of
preaching that Christianity is worn out as a social
impulse, and that the service of man has nothing to
do with the love of God. As plainly Paul's first triad
naturally leads to his third. When the spiritual life
realised its deepest secret it will be strong to mani-
self as vigorous in reference to the difficulties of
en that heart is blessed in its

Can we suppose that the Apostle here is going back
in thought to our Lord's profound teaching that every
good tree bringeth forth good fruit, but the corrupt
tree bringeth forth evil fruit? The obvious felicity of
that metaphor often conceals for us the drastic force
of its teaching, it regards all a man's conduct as but
the outcome of his character, and brushes aside as
trifling all attempts at altering products, whilst the
producer remains unaltered. Whether Paul was here
alluding to a known saying of Jesus or no, he was
insisting upon the very centre of Christian ethics, that
a man must first be good in order to do good   Our
Lord's words seemed to make an impossible demand—
'Make the tree good'—as the only way of securing good
fruit, and it was in accordance with the whole cast of the
Sermon on the Mount that the means of realising that
demand was left unexpressed. But Paul stood on this
side of Pentecost, and what was necessarily veiled in
Christ's earlier utterances stood forth a revealed and
blessed certainty to him. He had not to say 'Make the
tree good' and be silent as to how that process was to
be effected; to him the message had been committed,
'The Spirit also helpeth our infirmity.' There is but
one way by which a corrupt tree can be made good,
and that is by grafting into the wild briar stock a
'layer' from the rose. The Apostle had a double message
to proclaim, and the one part was built upon the other.
He had first to preach—and this day has first to believe
that God has sent His own Son in the likeness of sinful
flesh and as an offering for sin—and then he had
proclaim that, through that mission, it became possible
t   ordinance of the law might be fulfilled in
        ot after the flesh but after the spirit.'
        en, of all true goodness is to be sou

receiving into our corrupt natures the uncorrupted germs of the higher life, and it is only in the measure in which that Spirit of God moves in our spirits and, like the sap in the vine, permeates every branch and tendril, that fruit to eternal life will grow. Christian graces are the products of the indwelling divine life, and nothing else will succeed in producing them. All the preachings of moralists and all the struggles after self-improvement are reduced to impotence and vanity by the stern, curt sentence—'a corrupt tree cannot bring forth good fruit. Surely it should come to us all as a true gospel when we feel ourselves foiled by our own evil nature in our attempts to be better, that the first thing we have to do is not to labour at either of the two impossible tasks of the making our bad selves good, or of the getting good fruits from bad selves, but to open our spirits through faith in Jesus for the entrance into us of His Spirit which will change our corruption into incorruption, and cleanse us from all filthiness of flesh and spirit. Shall we not seek to become recipient of that new life, and having received it, should we not give diligence that it may in us produce all its natural effects?

These fruits, though they are the direct results of the indwelling Spirit and will never be produced without its presence, are none the less truly dependent upon our manner of receiving that Spirit and on our faithfulness and diligence in the use of its gifts. It is, alas! sadly too true, and matter of tragically common experience that instead of 'trees of righteousness, the planting of Lord' heavy with ruddy clusters, there are but fed and scrubby bushes which have scarcely life ep up a little sh w of n leaves a

Christian people would more earnestly and searchingly ask themselves why it is that, with such possibilities offered to them, their actual attainments should be so small. They have a power which is able to do for them exceeding abundantly above all that they can ask or think, and its actual effects on them are well on this side of both their petitions and their conceptions. · There need be no difficulty in answering the question why our Christian lives do not correspond more closely to the Spirit that inspires them. The plain answer is that we have not cultivated, used, and obeyed Him. The Lord of the vineyard would less often have to ask 'Wherefore when I looked that it should bring forth grapes, brought it forth wild grapes?' if we listened more obediently to the pathetic command which surely should touch a grateful heart—'Grieve not the holy Spirit of God whereby ye are sealed unto the day of redemption.'

IV. How this is the only worthy fruit.

We have already pointed out that the Apostle in the preceding context varies his terms, and catalogues the actions that come from the godless self as works, whilst those which are the outcome of the Spirit are fruit. The distinction thus drawn is twofold. Multiplicity is contrasted with unity and fruit with works. The deeds of the flesh have no consistency except that of evil; they are at variance with themselves—a huddled mob without regularity or order; and they are works indeed, but so disproportionate to the nature of the doer and his obligations that they do not deserve to be called fruit. It is not to attach too much importance to an accidental form of speech to insist upon this distinction as intended to be drawn, and as suggesting to us very solemn thoughts about many apparently very active lives. The man who lives to God truly lives; the busiest life which is not rooted in Him and directed towards Him has so far missed its aim as to have brought forth no good fruit, and therefore to have incurred the sentence that it is cut down and cast into the fire. There is a very remarkable expression in Scripture, 'The unfruitful works of darkness,' which admits the busy occupation and energy of the doers and denies that all that struggling and striving comes to anything. Done in the dark, they seemed to have some significance, when the light comes in they vanish. It is for us to determine whether our lives shall be works of the flesh, full, perhaps, of a time of 'sound and fury,' but 'signifying nothing,' or whether they shall be fruits of the Spirit, which we 'who have gathered shall eat in the courts of His holiness.' They will be so if, living in the Spirit, we walk in the Spirit, but if we 'sow to the flesh' we shall have a harder husbandry and a bitterer harvest when '.of the flesh we reap corruption,' and hear the awful and unanswerable question, 'What fruit had ye then of those things whereof ye are now ashamed?'

BURDEN-BEARING

'Bear ye one another's burdens, and so fulfil the law of Christ. . . . 5. For every man shall bear his own burden.'—GAL. vi. 2 5.

THE injunction in the former of these verses appears, ˌrst ˌight, to be inconsistent with the sta⋯⋯ ⋯r. But Paul has a way of ⋯

sentence, and couples together by a 'for,' these two
sayings: 'Work out your own salvation'; 'It is God
that worketh in you.' So here he has been exhorting
the Galatian Christians to restore a fallen brother.
That is one case to which the general commandment,
'Bear ye one another's burdens,' is applicable.

I cannot here enter on the intervening verses by
which he glides from the one to the other of these two
thoughts which I have coupled together, but I may
just point out in a word the outline of his course of
thought. 'Bear ye one another's burden,' says he; and
then he thinks, 'What is it that keeps men from bearing each other's burdens?' Being swallowed up with
themselves, and especially being conceited about their
own strength and goodness. And so he goes on: 'If
a man think himself to be something when he is nothing,
he deceives himself.' And what is the best cure for
all these fancies inside us of how strong and good we
are? To look at our work with an impartial and rigid
judgment. It is easy for a man to plume himself on
being good, and strong, and great; but let him look at
what he has done, and try that by a high standard,
and that will knock the conceit out of him. Or, if his
work stands the test, then 'he shall have rejoicing in
himself, and not' by comparing himself with other
people. Two blacks do not make a white, and we are
not to heighten the lustre of our own whiteness by
comparing it with our neighbour's blackness. Take
your act for what *it* is worth, apart altogether from
what other people are. Do not say, 'God! I thank
thee that I am not as other men are . . . or even
as the publican'; but look to yourself. There is an
occupation with self which is good, and is a help to
sympathy.'

And so the Apostle has worked round, you see, to almost an opposite thought from the one with which he started. 'Bear ye one another's burdens.' Yes, but a man's work is his own and nobody else's, and a man's character is his own and nobody else's, so 'every man shall bear his own burden.' The statements are not contradictory. They complete each other. They are the north and the south poles, and between them is the rounded orb of the whole truth. So then, let me point out that:

I. There are burdens which can be shared, and there are burdens which *cannot*.

Let us take the case from which the whole context has arisen. Paul was exhorting the Galatians, as I explained, in reference to their duty to a fallen brother; and he speaks of him—according to our version—as 'overtaken in a fault.' Now, that is scarcely his idea, I think. The phrase, as it stands in our Bibles, suggests that Paul is trying to minimise the gravity of the man's offence; but just in proportion as he minimised its gravity would he weaken his exhortation to restore him. But what he is really doing is not to make as little as possible of the sin, but to make as much of it as is consistent with the truth. The word 'overtaken' suggests that some sin, like a tiger in a jungle, springs upon a man and overpowers him by the suddenness of the assault. The word so rendered may perhaps be represented by some such phrase as 'discovered'; if I may use a 'colloquialism,' if a man be caught nded.' That is the idea. And Paul does not weak word 'fault,' but a very much stronger reputation; and all at once the curtain is thrown aside behind which he is working some wicked thing; and there the culprit stands, with the bull's-eye light flashed upon him, ashamed and trembling. Paul says, 'If you are a spiritual man'—there is irony there of the graver sort—'show your spirituality by going and lifting him up, and trying to help him.' When he says, 'Restore such an one,' he uses an expression which is employed in other connections in the New Testament, such as for mending the broken meshes of a net, for repairing any kind of damage, for setting the fractured bones of a limb. And that is what the 'spiritual' man has to do. He is to show the validity of his claim to live on high by stooping down to the man bemired and broken-legged in the dirt. We have come across people who chiefly show their own purity by their harsh con-demnation of others' sins. One has heard of women so very virtuous that they would rather hound a fallen sister to death than try to restore her; and there are saints so extremely saintly that they will not touch the leper to heal him, for fear of their own hands being ceremonially defiled. Paul says, 'Bear ye one another's burdens'; and especially take a lift of each other's sin.

I need not remind you how the same command applies in relation to pecuniary distress, narrow cir-cumstances, heavy duties, sorrows, and all the 'ills that flesh is heir to.' These can be borne by sympathy, by true loving outgoing of the heart, and by the rendering of such practical help as the circumstances require.

But there are burdens that cannot be borne by any but the man himself.

There is the awful burden of personal existence. It

is a solemn thing to be able to say 'I.' And that carries with it this, that after all sympathy, after all nestling closeness of affection, after the tenderest exhibition of identity of feeling, and of swift godlike readiness to help, each of us lives alone. Like the inhabitants of the islands of the Greek Archipelago, we are able to wave signals to the next island, and sometimes to send a boat with provisions and succour, but we are parted, 'with echoing straits between us thrown.' Every man, after all, lives alone, and society is like the material things round about us, which are all compressible, because the atoms that compose them are not in actual contact, but separated by slenderer or more substantial films of isolating air. Thus there is even in the sorrows which we can share with our brethren, and in all the burdens which we can help to bear, an element which cannot be imparted. 'The heart knoweth its own bitterness', and neither 'stranger' nor other 'intermeddleth' with the deepest fountains of 'its joy.'

Then again, there is the burden of responsibility which can be shared by none. A dozen soldiers may be turned out to make a firing party to shoot the mutineer, and no man knows who fired the shot, but one man did fire it. And however there may have been companions, it was his rifle that carried the bullet, and his finger that pulled the trigger. We say, 'The woman that Thou gavest me tempted me, and I did eat.' Or we say, 'My natural appetites, for which ⸺m not responsible, but Thou who madest me art, ⸺me aside, and I fell', or we may say, 'It was not ⸺ the other boy. And then there rises up in ⸺led form, and fr⸺ its ⸺tic assent—*Mea culpa ; mea maxima culpa*—'My fault, my exceeding great fault.' No man can bear that burden.

And then, closely connected with responsibility there is another—the burden of the inevitable consequences of transgression, not only away yonder in the future, when all human bonds of companionship shall be broken, and each man shall 'give account of himself to God,' but here and now ; as in the immediate context the Apostle tells us, 'Whatsoever a man soweth, that shall he also reap.' The effects of our evil deeds come back to roost; and they never make a mistake as to where they should alight. If I have sown, I, and no one else, will gather. No sympathy will prevent to-morrow's headache after to-night's debauch, and nothing that anybody can do will turn the sleuth-hounds off the scent. Though they may be slow-footed, they have sure noses and deep-mouthed fangs. 'If thou be wise thou shalt be wise for thyself, and if thou scornest thou alone shalt bear it.' So there are burdens which can, and burdens which cannot, be borne.

II. Jesus Christ is the Burden-bearer for both sorts of burdens.

'Bear ye one another's burdens, and so fulfil the law of Christ,' not only as spoken by His lips, but as set forth in the pattern of His life. We have, then, to turn to Him, and think of Him as Burden-bearer in even a deeper sense than the psalmist had discerned, who magnified God as 'He who daily beareth our burdens.'

Christ is the Burden-bearer of our sin. 'The Lord hath laid'—or made to meet—'upon Him the iniquity of us all.' The Baptist pointed his lean, ascetic finger at the young Jesus, and said, 'Behold the Lamb of God which beareth'—and beareth away—'the sin of the world.' How heavy the load, how real its pressure,

let Gethsemane witness, when He clung to human companionship with the unutterably solemn and plaintive
words, 'My soul is exceeding sorrowful even unto death.
Tarry ye here and watch with Me.' He bore the burden
of the world's sin.

Jesus Christ is the bearer of the burden of the consequences of sin, not only inasmuch as, in His sinless
humanity, He knew by sympathy the weight of the
world's sin, but because in that same humanity, by
identification of Himself with us, deeper and more
wonderful than our plummets have any line long
enough to sound the abysses of, He took the cup of
bitterness which our sins have mixed, and drank it all
when He said, 'My God! My God! Why hast Thou
forsaken Me?' Consequences still remain: thank God
that they do! 'Thou wast a God that forgavest them,
and Thou didst inflict retribution on their inventions.'
So the outward, the present, the temporal consequences
of transgression are left standing in all their power, in
order that transgressors may thereby be scourged from
their evil, and led to forsake the thing that has wrought
them such havoc. But the ultimate consequence, the
deepest of all, separation from God, has been borne by
Christ, and need never be borne by us.

I suppose I need not dwell on the other aspects of
this burden-bearing of our Lord, how that He, in a very
deep and real sense, takes upon Himself the sorrows
which we bear in union with, and faith on, Him. For
the griefs that still come to us, when so borne,
transmitted into 'light affliction which is but for
' 'In all their afflictio   affli

sustain you,' and sorrows borne in union with Him will change their character, and the very cross shall be wreathed in flowers.

Jesus bears the burden of that solemn solitude which our personal being lays upon us all. The rest of us stand round, and, as I said, hoist signals of sympathy, and sometimes can stretch a brotherly hand out and grasp the sufferer's hand. But their help comes from without; Christ comes in, and dwells in our hearts, and makes us no longer alone in the depths of our being, which He fills with the effulgence and peace of His companionship. And so for sin, for guilt, for responsibility, for sorrow, for holiness, Christ bears our burdens.

Yes! And when He takes ours on His shoulders, He puts His on ours. 'My yoke is easy, and My burden is light.' As the old mystics used to say, Christ's burden carries him that carries it. It may add a little weight, but it gives power to soar, and it gives power to progress. It is like the wings of a bird, it is like the sails of a ship.

III. Lastly, Christ's carrying our burdens binds us to carry our brother's!

'So fulfil the law of Christ.' There is a very biting sarcasm, and, as I said about another matter, a grave irony in Paul's use of that word 'law' here. For the whole of this Epistle has been directed against the Judaising teachers who were desirous of cramming Jewish law down Galatian throats, and is addressed to their victims in the Galatian churches who had fallen into the trap. Paul turns round on them here, and says, 'You want law, do you? Well, if you *will* have it, here it is—the law of Christ.' Christ's life is our law. Practical Christianity is doing what Christ did. The

Cross is not only the ground of our hope, but the pattern of our conduct.

And, says Paul in effect, the example of Jesus Christ, in all its sweep, and in all the depth of it, is the only motive by which this injunction that I am giving you will ever be fulfilled. 'Bear ye one another's burdens.' You will never do that unless you have Christ as the ground of your hope, and His great sacrifice as the example for your conduct. For the hindrance that prevents sympathy is self-absorption; and that natural selfishness which is in us all will never be exorcised and banished from us thoroughly, so as that we shall be awake to all the obligations to bear our brother's burdens, unless Christ has dethroned self, and is the Lord of our inmost spirits.

I rejoice as much as any man in the largely increased sense of mutual responsibility and obligation of mutual aid, which is sweetening society by degrees amongst us to-day, but I believe that no Socialistic or other schemes for the regeneration of society which are not based on the Incarnation and Sacrifice of Jesus Christ will live and grow. There is but one power that will cast out natural selfishness, and that is love to Christ, apprehending His Cross as the great example to which our lives are to be conformed. I believe that the growing sense of brotherhood amongst us, even where it is not consciously connected with any faith in Christianity, is, to a very large extent, the result of the diffusion rough society of the spirit of Christianity, even its body is rejected. Thank God, the river ter of life can percolate through many a mile reach the roots of trees far away, in the whence

be sure of this: it is the law of Christ that will fight
and conquer the natural selfishness which makes bearing our brother's burdens an impossibility for men.
Only, Christian people! let us take care that we are not
robbed of our prerogative of being foremost in all such
things, by men whose zeal has a less heavenly source
than ours ought to have. Depend upon it, heresy has
less power to arrest the progress of the Church than
the selfish lives of Christian professors.

So, dear friends, let us see to it that we first of all
cast our own burdens on the Christ who is able to bear
them all, whatever they are. And then let us, with
lightened hearts and shoulders, make our own the
heavy burdens of sin, of sorrow, of care, of guilt,
of consequences, of responsibility, which are crushing
down many that are weary and heavy laden. For be
sure of this, if we do not bear our brother's burdens,
the load that we thought we had cast on Christ will
roll back upon ourselves. He is able to bear both us
and our burdens, if we will let Him, and if we will fulfil
that law of Christ which was illustrated in all His life,
'Who, though He was rich, yet for our sakes became
poor,' and was written large in letters of blood upon
that Cross where there was 'laid on Him the iniquity
of us all.'

DOING GOOD TO ALL

'As we have therefore opportunity, let us do good unto all . . .'—GAL. vi. 10.

'   have therefore'—that points a finger ba
        has gone before. The Apostle has
        ried well-doing, on the grou

the certain coming of the harvest season. Now, there
is a double link of connection between the preceding
words and our text; for 'do good' looks back to 'well-
doing,' and the word rendered 'opportunity' is the
same as that rendered 'season.' So, then, two thoughts
arise—'well-doing' includes doing good to others, and
is not complete unless it does. The future, on the
whole, is the season of reaping; the present life on
the whole is the season of sowing; and while life as
a whole is the seed-time, in detail it is full of opportunities, openings which make certain good deeds
possible, and which therefore impose upon us the obligation to do them. If we were in the habit of looking
on life mainly as a series of opportunities for well-
doing, how different it would be; and how different we
should be!

Now, this injunction is seen to be reasonable by
every man, whether he obeys it or not. It is a
commonplace of morality, which finds assent in all
consciences, however little it may mould lives. But I
wish to give it a particular application, and to try to
enforce its bearing upon Christian missionary work.
And the thought that I would suggest is just this, that
no Christian man discharges that elementary obligation of plain morality, if he is indifferent to this great
enterprise. 'As we have an opportunity, let us do good
to all.' That is the broad principle, and one applica-
n is the duty of Christian men to diffuse the Gospel
hout the world.

me ask you to look at the obligation that is

d w ing is the ler, and doing

that virtue which is self-regarding, the culture which
is mainly occupied with self, is lame and imperfect,
and there is a great gap in it, as if some cantle had
been cut out of the silver disc of the moon. It is only
full-orbed when in well-doing, and as a very large con-
stituent element of it, there is included the doing good
to others. That is too plain to need to be stated. We
hear a great deal to-day about altruism. Well, Christianity preaches that more emphatically than any other
system of thought, morals, or religion does. And
Christianity brings the mightiest motives for it, and
imparts the power by which obedience to that great
law that every man's conscience responds to is made
possible.

But whilst thus we recognise as a dictate of elementary morality that well-doing must necessarily include
doing good to others, and feel, as I suppose we all do
feel, when we are true to our deepest convictions, that
possessions of all sorts, material, mental, and all others,
are given to us in stewardship, and not in absolute
ownership, in order that God's grace in its various
forms may fructify through us to all, my present point
is that, if that is recognised as being what it is, an
elementary dictate of morality enforced by men's
relationships to one another, and sealed by their own
consciences, there is no getting away from the obligation upon all Christian men which it draws after it, of
each taking his share in the great work of imparting
the gospel to the whole world.

For that gospel is our highest good, the best thin
that we can carry to anybody. We many of
recognise the obligation that is devolved upon us
t   sion of wealth, to use it for others as we
           s. We recognise, many of us, the ob

tion that is devolved upon us by the possession of
knowledge, to impart it to others as well as ourselves.
We are willing to give of our substance, of our time,
of our effort, to impart much that we have. But some
of us seem to draw a line at the highest good that we
have, and whilst responding to all sorts of charitable
and beneficent appeals made to us, and using our
faculties often for the good of other people, we take
no share and no interest in communicating the highest
of all goods, the good which comes to the man in
whose heart Christ rests. It is our highest good,
because it deals with our deepest needs, and lifts us to
the loftiest position. The gospel brings our highest
good, because it brings eternal good, whilst all other
benefits fade and pass, and are left behind with life
and the dead flesh. It is our highest good, because if
that great message of salvation is received into a
heart, or moulds the life of a nation, it will bring after
it, as its ministers and results, all manner of material
and lesser benefit. And so, giving Christ we give *our*
best, and giving Christ we give the highest gift that a
weary world can receive.

Remember, too, that the impartation of this highest
good is one of the main reasons why we ourselves
possess it. Jesus Christ can redeem the world alone,
but it cannot become a redeemed world without the
help of His servants. He needs us in order to carry
into all humanity the energies that He brought into
the midst of mankind by His Incarnation and Sacrifice;
and the cradle of Bethlehem and the Cross of Cavalry
are not sufficient for the accomplishment of the purpose for which they respectively came to pass, without
the co-operation and ministry of Christian people. It
is, amongst others, that each of us who

have received that great gift into our hearts have been
enriched by it. The river is fed from the fountains of
the hills, in order that it may carry verdure and life
whithersoever it goes. And you and I have been
brought to the Cross of Christ, and made His disciples,
not only in order that we ourselves might be blessed
and quickened by the gift unspeakable, but in order
that through us it may be communicated, just as each
particle when leavened in the mass of the dough com-
municates its energy to its adjacent particle until the
whole is leavened.

I am afraid that indifference to the communication
of the highest good, which marks sadly too many
Christian professors in all ages, and in this age, is a
suspicious indication of a very slight realisation of the
good for themselves. Luther said that justification
was the article of a standing or a falling church. That
may be true in the region of theology, but in the region
of practical life I do not know that you will find a test
more reliable and more easy of application than this,
Does a man care for spreading amongst his fellows the
gospel that he himself has received? If he does not,
let him ask himself whether, in any real sense, he has
it. 'Well-doing' includes doing good to others, and
the possession of Christ will make it certain that we
shall impart Him.

II. Notice the bearing of this elementary injunction
upon the scope of the obligation.

'Let us do good to all men.' It was Christianity that
invented the word 'humanity'; either in its meaning
of the aggregate of men or its meaning of a gracio
a   le towards them. And it invented the w
        it revealed the thing on which it
        od' is the sequel of 'Fatherhood,' an

conception of mankind, beneath all diversities of race
and culture and the like, as being an organic whole,
knit together by a thousand mystical bands, and each
atom of which has connection with, and obligations to,
every other—that is a product of Christianity, however it may have been in subsequent ages divorced
from a recognition of its source.   So, then, the gospel
rises above all the narrow distinctions which call themselves patriotism and are parochial, and it says that
there is 'neither circumcision nor uncircumcision, Jew
nor Greek, Barbarian, Scythian, bond nor free,' but all
are one. Get high enough up upon the hill, and the
hedges between the fields are barely perceptible. Live
on the elevation to which the Gospel of Jesus Christ
lifts men, and you look down upon a great prairie,
without a fence or a ditch or a division. So my text
comes with profound significance, 'Let us do good to
all,' because all are included in the sweep of that great
purpose of love, and in the redeeming possibilities of
that great death on the Cross. Christ has swept the
compass, if I may say so, of His love and work all
round humanity; and are we to extend our sympathies
or our efforts less widely? The circle includes the
world; our sympathies should be as wide as the circle
that Christ has drawn.

Let me remind you, too, that only such a world-wide
communication of the highest good that has blessed
elves will correspond to the proved power of that
l which treats as of no moment diversities that
ial, and can grapple with and overcome,
f as a   n of   variety of

an exotic everywhere, because it came down from
heaven, but it can grow in all soils, and it can bring
forth fruit unto eternal life everywhere amongst mankind. So 'let us do good to all.'

And then we are met by the old objection, 'The eyes
of a fool are in the ends of the earth. Keep your
work for home, that wants it.' Well! I am perfectly
ready to admit that in Christian work, as in all others,
there must be division of labour, and that one man's
tastes and inclinations will lead him to one sphere and
one form of it; and another man's to another; and I
am quite ready, not to admit, but strongly to insist,
that, whatever happens, home is not to be neglected.
'All men' includes the slums in England as well as the
savages in Africa, and it is no excuse for neglecting
either of these departments that we are trying to do
something in the other. But it is not uncharitable to
say that the objection to which I am referring is most
often made by one or other of two classes, either by
people who do not care about the Gospel, nor recognise
the 'good' of it at all, or by people who are ingenious
in finding excuses for not doing the duty to which they
are at the moment summoned. The people that do
the one are the people that do the other. Where do
you get your money from for home work? Mainly
from the Christian Churches. Who is it that keeps
up missionary work abroad? Mainly the Christian
Churches. There is a vast deal of unreality in that
objection. Just think of the disproportion between
the embarrassment of riches in our Christian appli-
ances here in England and the destitution in these
d   nds. Here the ships are crammed into
            inst one another, rubbing their ya
            away out yonder on the w

there are leagues of loneliness, where never a sail is
seen. Here, at home, we are drenched with Christian
teaching, and the Churches are competing with each
other, often like rival tradespeople for their customers;
and away out yonder a man to half a million is considered a fair allowance. 'Let us do good to all.'

III. Lastly, note the bearing of this elementary precept on the occasions that rise for the discharge of the
duty.

'As we have opportunity.' As I have already said,
the Christian way to look at our circumstances is to
regard them as openings for the exercise of Christian
virtue, and therefore summonses to its discharge. And
if we regarded our own position individually, so we
should find that there were many, many doors that
had long been opened, into which we had been too
blind or too lazy, or too selfishly absorbed in our own
concerns, to enter. The neglected opportunities, the
beckoning doors whose thresholds we have never
crossed, the good that we might have done and have
not done — these are as weighty to sink us as the
positive sins, the opportunities for which have appealed
to our worse selves.

But I desire to say a word, not only about the opportunities offered to us individually, but about those
ffered to England for this great enterprise. The pro-
et of old represented the proud Assyrian conqueror
oasting, 'My hand hath gathered as a nest the
of the peoples . . . and there was none that
wing, or opened the mouth, or p ed.' It

given to us the wide dominion that we possess. I
know that England has not climbed to her place without many a crime, and that in her 'skirts is found the
blood of poor innocents,' but yet we have that connection, for good or for evil, with subject races all
over the earth. And I ask whether or not that is an
opportunity that the Christian Church is bound to
make use of. What have we been intrusted with it
for? Commerce, dominion, the impartation of Western
knowledge, literature, laws? Yes! Is that all? Are
you to send shirting and not the Gospel? Are you to
send muskets that will burst, and gin that is poison,
and not Christianity? Are you to send Shakespeare,
and Milton, and modern science, and Herbert Spencer,
and not Evangelists and the Gospels? Are you to
send the code of English law and not Christ's law of
love? Are you to send godless Englishmen, 'through
whom the name of God is blasphemed amongst the
Gentiles,' and are you not to send missionaries of the
Cross? A Brahmin once said to a missionary, 'Look
here! Your Book is a good Book. If you were as
good as your Book you would make India Christian in
ten years.'

Brethren! the European world to-day is fighting and
scrambling over what it calls the unclaimed corners of
the world; looking upon all lands that are uncivilised
by Western civilisation either as markets, or as parts
of their empire. Is there no other way of looking at
the heathen world than that? How did Christ look at
it? He was moved when He saw the multitudes as
'sheep having no shepherd.' Oh! if Christian men, as
members of this nation, would rise to the height of
the grace of vision, and would look at the world
, what a difference it would make!

appeal to you, Christian men and women, as members
of this nation, and therefore responsible, though it
may be infinitesimally, for what this nation is doing
in the distant corners of the world, and urge on you
that you are bound, so far as your influence goes, to
protest against the way of looking at these heathen
lands as existing to be exploited for the material
benefit of these Western Powers. You are bound to
lend your voice, however weak it may be, to the
protests against the savage treatment of native races
—against the drenching of China with narcotics, and
Africa with rum; to try to look at the world as Christ
looked at it, to rise to the height of that great vision
which regards all men as having been in His heart
when He died on the Cross, and refuses to recognise
in this great work ' Barbarian, Scythian, bond or free.'
We have awful responsibilities; the world is open to
us. We have the highest good. How shall we obey
this elementary principle of our text, unless we help as
we can in spreading Christ's reign? Blessed shall we
be if, and only if, we fill the seed-time with delightful
work, and remember that well-doing is imperfect unless it includes doing good to others, and that the best
good we can do is to impart the Unspeakable Gift to
the men that need it.

THE OWNER'S BRAND

'I bear in my body the marks of the Lord Jesus.'—GAL. vi. 17.

old times criminals, and certain classes of Temple servants, and sometimes soldiers, were also so marked, but it is most in accordance with the Apostle's way of thinking that he here has reference to the first class, and would represent himself as the *slave* of Jesus Christ, designated as His by the scars and weaknesses which were the consequences of his apostolic zeal. Imprisonment, beating by the Jewish rod, shipwrecks, fastings, weariness, perils, persecutions, all these he sums up in another place as being the tokens by which he was approved as an apostle of Jesus Christ. And here he, no doubt, has the same thought in his mind, that his bodily weakness, which was the direct issue of his apostolic work, showed that he was Christ's. The painful infirmity under which, as we learn, he was more especially suffering, about the time of writing this letter, may also have been in his mind.

All through this Epistle he has been thundering and lightning against the disputers of this apostolic authority. And now at last he softens, and as it were, bares his thin arm, his scarred bosom, and bids these contumacious Galatians look upon them, and learn that he has a right to speak as the representative and messenger of the Lord Jesus.

So we have here two or three points, I think, worth considering. First, think for a moment of the slave of Christ; then of the brands which mark the ownership; then of the glory in the servitude and the sign; and then of the immunity from human disturbances which that service gives. 'From henceforth let no man trouble me. I bear in my body the marks of the Lord J

a word or two about that concep

st.

It is a pity that our Bible has not rendered the
title which Paul ever gives himself at the beginning
of his letters, by that simple word 'slave,' instead of
the feebler one, 'servant.' For what he means when
he calls himself the 'servant of Jesus Christ' is not
that he bore to Christ the kind of relation which servants among us bear to those who have hired and paid
them, and to whom they have come under obligations
of their own will which they can terminate at any
moment by their own caprice; but that he was in the
roughest and simplest sense of the word, Christ's slave.

What lies in that metaphor? Well, it is the most
uncompromising assertion of the most absolute
authority on the one hand, and claim of unconditional
submission and subjection on the other.

The slave belonged to his master; the master could
do exactly as he liked with him. If he killed him
nobody had anything to say. He could set him to
any task; he could do what he liked with any little
possession or property that the slave seemed to have.
He could break all his relationships, and separate him
from wife and kindred.

All that is atrocious and blasphemous when it is
applied to the relations between man and man, but it
a blessed and magnificent truth when it is applied to
relations between a man and Christ. For this
has absolute authority over us, and He can do
likes with everything that belongs to us; and

which is blasphemous presumption when it is required
by a man, that which is impossible, in its deepest
reality, as between man and man, is possible, is blessed,
is joyful and strong when it is required by, and
rendered to, Jesus Christ. We are His slaves if we
have any living relationship to Him at all. Where,
then, in the Christian life, is there a place for self-will;
where a place for self-indulgence; where for murmuring or reluctance; where for the assertion of any rights
of my own as against that Master? We owe absolute
obedience and submission to Jesus Christ.

And what does the metaphor carry as to the basis
on which this authority rests? How did men acquire
slaves? Chiefly by purchase. The abominations of
the slave market are a blessed metaphor for the deep
realities of the Christian life. Christ has bought you
for His own. The only thing that gives a human soul
the right to have any true authority over another
human soul is that it shall have yielded itself to the
soul whom it would control. We must first of all give
ourselves away before we have the right to possess,
and the measure in which we give ourselves to another
is the measure in which we possess another. And so
Christ our Lord, according to the deep words of one of
Paul's letters, 'gives Himself for us, that He might
purchase unto Himself a people for His possession.'
'Ye are not your own; ye are bought with a
price.'

Therefore the absolute authority, and unconditional
surrender and submission which are the very essence
of the Christian life, at bottom are but the corre-
s   and twofold effects of one thing, and that
          there is no possession of man by man
          is based on love. And there

submission of man to man worth calling so except that which is also based therein.

'Thou hearts alone wouldst move;
Thou only hearts dost love.'

The relation in both its parts, on the side of the Master and on the side of the captive bondsman, is the direct result and manifestation of that love which knits them together.

Therefore the Christian slavery, with its abject submission, with its utter surrender and suppression of mine own will, with its complete yielding up of self to the control of Jesus, who died for me; because it is based upon His surrender of Himself to me, and in its inmost essence it is the operation of love, is therefore co-existent with the noblest freedom.

This great Epistle to the Galatians is the trumpet call and clarion proclamation of Christian liberty. The breath of freedom blows inspiringly through it all. The very spirit of the letter is gathered up in one of its verses, 'I have been called unto liberty,' and in its great exhortation, 'Stand fast therefore in the liberty wherewith Christ hath made you free.' It is then sufficiently remarkable and profoundly significant that in this very letter, which thus is the protest of the free Christian consciousness against all limitations and outward restrictions, there should be this most emphatic declaration that the liberty of the Christian ... ery and the slavery of the Christian is freedom.

loosed my bands.' 'I bear in my body' the charter of my liberty, for I bear in my body the 'brand of the Lord Jesus.'

II. And so now a word in the next place about these marks of ownership.

As I have said, the Apostle evidently means thereby distinctly the bodily weaknesses, and possibly diseases, which were the direct consequences of his own apostolic faithfulness and zeal. He considered that he proved himself to be a minister of God by his stripes, imprisonments, fastings, by all the pains and sufferings and their permanent consequences in an enfeebled constitution, which he bore because he had preached the Cross of Christ. He knew that these things were the result of his faithful ministry. He believed that they had been sent by no blundering, blind fate; by no mere secondary causes; but by his Master Himself, whose hand had held the iron that branded into the hissing flesh the marks of His ownership. He felt that by means of these he had been drawn nearer to his Master, and the ownership had been made more perfect. And so in a rapture of contempt of pain, this heroic soul looks upon even bodily weakness and suffering as being the signs that he belonged to Christ, and the means of that possession being made more perfect.

Now, what is all that to us Christian people who have no persecutions to endure, and none of whom I am afraid have ever worked hard enough for Christ to have damaged our health by it? Is there anything in this text that may be of general application to us all? Yes! I think so. Every Christian man or woman ought to bear, in his or her body, in a plain, literal sense, the tokens that he or she belongs to Je

Christ. You ask me how? 'If thy foot or thine hand offend thee, cut it off, and cast it from thee.'

There are things in your physical nature that you have to suppress; that you have always to regulate and coerce; that you have sometimes entirely to cast away and to do without, if you mean to be Jesus Christ's at all. The old law of self-denial, of subduing the animal nature, its passions, appetites, desires, is as true and as needful to-day as it ever was; and for us all it is essential to the loftiness and purity of our Christian life that our animal nature and our fleshly constitution should be well kept down under heel and subdued. As Paul himself said in another place, 'I bring under my body, and I keep it in subjection, lest by any means I should myself, having proclaimed to others the laws of the contest, be rejected from the prize.' Oh, you Christian men and women! if you are not living a life of self-denial, if you are not crucifying the flesh, with its affections and lusts, if you are not bearing 'about in the body the dying of the Lord Jesus, that the life also of Christ may be manifested in your mortal body,' what tokens are there that you are Christ's slaves at all?

Then, besides this, we may expand the thought even further, and say that, in a very real sense, all the pains and sorrows and disappointments and afflictions that mainly touch our mortal part should be taken by us as, and made by us to be, the tokens that we belong to the Master.

But it is not only in limitations and restrictions and self-denials and pains that Christ's ownership of us ought to be manifested in our daily lives, and so by means of our mortal bodies, but if there be in our hearts a deep indwelling possession of the grace and

sweetness of Christ, it will make itself visible, ay! even
in our faces, and 'beauty born of' our communion
with Him 'shall pass into' and glorify even rugged
and care-lined countenances. There may be, and there
ought to be, in all Christian people, manifestly visible
the tokens of the indwelling serenity of the indwelling
Christ. And it should not be left to some moment of
rapture at the end of life, for men to look upon us, to
behold our faces, ' as it had been the face of an angel,'
but by our daily walk, by our countenances full of a
removed tranquillity, and a joy that rises from within,
men ought to take knowledge of us that we have been
with Jesus, and it should be the truth—I bear in my
body the tokens of His possession.

III. Now, once more notice the glorying in the
slavery and its signs.

' I bear,' says Paul; and he uses, as many of you may
know, a somewhat remarkable word, which does not
express mere bearing in the sense of toleration and
patient endurance, although that is much; nor mere
bearing in the sense of carrying, but implies bearing
with a certain triumph as men would do who, coming
back victorious from conflict, and being received into
the city, were proud to show their scars, the honourable signs of their courage and constancy. So, with a
triumph that is legitimate, the Apostle solemnly and
proudly bears before men the marks of the Lord
Jesus. Just as he says in another place :—'Thanks be
unto God, which always leadeth us about in triumph
in Jesus Christ.' He was proud of being dragged
the conqueror's chariot wheels, chained to them by th
cords of love; and so he was proud of being the sl
of Christ.

It   dation to a man to yield abject su

sion, unconditional service to another man. It is the highest honour of our natures so to bow before that dear Lord. To prostrate ourselves to Him is to lift ourselves high in the scale of being. The King's servant is every other person's master. And he that feels that he is Christ's, may well be, not proud but conscious, of the dignity of belonging to such a Lord. The monarch's livery is a sign of honour. In our old Saxon kingdom the king's menials were the first nobles. So it is with us. The aristocracy of humanity are the slaves of Jesus Christ.

And let us be proud of the marks of the branding iron, whether they come in the shape of sorrows and pains, or otherwise. It is well that we should have to carry these. It is blessed, and a special mark of the Master's favour that He should think it worth His while to mark us as His own, by any sorrow or by any pain. Howsoever hot may be the iron, and howsoever deeply it may be pressed by His firm, steady, gentle hand upon the quivering flesh and the shrinking heart, let us be thankful if He, even by it, impresses on us the manifest tokens of ownership. Oh, brethren! if we could come to look upon sorrows and losses with this clear recognition of their source, meaning and purpose, they change their nature, the paradox is fulfilled that we do 'gather grapes of thorns and figs thistles.' 'I bear in my body,' with a solemn tri- h and patient hope, 'the marks of the Lord Jesus.'

d now, lastly, the immunity from any dis-
men can bring which

give him a sacredness in their eyes; that henceforth
there should be no rebellion against his teaching and
his word.   We may expand the thought to apply more
to ourselves, and say that, in the measure in which we
belong to Christ, and bear the marks of His possession
of us, in that measure are we free from the disturbance
of earthly influences and of human voices; and from
all the other sources of care and trouble, of perturba-
tion and annoyance, which harass and vex other men's
spirits.   'Ye are bought with a price,' says Paul elsewhere.   'Be not the servants of men.'   Christ is your
Master; do not let men trouble you.   Take your
orders from Him; let men rave as they like.   Be
content to be approved by Him; let men think of you
as they please.   The Master's smile is life, the Master's
frown is death to the slave; what matters it what
other people may say?   'He that judgeth me is the
Lord.'   So keep yourselves above the cackle of 'public
opinion'; do not let your creed be crammed down
your throats even by a consensus of however venerable and grave human teachers.   Take your directions
from your Master, and pay no heed to other voices if
they would command.   Live to please Him, and do
not care what other people think.   You are Christ's
servant; 'let no man trouble' you.

And so it should be about all the distractions and
petty annoyances that disturb human life and harass
our hearts.   A very little breath of wind will ruffle all
the surface of a shallow pond, though it would swee
across the deep sea and produce no effect.   Deep
your natures by close union with Christ, and absolu
submission to Him, and there will be a great calm
d cares and sorrows, and all the exte
ty, far away, down there beneath

feet, will 'show scarce so gross as beetles,' whilst you
stand upon the high cliff and look down upon them
all. 'From henceforth no man shall trouble me.' 'I
bear in my body the marks of the Lord Jesus.'

My brother! Whose marks do you bear? There are
only two masters. If an eye that could see things as
they are, were to go through this congregation, whose
initials would it discern in your faces? There are
some of us, I have no doubt, who in a very horrid
sense bear in our bodies the marks of the idol that we
worship. Men who have ruined their health by
dissipation and animal sensualism—are there any of
them here this morning? Are there none of us whose
faces, whose trembling hands, whose diseased frames,
are the tokens that they belong to the flesh and the
world and the devil? Whose do *you* bear?

Oh! when one looks at all the faces that pass one
upon the street—this all drawn with avarice and
earthly-mindedness; that all bloated with self-indulgence and loose living—when one sees the mean faces,
the passionate faces, the cruel faces, the vindictive
faces, the lustful faces, the worldly faces, one sees how
many of us bear in our bodies the marks of *another*
lord. They have no rest day nor night who worship
the beast; and whosoever receiveth the mark of his
name.

I pray you, yield yourselves to your true Lord, so on
you may bear the beginnings of the likeness
ps you His, and hereafter
ll do

PHILIPPIANS

LOVING GREETINGS

'Paul and Timothy, servants of Christ Jesus, to all the saints in Christ Jesus which are at Philippi, with the bishops and deacons: 2. Grace to you and peace from God our Father and the Lord Jesus Christ. 3. I thank my God upon all my remembrance of you, 4. Always in every supplication of mine on behalf of you all making my supplication with joy, 5. For your fellowship in furtherance of the gospel from the first day until now; 6. Being confident of this very thing, that He which began a good work in you will perfect it until the day of Jesus Christ: 7. Even as it is right for me to be thus minded on behalf of you all, because I have you in my heart, inasmuch as, both in my bonds and in the defence and confirmation of the gospel, ye all are partakers with me of grace. 8. For God is my witness, how I long after you all in the tender mercies of Christ Jesus.'– PHIL. i. 1-8 (R.V.).

THE bond between Paul and the church at Philippi was peculiarly close. It had been founded by himself, as is narrated at unusual length in the book of Acts. It was the first church established in Europe. Ten years had elapsed since then, possibly more. Paul is now a prisoner in Rome, not suffering the extremest rigour of imprisonment, but still a prisoner in his own hired house, accessible to his friends and able to do work for God, but still in the custody of soldiers, chained and waiting till the tardy steps of Roman law should come up to him, or perhaps till the caprice of Nero should deign to hear his cause. In that imprisonment we have his letters to the Philippians, Ephesians, Colossians, and Philemon, which latter three are closely connected in time, the two former in subject, and the latter in destination. This letter stands apart from the great Asiatic churches.

Its tone and general cast are unlike those of most of his letters. It contains no doctrinal discussions and no rebukes of evil, but is an outpouring of happy love and confidence. Like all Paul's epistles it begins with salutations, and like most of them with prayer, but from the very beginning is a long gush of love. These early verses seem to me very beautiful if we regard them either as a revelation of the personal character of the Apostle, or as a picture of the relation between teacher and taught in its most blessed and undisturbed form, or as a lovely ideal of friendship and love in any relation, hallowed and solemnised by Christian feeling.

Verses one and two contain the apostolic greeting. In it we note the senders. Timothy is associated with Paul, according to his custom in all his letters even when he goes on immediately to speak in the singular. He ever sought to hide his own supremacy and to bring his friends into prominence. He was a great, lowly soul, who had no pride in the dignity of his position but felt the weight of its responsibility and would fain have had it shared. He calls Timothy and himself the slaves of Christ. He regarded it as his highest honour to be Christ's born servant, bound to absolute submission to the all-worthy Lord who had died to win him. It is to be noted that there is no reference here to apostolic authority, and the contrast is very remarkable in this respect with the Epistle to the Galatians, where with nful emphasis he asserts it as bestowed 'not from ither through man, but through Jesus Christ the Father.' In this desi but rather personally. There is a similar omission in Philemon and a pathetic substitution there of the 'prisoner of Jesus Christ' for the 'slave of Christ Jesus.'

The persons addressed are 'all the saints in Christ Jesus.' As he had not called himself an apostle, so he does not call them a church. He will not lose in an abstraction the personal bond which unites them. They are saints, which is not primarily a designation of moral purity, but of consecration to God, from whom indeed purity flows. The primitive meaning of the word is *separation*; the secondary meaning is *holiness*, and the connection between these two meanings contains a whole ethical philosophy. They are saints in Christ Jesus; union with Him is the condition both of consecration and of purity.

The Philippian community had an organisation primitive but sufficient. We do not enter on the discussion of its two offices further than to note that the bishops are evidently identical with the elders, in the account in Acts **xx.** of Paul's parting with the Ephesian Christians, where the same persons are designated by both titles, as is also the case in Titus i. 5 and 7; the one name (elder) coming from the Hebrew and designating the office on the side of dignity, the other (bishop) being of Greek origin and representing it in terms of function. We note that there were several elders then in the Philippian church, and that their place in the salutation negatives the idea of hierarchical supremacy.

The benediction or prayer for grace and peace is couched in the form which it assumes in all Paul's letters. It blends Eastern and Western forms of greeting, 'Grace' being the Greek and 'Peace' the Hebrew form of salutation. So Christ fuses and fulfils th w   s. The grace which He gives is the

imparting love of God, the peace which He gives is its
consequence, and the salutation is an unmistakable
evidence of Paul's belief in Christ's divinity.

This salutation is followed by a great burst of
thankful love, for the full apprehension of which we
must look briefly at the details of these verses. We
have first Paul's thankfulness in all his remembrance
of the Philippians, then he further defines the times of
his thankfulness as 'always in every supplication of
mind on behalf of you all making my supplication with
joy.' His gratitude for them is expressed in all his
prayers which are all thank-offerings. He never thinks
of them nor prays for them without thanking God for
them. Then comes the reason for his gratitude—their
fellowship in furtherance of the gospel, from the first
day when Lydia constrained him to come into her
house, until this moment when now at the last their care
of him had flourished again. The Revised Version's
rendering 'fellowship in furtherance of' instead of
'fellowship in' conveys the great lesson which the
other rendering obscures—that the true fellowship is
not in enjoyment but in service, and refers not so
much to a common participation in the blessedness as
in the toils and trials of Christian work. This is
apparent in an immediately following verse where the
Philippians' fellowship with Christ is again spoken of
consisting in sharing both in His bonds and in the
le work of defending the gospel from gainsayers
positively proclaiming it. Very beautifully in
ion does he designate that wor   toil

thanksgivings. And such confidence becomes him because he has them in his heart, and 'love hopeth all things' and delights to believe in and anticipate all good concerning its object. He has them in his heart because they faithfully share with him his honourable, blessed burdens. But that is not all, it is 'in the tender mercies' of Christ that he loved them. His love is the love of Christ in him; his being is so united to Jesus that his heart beats with the same emotion as throbs in Christ's, and all that is merely natural and of self in his love is changed into a solemn participation in the great love which Christ has to them. This, then, being the general exposition of the words, let us now dwell for a little while on the broad principles suggested by them.

I. Participation in the work of Christ is the noblest basis for love and friendship.

Paul had tremendous courage and yet hungered for sympathy. He had no outlets for his love but his fellow Christians. There had, no doubt, been a wrenching of the ties of kindred when he became a Christian, and his love, dammed back and restrained, had to pour itself on his brethren.

The Church is a workshop, not a dormitory, and every Christian man and woman is bound to help in the common cause. These Philippians help Paul by sympathy and gifts, indeed, but by their own direct work as well, and things are not right with us unless leaders can say, 'Ye all are partakers of my grace.' There are other real and sweet bonds of love and friendship, but the most real and sweetest is to be found in our common relation to Jesus Christ and in our co-opera tion in the work which is ours because it is His

II. Thankful, glad prayer flows from such co-opera·
tion.

The prisoner in his bonds in the alien city had the
remembrance of his friends coming into his chamber
like fresh, cool air, or fragrance from far-off gardens. A
thrill of gladness was in his soul as often as he thought
on them.   It is blessed if in our experience teacher
and taught are knit together thus; without some such
bond of union no good will be done.   The relation of
pastor and people is so delicate and spiritual, the
purpose of it so different from that of mere teaching,
the laws of it so informal and elastic, the whole power
of it, therefore, so dependent on sympathy and mutual
kindliness that, unless there be something like the bond
which united Paul and the Philippians, there will be
no prosperity or blessing. The thinnest film of cloud
prevents deposition of dew.   If all men in pulpits could
say what Paul said of the Philippians, and all men in
pews could deserve to have it said of them, the world
would feel the power of a quickened Church.

III. Confidence is born of love and common service.

Paul delights to think that God will go on because
God has already begun a good work in them, and Paul
delights to think of their perfection because he loves
them.   'God is not a man that He should lie, or the
son of man that He should repent.'   His past is the
guarantee for His future; what He begins He finishes.

IV. Our love is hallowed and greatened in the love
Christ.

lived, yet not he, but Christ lived in him.   It is
tration of the principle of his being th
of

the true consecration of love when we live and love in
the Lord; when we will as Christ does, think as He
does, love as He does, when the mind that was in Christ
Jesus was in us. It is needful to guard against the
intrusion of mere human affection and regard into our
sacred relations in the Church; it is needful to guard
against it in our own personal love and friendship.
Let us see that we ourselves know and believe the love
wherewith Christ hath loved us, and then let us see
that that love dwells in us informing and hallowing
our hearts, making them tender with His great tenderness, and turning all the water of our earthly affections
into the new wine of His kingdom. Let the law for
our hearts, as well as for our minds and wills, be 'I live,
yet not I but Christ liveth in me.'

A COMPREHENSIVE PRAYER

'And this I pray, that your love may abound yet more and more in knowledge
and all discernment; 10. So that ye may approve the things that are excellent;
that ye may be sincere and void of offence unto the day of Christ; 11. Being
filled with the fruits of righteousness, which are through Jesus Christ, unto the
glory and praise of God.'—PHIL. i. 9-11 (R.V.).

WHAT a blessed friendship is that of which the natural
language is prayer! We have many ways, thank God,
of showing our love and of helping one another, but
the best way is by praying for one another. All that
is selfish and low is purged out of our hearts in the act,
suspicions and doubts fade away when we pray for
those whom we love. Many an alienation would have
melted like morning mists if it had been prayed about,
added tenderness and delicacy come to our friendship
so like the bloom on ripening grapes. We may t
is simple criterion—Can we pray

them? If not, should we have them? Are they blessings to us or to others?

This prayer, like all those in Paul's epistles, is wonderfully full. His deep affection for, and joy in, the Philippian church breathes in every word of it. Even his jealous watchfulness saw nothing in them to desire but progress in what they possessed. Such a desire is the highest that love can frame. We can wish nothing better for one another than growth in the love of God. Paul's estimate of the highest good of those who were dearest to him was that they should be more and more completely filled with the love of God and with its fruits of holiness and purity, and what was his supreme desire for the Philippians is the highest purpose of the gospel for us all, and should be the aim of our effort and longing, dominating all others as some sovereign mountain peak towers above the valleys. Looking then at this prayer as containing an outline of true progress in the Christian life, we may note:

I. The growth in keenness of conscience founded on growth in love.

Paul does not merely desire that their love may abound, but that it may become more and more 'rich in knowledge and all discernment.' The former is perhaps accurate knowledge, and the latter the application of it. 'Discernment' literally means 'sense,' and here, of course, when employed about spiritual and moral it means the power of apprehending good and . It is, I suppose, sub

that differ.' It is a process of discrimination and testing that is meant, which is, I think, fairly represented
by the more modern expression which I have used—
keenness of conscience.

I need spend little time in remarking on the absolute
need of such a process of discrimination. We are surrounded by temptations to evil, and live in a world
where maxims and principles not in accordance with
the gospel abound. Our own natures are but partially
sanctified. The shows of things must be tested.
Apparent good must be proved. The Christian life is
not merely to unfold itself in peace and order, but
through conflict. We are not merely to follow impulses,
or to live as angels do, who are above sin, or as animals
do who are beneath it. When false coin is current it
is folly to accept any without a test. All around us
there is glamour, and so within us there is need for
careful watchfulness and quick discrimination.

This keenness of conscience follows on the growth of
love. Nothing makes a man more sensitive to evil
than a hearty love to God. Such a heart is keener to
discern what is contrary to its love than any ethical
maxims can make it. A man who lives in love will be
delivered from the blinding influence of his own evil
tastes, and a heart steadfast in love will not be swayed
by lower temptations. Communion with God will,
from its very familiarity with Him, instinctively discern the evil of evil, as a man coming out of pure air
is conscious of vitiated atmosphere which those who
dwell in it do not perceive. It used to be said th
Venice glass would shiver into fragments if poison w
poured into the cup. As evil spirits were suppose
by the presence of an innocent child
he ugly shapes that sometimes t

us by assuming fair disguises will be shown in their native hideousness when confronted with a heart filled with the love of God.

Such keenness of judgment is capable of indefinite increase. Our consciences should become more and more sensitive: we should always be advancing in our discovery of our own evils, and be more conscious of our sins, the fewer we have of them. Twilight in a chamber may reveal some foul things, and the growing light will disclose more. 'Secret faults' will cease to be secret when our love abounds more and more in knowledge, and in all discernment.

II. The purity and completeness of character flowing from this keenness of conscience.

The Apostle desires that the knowledge which he asks for his Philippian friends may pass over into character, and he describes the sort of men which he desires them to be in two clauses, 'sincere and void of offence' being the one, 'filled with the fruits of right-eousness' being the other. The former is perhaps pre-dominantly negative, the latter positive. That which is sincere is so because when held up to the light it shows no flaws, and that which is without offence is so because the stones in the path have been cleared away by the power of discrimination, so that there is no stumbling. The life which discerns keenly will bring forth the fruit which consists of righteousness, and ⟨tha⟩t fruit is to fill the whole nature so that no part ⟨can⟩ be without it.

⟨Nothing⟩ lower than this is the lofty standard towards ⟨which the Ch⟩ristian ⟨life⟩ is to ai⟨m an⟩d to ⟨w⟩hich it ⟨c⟩an no flaws in the weaving, and no threads dropped or broken. There must also be the actual presence of positive righteousness filling life in all its parts. That lofty standard is pressed upon us by a solemn motive, 'unto the day of Christ.' We are ever to keep before us the thought that in that coming day all our works will be made manifest, and that all of them should be done, so that when we have to give account of them we shall not be ashamed.

The Apostle takes it for granted here that if the Philippian Christians know what is right and what is wrong, they will immediately choose and do the right. Is he forgetting the great gulf between knowledge and practice? Not so, but he is strong in the faith that love needs only to know in order to do. The love which abounds more and more in knowledge and in all discernment will be the soul of obedience, and will delight in fulfilling the law which it has delighted in beholding. Other knowledge has no tendency to lead to practice, but this knowledge which is the fruit of love has for its fruit righteousness.

III. The great Name in which this completeness is secured.

The Apostle's prayer dwells not only on the way by which a Christian life may increase itself, but in its close reaches the yet deeper thought that all that growth comes 'through Jesus Christ.' He is the Giver of it all, so that we are not so much called to a painful toil as to a glad reception. Our love fills us with the fruits of righteousness, because it takes all these from His hands. It is from His gift that conscience derive its sensitiveness. It is by His inspiration that co s becomes strong enough to determine act our dull hearts are quickened into a

of desiring to have in our lives, the law of the spirit of
life, that was in Christ Jesus, and to make our own all
that we see in Him of 'things that are lovely and of
good report.'

The prayer closes with a reference to the highest
end of all our perfecting—the glory and praise of God;
the former referring rather to the transcendent
majesty of God in itself, and the latter to the exaltation of it by men.   The highest glory of God comes
from the gradual increase in redeemed men's likeness
to Him.   They are 'the secretaries of His praise,' and
some portion of that great honour and responsibility
lies on each of us.   If all Christian men were what
they all might be and should be, swift and sure in their
condemnation of evil and loyal fidelity to conscience,
and if their lives were richly hung with ripened clusters
of the fruits of righteousness, the glory of God would
be more resplendent in the world, and new tongues
would break into praise of Him who had made men so
like Himself.

A PRISONER'S TRIUMPH

'Now I would have you know, brethren, that the things which happened unto
me have fallen out rather unto the progress of the gospel; 13. So that my
bonds became manifest in Christ throughout the whole praetorian guard, and to
all the rest; 14. And that most of the brethren in the Lord, being confident through
my bonds, are more abundantly bold to speak the word of God without fear.
15. Some indeed preach Christ even of envy and strife; and some also of good
w   : 16. The one do it of love, knowing that I am set for the defence of the
el: 17. But the other proclaim Christ of faction, not sincerely, thinking to
p affliction for me in my bonds. 18. What then? only that in every way,
r in pretence or in truth, Christ is proclaimed; and th   I rejoice, yea,
ice. 19. For I know that this sha   turn to
n and   e supply of the Spirit o

interpenetration of his whole nature with his religion.
His theology was but the generalisation of his experience. He has felt and verified all that he has to say.
But the personal experiences of this sunny letter to his
favourite church have a character all their own. In
that atmosphere of untroubled love and sympathy a
shyer heart than Paul's would have opened: his does so
in tenderness, gladness, and trust. We have here the
unveiling of his inmost self in response to what he
knew would be an eager desire for news of his welfare.
This whole section appears to me to be a wonderful
revelation of his prison thoughts, an example of what
we may call the ennobling power of a passionate
enthusiasm for Christ. Remember that he is a
prisoner, shut out from his life's work, waiting to be
tried before Nero, whose reign had probably, by this
time, passed from its delusive morning of dewy promise
to its lurid noon. The present and the future were
dark for him, and yet in spite of them all comes forth
this burst of undaunted courage and noble gladness.
We simply follow the course of the words as they lie,
and we find in them,

I. An absorbing purpose which bends all circumstances to its service and values them only as
instruments.

The things which happened unto me; that is Paul's
minimising euphemism for the grim realities of imprisonment, or perhaps for some recent ominous turns in
his circumstances. To him they are not worth dwelling on further, nor is their personal incidence worth
taking into account; the only thing which is important
is to say how these things have affected his life's work.
It is enough for him, and he believes that it will be
en even for his loving friends at Philippi to kn

that, instead of their being as they might have feared, and as he sometimes when he was faithless expected, hindrances to his work, they have turned out rather to 'the furtherance of the gospel.' Whether he has been comfortable or not is a matter of very small importance, the main thing is that Christ's work has been helped, and then he goes on to tell two ways in which his imprisonment had conduced to this end.

'My bonds became manifest in Christ.' It has been clearly shown why I was a prisoner; all the Prætorian guard had learned what Paul was there for. We know from Acts that he was 'suffered to abide by himself with the soldier that kept him.' He has no word to say of the torture of compulsory association, night and day, with the rude legionaries, or of the horrors of such a presence in his sweetest, sacredest moments of communion with his Lord. These are all swallowed up in the thought as they were in the fact, that each new guard as he came to sit there beside Paul was a new hearer, and that by this time he must have told the story of Christ and His love to nearly the whole corps. That is a grand and wonderful picture of passionate earnestness and absorbed concentration in one pursuit. Something of the same sort is in all pursuits, the condition of success and the sure result of real interest. We have all to be specialists if we would succeed in any calling. The river that spreads wide ... s slow, and if it is to have a scour in its current it ... be kept between high banks. We have to bring ... to a point and to see that the p...nt is ...d-... ...an to bore with it. ...

scholar, the craftsman, all need to take for their motto 'This one thing I do.' I suppose that a man would not be able to make a good button unless he confined himself to button-making. We see round us abundant examples of men who, for material aims and almost instinctively, use all circumstances for one end and appraise them according to their relations to that, and they are quoted as successful, and held up to young souls as patterns to be imitated. Yes! But what about the man who does the same in regard to Christ and His work? Is he thought of as an example to be imitated or as a warning to be avoided? Is not the very same concentration when applied to Christian work and living thought to be fanatical, which is welcomed with universal applause when it is directed to lower pursuits? The contrast of our eager absorption in worldly things and of the ease with which any fluttering butterfly can draw us away from the path which leads us to God, ought to bring a blush to all cheeks and penitence to all hearts. There was no more obligation on Paul to look at the circumstances of his life thus than there is on every Christian to do so. We do not desire that all should be apostles, but the Apostle's temper and way of looking at 'the things which happened unto' him should be our way of looking at the things which happen unto us. We shall estimate them rightly, and as God estimates them, only when we estimate them according to their power to serve our souls and to further Christ's kingdom.

II. The magnetism or contagion of enthusiasm.

The second way by which Paul's circumstance furthered the gospel was 'that most of the breth being confident through my bonds, are more abunda bold to speak the word of God.' His constancy courage stirred them up. Moved by good-will and love, they were heartened to preach because they saw in him one 'appointed by God for the defence of the gospel.' A soul all on flame has power to kindle others. There is an old story of a Scottish martyr whose constancy at the stake touched so many hearts that 'a merry gentleman' said to Cardinal Beaton, 'If ye burn any more you should burn them in low cellars, for the reek (smoke) of Mr. Patrick Hamilton has infected as many as it blew upon.'

It is not only in the case of martyrs that enthusiasm is contagious. However highly we may estimate the impersonal forces that operate for 'the furtherance of the gospel' we cannot but see that in all ages, from the time of Paul down to to-day, the main agents for the spread of the gospel have been individual souls all aflame with the love of God in Christ Jesus and filled with the life of His Spirit. The history of the Church has largely consisted in the biographies of its saints, and every great revival of religion has been the flame kindled round a flaming heart. Paul was impelled by his own love; the brethren in Rome were in a lower state as only reflecting his, and it ought to be the prerogative of every Christian to be a centre and source of kindling influence rather than a mere recipient of it. It is a question which may well be asked by each of about ourselves—would anybody find quickening to divine life and Christian service coming or do we simply serve to keep others' coldness ce? It was said of old of Jesus Christ, been plunged into ice-cold water than into fire, and their coldness is as contagious as Paul's radiant enthusiasm was. Let us try, for our parts, to radiate out the warmth of the love of God, that it may kindle in others the flame which it has lighted in ourselves, and not be like icebergs floating southwards and bringing down the temperature of even the very temperate seas in which we find ourselves.

III. The wide tolerance of such enthusiasm.

It is stigmatised as 'narrow,' which to-day is the sin of sins, but it is broad with the true breadth. Such enthusiasm lifts a man high enough to see over many hedges and to be tolerant even of intolerance, and of the indifference which tolerates everything but earnestness. Paul here deals with a class amongst the Roman Christians who were 'preaching of envy and strife,' with the malicious calculation that so they would annoy him and 'add affliction' to his bonds. It is generally supposed that these were Judaising Christians against whom Paul fulminates in all his letters, but I confess that, notwithstanding the arguments of authoritative commentators, I cannot believe that they are the same set of men preaching the same doctrines which in other places he treats as destructive of the whole gospel. The change of tone is so great as to require the supposition of a change of subjects, and the Judaisers with whom the Apostle waged a never-ending warfare, never did evangelistic work amongst the heathen as these men seem to have done, but confined themselves to trying to pervert conve already made. It was not their message but th spirit that was faulty. With whatever purpose annoyance they were animated, they did 'p Paul superbly brushes aside all tha antagonistic to him personally, in his triumphant recognition that the one thing needful *was* spoken, even from unworthy motives and with a malicious purpose. The situation here revealed, strange though it appears with our ignorance of the facts, is but too like much of what meets us still. Do we not know denominational rivalries which infuse a bitter taint of envy and strife into much evangelistic earnestness, and is the spectacle of a man preaching Christ with a taint of sidelong personal motives quite unknown to this day? We may press the question still more closely home and ask ourselves if we are entirely free from the influence of such a spirit. No man who knows himself and has learned how subtly lower motives blend themselves with the highest will be in haste to answer these questions with an unconditional ' No,' and no man who looks on the sad spectacle of competing Christian communities and knows anything of the methods of competition that are in force, will venture to deny that there are still those who preach Christ of envy and strife.

It comes, then, to be a testing question for each of us, have we learned from Paul this lesson of tolerance, which is not the result of cold indifference, but the outcome of fiery enthusiasm and of a clear recognition of the one thing needful? Granted that there is preaching from unworthy motives and modes of work which offend our tastes and prejudices, and that there ypes of evangelistic earnestness which have errors up with them, are we inclined to say 'Never- ist is proclaimed, and therein I rejoice, Yea, '? Much chaff may be blended with the carelessness which comes from languid indifference. The one does not mind what a man preaches because it has no belief in any of the things preached, and to it one thing is as good as another, and none are of any real consequence. The other proceeds from a passionate belief that the one thing which sinful men need to hear is the great message that Christ has lived and died for them, and therefore, it puts all else on one side and cares nothing for jangling notes that may come in, if only above them the music of His name sounds out clear and full.

IV. The calm fronting of life and death as equally magnifying Christ.

The Apostle is sure that all the experiences of his prison will turn to his ultimate salvation, because he is sure that his dear friends in Philippi will pray for him, and that through their prayers he will receive a 'supply of the Spirit of Jesus Christ,' which shall be enough to secure his steadfastness. His expectation is not that he will escape from prison or from martyrdom, both of which stand only too clearly before him, but that whatever may be waiting for him in the future, 'all boldness' will be granted him, so that whether he lives he will live to the Lord, or whether he dies, he will die to the Lord. He had so completely accepted it as his life's purpose to magnify Jesus, that the extremest possible changes of condition came to be insignificant to him. He had what we may have, the true anæsthetic which will give us a 'solemn scorn of ills' and make even the last and greatest change from life death of little account. If we magnify Christ in lives with the same passionate earnestness and c absorption as Paul had, our lives like ll-laid rails will enter upon the b across the valley with scarce a jolt. With whatever differences—and the differences are to us tremendous— the same purpose will be pursued in life and in death, and they who, living, live to the praise of Christ, dying will magnify Him as their last act in the body which they leave. What was it that made possible such a passion of enthusiasm for a man whom Paul had never seen in the flesh ? What changed the gloomy fuliginous fanaticism of the Pharisee, at whose feet were laid the clothes of the men who stoned Stephen, into this radiant light, all aflame with a divine splendour ? The only answer is in Paul's own words, 'He loved me and gave Himself for me.' That answer is as true for each of us as it was for him. Does it produce in us anything like the effects which it produced in him ?

A STRAIT BETWIXT TWO

To me to live is Christ, and to die is gain. 22. But if I live in the flesh, this is the fruit of my labour : yet what I shall choose I wot not. 23. For I am in a strait betwixt two, having a desire to depart, and to be with Christ ; which is far better : 24. Nevertheless to abide in the flesh is more needful for you. 25. And having this confidence, I know that I shall abide and continue with you all for your furtherance and joy of faith.'—PHIL. i. 21-25.

A PREACHER may well shrink from such a text. Its elevation of feeling and music of expression make all sermons on it sound feeble and harsh, like some poor shepherd's pipe after an organ. But, though this be true, it may not be useless to attempt, at least, to point the course of thought in these grand words. They are a great river, which springs at first with a from some deep cave, then is torn and chafed we have the clear, unhesitating statement of the comparative advantages of life and death to a Christian man, when thought of as affecting himself alone. The one is Christ, the other gain. But we neither live nor die to ourselves; and no man has a right to think of life or death only from the point of view of his own advantage. So the problem is not so simple as it looked. Life here is the condition of fruitful labour here. There are his brethren and his work to think of. These bring him to a stand, and check the rising wish. He knows not which state to prefer. The stream is dammed back between rocks, and it chafes and foams and seems to lose its way among them. Then comes a third bend in the flow of thought and feeling, and he gladly apprehends it as his present duty to remain at his work. If his own joy is thereby less, his brethren's will be more. If he is not to depart and be with Christ, he will remain and be with Christ's friends, which is, in some sort, being with Him too. If he may not have the gain of death, he will have the fruit of work in life.

Let us try to fill up, somewhat, this meagre outline of the warm stream that pours through these great words.

I. The simplicity of the comparison between life and death to a Christian thinking of himself alone.

'To me' is plainly emphatic. It means more than 'in my judgment' or even 'in my case.' It is equal to 'To me personally, if I stood alone, and had no one to consider but myself.' 'To live' refers mainly here to outward practical life of service, and 'to die' shoul perhaps, rather be 'to be dead,' referring, not to t solution, but to the state after; not to e er, but to the palace to which it a re grandly set forth the simplicit

unity of the Christian life. While the words probably
refer mainly to outward life, they presuppose an inward, of which that outward is the expression. In
every possible phase of the word 'life,' Christ is the
life of the Christian. To live is Christ, for He is the
mystical source from whom all ours flows. 'With
Thee is the fountain of life,' and all life, both of body
and spirit, is from Him, by Him, and in Him. 'To live
is Christ,' for He is the aim and object, as well as the
Lord, of it all, and no other is worth calling life, but
that which is *for* Him by willing consecration, as well
as *from* Him by constant derivation. 'To live is Christ,'
for He is the model of all our life, and the one all-
sufficient law for us is to follow Him.

Life is to be *as* Christ, *for* Christ, *by*, *in*, and *from*
Christ. So shall there be strength, peace, and freedom
in our days. The unity brought into life thereby will
issue in calm blessedness, contrasted wondrously with
the divided hearts and aims which fritter our days into
fragments, and make our lives heaps of broken links
instead of chains.

Surely this is the charm which brings rest into the
most troubled history, and nobleness into the lowliest
duties. There is nothing so grand as the unity breathed
into our else distracted days by the all-pervading
reference to and presence of Christ. Without that,
we are like the mariners of the old world, who crept
timidly from headland to headland, making each their
for a while, and leaving each inevitably behind,
losing sight of shore, nor ever knowing the
of the deep and all the majesty of mid-ocean,
the happy shores beyond, which th
ss th

Then comes the other great thought, that where life is simply Christ, death will be simply gain.

Paul, no doubt, shrank from the act of death, as we all do. It was not the narrow passage which attracted him, but the broad land beyond. Every other aspect of that was swallowed up in one great thought, which will occupy us more at length presently. But that word 'gain' suggests that to Paul's confident faith death was but an increase and progression in all that was good here. To him it was no loss to lose flesh and sense and all the fleeting joys with which they link us. To him death was no destruction of his being, and not even an interruption of its continuity. Everything that was of any real advantage to him was to be his after as before. The change was clear gain. Everything good was to be just as it had been, only better. Nothing was to be dropped but what it was progress to lose, and whatever was kept was to be heightened.

How strongly does that view express the two thoughts of the *continuity* and *intensifying* of the Christian life beyond the grave! And what a contrast does that simple, sublime confidence present to many another thought of death! To how many men its blackness seems to be the sudden swallowing up of the light of their very being! To how many more does it seem to put an end to all their occupations, and to shear their lives in twain, as remorselessly as the fall of the guillotine severs the head from the body. How are the light butterfly wings of the trivialities in which many men and women spend their days to carry them across the awful gulf? What are the people to do on the other side whose lives have all been given to purposes and tasks that stop on this side? Are there she and mills, or warehouses and drawing-rooms, or stu and lecture-halls, over there? Will the lives which have not struck their roots down through all the surface soil to the rock, bear transplanting? Alas! for the thousands landed in that new country, as unfit for it by the tenor of their past occupations, as some pale artisan, with delicate fingers and feeble muscles, set down as a colonist to clear the forest!

This Paul had a work here which he could carry on hereafter. There would be no reversal of view, no change in the fundamental character of his occupations. True, the special forms of work which he had pursued here would be left behind, but the principle underlying them would continue. It matters very little to the servant whether he is out in the cold and wet 'ploughing and tending cattle,' or whether he is waiting on his master at table. It is service all the same, only it is warmer and lighter in the house than in the field, and it is promotion to be made an indoor servant.

So the direction of the life, and the source of the life, and the fundamentals of the life continue unchanged. Everything is as it was, only in the superlative degree. To other men the narrow plain on which their low-lying lives are placed is rimmed by the jagged, forbidding white peaks. It is cold and dreary on these icy summits where no creature can live. Perhaps there is land on the other side; who knows? The pale barrier separates all here from all ; we know not what may be on the other side. we feel that the journey is long and chill, that the barren stone appal that we never believed, without 'break of gauge,' and would pass through the darkness, scarcely knowing when it came, and certainly unchecked for even a moment, right on to the other side where he would come out, as travellers to Italy do, to fairer plains and bluer skies, to richer harvests and a warmer sun. No jolt, no pause, no momentary suspension of consciousness, no reversal, nor even interruption in his activity, did Paul expect death to bring him, but only continuance and increase of all that was essential to his life.

He has calmness in his confidence. There is nothing hysterical or overwrought or morbid in these brief words, so peaceful in their trust, so moderate and restrained in their rapture. Are our anticipations of the future moulded on such a pattern? Do we think of it as quietly as this man did? Are we as tranquilly sure about it? Is there as little mist of uncertainty about the clearly defined image to our eye as there was to his? Is our confidence so profound that these brief monosyllables are enough to state it? Above all, do we know that to die will be gain, because we can honestly say that to live is Christ? If so, our hope is valid, and will not yield when we lean heavily upon it for support in the ford over the black stream. If our hope is built on anything besides, it will snap then like a rotten pole, and leave us to stumble helpless among the slippery stones and the icy torrent.

II. The second movement of thought here, which troubles and complicates this simple decision, as to what is the best for Paul himself, is the hesitation springing from the wish to help his brethren.

As we said, no man has a right to forget others settling the question whether he would live or the Apostle here brought to a stand by conflicting currents of feelings. For himself he would gladly go, for his friends' sake he is drawn to the opposite choice. He has 'fallen into a place where two seas meet,' and for a minute or two his will is buffeted from side to side by the 'violence of the waves.' The obscurity of his language, arising from its broken construction, corresponds to the struggle of his feelings. As the Revised Version has it, 'If to live in the flesh—if this is the fruit of my work, then what I shall choose, I wot not.' By which fragmentary sentence, rightly representing as it does the roughness of the Greek, we understand him to mean that if living on in this life is the condition of his gaining fruit from his toil, then he has to check the rising wish, and is hindered from decisive preference either way. Both motives act upon him, one drawing him deathward, the other holding him firmly here. He is in a dilemma, pinned in, as it were, between the two opposing pressures. On the one hand he has the desire (not 'a desire,' as the English Bible has it, as if it were but one among many) turned towards departing to be with Christ; but on the other, he knows that his remaining here is for the present all but indispensable for the immature faith of the churches which he has founded. So he stands in doubt for a moment, and the picture of his hesitation may well be studied by us.

Such a reason for wishing to die in conflict with such a reason for wishing to live, is as noble as it is rare,
, thank God, as imitable as it is noble.
ice the aspect which death wore to his faith. He
f it as 'departing,' a metaphor which does not,
of the flattering appellations which men

calls him gentle names, because he fears him not at all. To him all the dreadfulness, the mystery, the pain and the solitude have melted away, and death has become a mere change of place. The word literally means *to unloose*, and is employed to express pulling up the tent-pegs of a shifting encampment, or drawing up the anchor of a ship. In either case the image is simply that of removal. It is but striking the earthly house of this tent; it is but one more day's march, of which we have had many already, though this is over Jordan. It is but the last day's journey, and to-morrow there will be no packing up in the morning and resuming our weary tramp, but we shall be at home, and go no more out. So has the awful thing at the end dwindled, and the brighter and greater the land behind it shines, the smaller does it appear.

The Apostle thinks little of dying because he thinks so much of what comes after. Who is afraid of a brief journey if a meeting with dear friends long lost is at the end of it? The narrow avenue seems short, and its roughness and darkness are nothing, because Jesus Christ stands with outstretched arms at the other end, beckoning us to Himself, as mothers teach their children to walk. Whosoever is sure that he will be with Christ can afford to smile at death, and call it but a shifting of place. And whosoever feels the desire to be with Christ will not shrink from the means by which that desire is fulfilled, with the agony of revulsion that it excites in many an imagination. It will always be solemn, and its physical accompaniments of pain and struggle will always be more or less of a terror, and the parting, even for a time, from our dear one will always be loss, but nevertheless if we see Ch__ a__ __ __gulf, and know that one struggle more

we shall clasp Him with 'inseparable hands with joy
and bliss in over measure for ever,' we shall not dread
the leap.

One thought about the future should fill our minds,
as it did Paul's, that it is to be with Christ. How
different that nobly simple expectation, resolving all
bliss into the one element, is from the morbid curiosity
as to details, which vulgarises and weakens so much
of even devout anticipation of the future. To us as to
him Heaven should be Christ, and Christ should be
Heaven. All the rest is but accident. Golden harps
and crowns, and hidden manna and white robes and
thrones, and all the other representations, are but
symbols of the blessedness of union with Him, or consequences of it. Immortal life and growth in perfection,
both of mind and heart, and the cessation of all that
disturbs, and our investiture with glory and honour,
flung around our poor natures like a royal robe over
a naked body, are all but the many-sided brightnesses
that pour out from Him, and bathe in their rainbowed
light those who are with Him.

To be with Christ is all we need. For the loving
heart to be near Him is enough.

> ' I shall clasp thee again, O soul of my soul,
> And with God be the rest.'

Let us not fritter away our imaginations and our hopes
on the subordinate and non-essential accompaniments,
but concentrate all their energy on the one central
t. Let us not lose this gracious image in a
symbols, that, though precious, are secondary.
nquire, with curiosity that will find no

ing. Let us not acquire the habit of thinking of the future as the perfecting of our humanity, without connecting all our speculations with Him, whose presence will be all of heaven to us all. But let us keep His serene figure ever clear before our imaginations in all the blaze of the light, and try to feed our hopes and stay our hearts on this aspect of heavenly blessedness as the all-embracing one, that all, each for himself, shall be for ever conscious of Christ's loving presence, and of the closest union with Him, a union in comparison with which the dearest and sacredest blendings of heart with heart and life with life are cold and distant. For the clearness of our hope the fewer the details the better: for the willingness with which we turn from life and face the inevitable end, it is very important that we should have that one thought disengaged from all others. The one full moon, which dims all the stars, draws the tides after it. These lesser lights may gem the darkness, and dart down white shafts of brilliance in quivering reflections on the waves, but they have no power to move their mass. It is Christ and Christ only who draws us across the gulf to be with Him, and reduces death to a mere shifting of our encampment.

This is a noble and worthy reason for wishing to die; not because Paul is disappointed and sick of life, not because he is weighed down with sorrow, or pain, or loss, or toil, but because he would like to be with his Master. He is no morbid sentimentalist, he i cherishing no unwholesome longing, he is not wea of work, he indulges in no hysterical raptures desire. What an eloquent simplicity is in that q 've far better!' It goes straight to one's heart re than paragraphs of falsetto year

There is nothing in such a wish to die, based on such a reason, that the most manly and wholesome piety need be ashamed of. It is a pattern for us all.

The attraction of life contends with the attraction of heaven in these verses. That is a conflict which many good men know something of, but which does not take the shape with many of us which it assumed with Paul. Drawn, as he is, by the supreme desire of close union with his Master, for the sake of which he is ready to depart, he is tugged back even more strongly by the thought that, if he stays here, he can go on working and gaining results from his labour. It does not follow that he did not expect service if he were with Christ. We may be very sure that Paul's heaven was no idle heaven, but one of happy activity and larger service. But he will not be able to help these dear friends at Philippi and elsewhere who need him, as he knows. So love to them drags at his skirts, and ties him here.

One can scarcely miss the remarkable contrast between Paul's 'To abide in the flesh is more needful for you,' and the saying of Paul's Master to people who assuredly needed His presence more than Philippi needed Paul's, 'It is expedient for you that I go away.' This is not the place to work out the profound significance of the contrast, and the questions which it raises as to whether Christ expected His work to be finished and His helpfulness ended by His death, as Paul did by his. ... ust suffice to have suggested the comparison.

...rning to our text, such a reason for wishing to ...in check and overcome by such a reason for ...e, is ... and noble. There are few of personally, if we were free to think only of ourselves, we should be glad to go, because we should be closer to Christ, but that we hesitate for the sake of others whom we think we can help! Many of us cling to life with a desperate clutch, like some poor wretch pushed over a precipice and trying to dig his nails into the rock as he falls. Some of us cling to it because we dread what is beyond, and our longing to live is the measure of our dread to die. But Paul did not look forward to a thick darkness of judgment, or to nothingness. He saw in the darkness a great light, the light in the windows of his Father's house, and yet he turned willingly away to his toil in the field, and was more than content to drudge on as long as he could do anything by his work. Blessed are they who share his desire to depart, and his victorious willingness to stay here and labour! They shall find that such a life in the flesh, too, is being with Christ.

III. Thus the stream of thought passes the rapids and flows on smoothly to its final phase of peaceful acquiescence.

That is expressed very beautifully in the closing verse, 'Having this confidence, I know that I shall abide and continue with you all, for your furtherance and joy in faith.' Self is so entirely overcome that he puts away his own desire to enter into their joy, and rejoices with them. He cannot yet have for himself the blessedness which his spirit seeks. Well, be it so, he will stop here and find a blessedness in seeing the growing in confidence and knowledge of Christ and the gladness that comes from it. He gives up the higher companionship with Jesus which ily. Well, be it so; he will have brethren and 'abiding w all' may haply find, even before the day of final account, that to 'visit' Christ's little ones is to visit Christ. Therefore he fuses his opposing wishes into one. He is no more in a strait betwixt two, or unwitting what he shall choose. He chooses nothing, but accepts the appointment of a higher wisdom. There is rest for him, as for us, in ceasing from our own wishes, and laying our wills silent and passive at His feet.

The true attitude for us in which to face the unknown future, with its dim possibilities, and especially the supreme alternative of life or death, is neither desire nor reluctance, nor a hesitation compounded of both, but trustful acquiescence. Such a temper is far from indifference, and as far from agitation. In all things, and most of all in regard to these matters, it is best to hold desire in equilibrium till God shall speak. Torture not yourself with hopes or fears. They make us their slaves. Put your hand in God's hand, and let Him guide you as He will. Wishes are bad steersmen. We are only at peace when desires and dreads are, if not extinct, at all events held tightly in. Rest, and wisdom, and strength come with acquiescence. Let us say with Richard Baxter, in his simple, noble words:

'Lord, it belongs not to my care
    Whether I die or live;
To love and serve Thee is my share,
    And that Thy grace must give.'

We may learn, too, that we may be quite sure that we shall be left here as long as we are needed. Paul knew that his stay was needful, so he could say, 'I know that I shall abide with you.' We do not, but we may be sure that if our stay is needful we shall abide. We are always tempted to think ourselves indispensable, but, thank God, nobody is necessary. There are no irreparable losses, hard as it is to believe it. We look at our work, at our families, our business, our congregations, our subjects of study, and we say to ourselves, 'What will become of them when I am gone? Everything would fall to pieces if I were withdrawn.' Do not be afraid. Depend on it, you will be left here as long as you are wanted. There are no incomplete lives and no premature removals. To the eye of faith the broken column in our cemeteries is a sentimental falsehood. No Christian life is broken short off so, but rises in a symmetrical shaft, and its capital is garlanded with amaranthine flowers in heaven. In one sense all our lives are incomplete, for they and their issues are above, out of our sight here. In another none are, for we are 'immortal till our work is done.'

The true attitude, then, for us is patient service till He withdraws us from the field. We do not count him a diligent servant who is always wearying for the hour of leaving off to strike. Be it ours to labour where He puts us, patiently waiting till 'death's mild curfew' sets us free from the long day's work, and sends us home.

Brethren! there are but two theories of life; two corresponding aspects of death. The one says, 'To me to live is Christ, and to die gain'; the other, 'To me to live is self, and to die is loss and despair.' One or other must be your choice. Which?

CITIZENS OF HEAVEN

'Only let your conversation be as it becometh the gospel of Christ: that whether I come and see you, or else be absent, I may hear of your affairs, that ye stand fast in one spirit, with one mind striving together for the faith of the gospel; 28. And in nothing terrified by your adversaries.'—PHIL. i. 27, 28.

WE read in the Acts of the Apostles that Philippi was the chief city of that part of Macedonia, and a 'colony.' Now, the connection between a Roman colony and Rome was a great deal closer than that between an English colony and England. It was, in fact, a bit of Rome on foreign soil.

The colonists and their children were Roman citizens. Their names were enrolled on the lists of Roman tribes. They were governed not by the provincial authorities, but by their own magistrates, and the law to which they owed obedience was not that of the locality, but the law of Rome.

No doubt some of the Philippian Christians possessed these privileges. They knew what it was to live in a community to which they were less closely bound than to the great city beyond the sea. They were members of a mighty polity, though they had never seen its temples nor trod its streets. They lived in Philippi, but they belonged to Rome. Hence there is a peculiar significance in the first words of our text. The rendering, 'conversation,' was inadequate even when it was made. It has become more so now. The word then meant 'conduct.' It now means little more than words. though the phrase may express loosely the general idea, it loses entirely the stri der which it is couched. The Rev rendering which disregards the figure in the word, and contents itself with the less picturesque and vivid phrase—'let your manner of life be worthy.' But there seems no reason for leaving out the metaphor; it entirely fits in with the purpose of the Apostle and with the context.

The meaning is, Play the citizen in a manner worthy of the Gospel. Paul does not, of course, mean, Discharge your civic duties as Christian men, though some Christian Englishmen need that reminder; but the city of which these Philippians were citizens was the heavenly Jerusalem, the metropolis, the mother city of us all. He would kindle in them the consciousness of belonging to another order of things than that around them. He would stimulate their loyalty to obedience to the city's laws. As the outlying colonies of Rome had sometimes entrusted to them the task of keeping the frontiers and extending the power of the imperial city, so he stirs them up to aggressive warfare; and as in all their conflicts the little colony felt that the Empire was at its back, and therefore looked undaunted on shoals of barbarian foes, so he would have his friends at Philippi animated by lofty courage, and ever confident of final victory.

Such seems to be a general outline of these eager exhortations to the citizens of heaven in this outlying colony of earth. Let us think of them briefly in order now.

I. Keep fresh the sense of belonging to the mother city.

Paul was not only writing *to* Philippi, but *fro...* Rome, where he might see how, even in degenera... days, the consciousness of being a Roman gave digni... to a man, and how the idea became almost a reli... ... kindle a similar feeling in Christians.

We do belong to another polity or order of things than that with which we are connected by the bonds of flesh and sense. Our true affinities are with the mother city. True, we are here on earth, but far beyond the blue waters is another community, of which we are really members, and sometimes in calm weather we can see, if we climb to a height above the smoke of the valley where we dwell, the faint outline of the mountains of that other land, lying bathed in sunlight and dreamlike on the opal waves.

Therefore it is a great part of Christian discipline to keep a vivid consciousness that there is such an unseen order of things at present in existence. We speak popularly of ' the future life,' and are apt to forget that it is also the *present* life to an innumerable company. In fact, this film of an earthly life floats in that greater sphere which is all around it, above, beneath, touching it at every point.

It is, as Peter says, 'ready to be unveiled.' Yes, behind the thin curtain, through which stray beams of the brightness sometimes shoot, that other order stands, close to us, parted from us by a most slender division, only a woven veil, no great gulf or iron barrier. And before long His hand will draw it back, rattling with its rings as it is put aside, and *there* will blaze out what has always been, though we saw it not. It is so close, so real, so bright, so solemn, that it is worth while to try to feel its nearness; and we are so blind, and such foolish slaves of mere sense, shaping on the legal maxim that things which are non-

we belong to it in the measure in which we are
Christians.   All these figurative expressions about our
citizenship being in heaven and the like, rest on the
simple fact that the life of Christian men on earth and
in heaven is fundamentally the same.   The principles
which guide, the motives which sway, the tastes and
desires, affections and impulses, the objects and aims,
are substantially one.   A Christian man's true affinities
are with the things not seen, and with the persons
there, however his surface relationship knit him to the
earth.   In the degree in which he is a Christian, he is
a stranger here and a native of the heavens.   That
great City is, like some of the capitals of Europe, built
on a broad river, with the mass of the metropolis on
the one bank, but a wide-spreading suburb on the
other.   As the Trastevere is to Rome, as Southwark to
London, so is earth to heaven, the bit of the city on
the other side the bridge.   As Philippi was to Rome,
so is earth to heaven, the colony on the outskirts of
the empire, ringed round by barbarians, and separated
by sounding seas, but keeping open its communications,
and one in citizenship.

Be it our care, then, to keep the sense of that city
beyond the river vivid and constant.   Amid the shows
and shams of earth look ever onward to the realities,
'the things which *are*,' while all else only seems to be.
The things which are seen are but smoke wreaths,
floating for a moment across space, and melting into
nothingness while we look.   We do not belong to them
or to the order of things to which they belong.   There
is no kindred between us and them.   Our true relatie
ships are elsewhere.   In this present visible world
other creatures find their sufficient and home
abode.   'Foxes have holes, and birds their roos

places'; but man alone has not where to lay his head, nor can he find in all the width of the created universe a place in which and with which he can be satisfied. Our true *habitat* is elsewhere. So let us set our thoughts and affections on things above. The descendants of the original settlers in our colonies talk still of coming to England as going 'home,' though they were born in Australia, and have lived there all their lives. In like manner we Christian people should keep vigorous in our minds the thought that our true home is there where we have never been, and that here we are foreigners and wanderers.

Nor need that feeling of detachment from the present sadden our spirits, or weaken our interest in the things around us. To recognise our separation from the order of things in which we 'move,' because we belong to that majestic unseen order in which we really 'have our being,' makes life great and not small. It clothes the present with dignity beyond what is possible to it if it be not looked at in the light of its connection with 'the regions beyond.' From that connection life derives all its meaning. Surely nothing can be conceived more unmeaning, more wearisome in its monotony, more tragic in its joy, more purposeless in its efforts, than man's life, if the life of sense and time be all. Truly it is 'like a tale told by an idiot, full of sound and fury, signifying nothing.' 'The white radiance of eternity,' streaming through it from above, all its beauty to the 'dome of many-coloured ich men call life. They who feel most their most intelligently and most nobly, in the homeliest and smallest of the tasks and concerns of the present.

So, in all things, act as citizens of the great Mother of heroes and saints beyond the sea. Ever feel that you belong to another order, and let the thought, 'Here we have no continuing city,' be to you not merely the bitter lesson taught by the transiency of earthly joys and treasures and loves, but the happy result of 'seeking for the city which hath the foundations.'

II. Another exhortation which our text gives is, Live by the laws of the city.

The Philippian colonists were governed by the code of Rome. Whatever might be the law of the province of Macedonia, they owed no obedience to it. So Christian men are not to be governed by the maxims and rules of conduct which prevail in the province, but to be governed from the capital. We ought to get from on-lookers the same character that was given to the Jews, that we are 'a people whose laws are different from all people that be on earth,' and we ought to reckon such a character our highest praise. Paul would have these Philippian Christians act 'worthy of *the gospel*.' That is our law.

The great good news of God manifest in the flesh, and of our salvation through Christ Jesus, is not merely to be believed, but to be obeyed. The gospel is not merely a message of deliverance, it is also a rule of conduct. It is not merely theology, it is also ethics. Like some of the ancient municipal charters, the grant of privileges and proclamation of freedom is also the sovereign code which imposes duties and shapes life. A gospel of laziness and mere exemption from hell was not Paul's gospel. A gospel of doctrine to be investigated, spun into a system of theology,

accepted by the understanding, and there an end, was
not Paul's gospel. He believed that the great facts
which he proclaimed concerning the self-revelation of
God in Christ would unfold into a sovereign law of life
for every true believer, and so his one all-sufficient precept and standard of conduct are in these simple words,
'worthy of the gospel.'

That law is all-sufficient. In the truths which constituted Paul's gospel, that is to say, in the truths of
the life, death, and resurrection of Jesus Christ, lies all
that men need for conduct and character. In Him we
have the 'realised ideal,' the flawless example, and
instead of a thousand precepts, for us all duty is
resolved into one—be like Christ. In Him we have the
mighty motive, powerful enough to overcome all forces
that would draw us away, and like some strong spring
to keep us in closest contact with right and goodness.
Instead of a confusing variety of appeals to manifold
motives of interest and conscience, and one knows not
what beside, we have the one all-powerful appeal, 'If ye
love Me, keep My commandments,' and that draws all
the agitations and fluctuations of the soul after it, as the
rounded fulness of the moon does the heaped waters
in the tidal wave that girdles the world. In Him we
have all the helps that weakness needs, for He Himself
will come and dwell with us and in us, and be our
righteousness and our strength.

e 'worthy of the gospel,' then. How grand the
and simplicity thus breathed into our duties and
our lives! All duties are capable of redu

shall joyfully learn how much mightier and happier is
the life which is shaped by one fruitful principle, than
that which is hampered by a thousand regulations.

Nor is such an all-comprehensive precept a mere
toothless generality. Let a man try honestly to shape
his life by it; and he will find soon enough how close
it grips him, and how wide it stretches, and how deep
it goes. The greatest principles of the gospel are to
be fitted to the smallest duties. Indeed that combination—great principles and small duties—is the secret
of all noble and calm life, and nowhere should it be so
beautifully exemplified as in the life of a Christian
man. The tiny round of the dew-drop is shaped by the
same laws that mould the giant sphere of the largest
planet. You cannot make a map of the poorest grass-
field without celestial observations. The star is not
too high nor too brilliant to move before us and guide
simple men's feet along their pilgrimage. 'Worthy of
the gospel' is a most practical and stringent law.

And it is an exclusive commandment too, shutting
out obedience to other codes, however common and
fashionable they may be. We are governed from
home, and we give no submission to provincial
authorities. Never mind what people say about you,
nor what may be the maxims and ways of men around
you. These are no guides for you. Public opinion
(which only means for most of us the hasty judgments of the half-dozen people who happen to be
nearest us), use and wont, the customs of our set, the
notions of the world about duty, with all these
have nothing to do. The censures or the praise
men need not move us. We report to headquar
di es' estimate need be nothing to
'With me it very small

that I should be judged of men's judgment. He that judgeth me is the Lord.'   When we may be mis-understood or harshly dealt with, let us lift our eyes to the lofty seat where the Emperor sits, and remove ourselves from men's sentences by our 'appeal unto Cæsar'; and, in all varieties of circumstances and duty, let us take the Gospel which is the record of Christ's life, death, and character, for our only law, and labour that, whatever others may think of us, we 'may be well pleasing to Him.'

III. Further, our text bids the colonists fight for the advance of the dominions of the City.

Like the armed colonists whom Russia and other empires had on their frontier, who received their bits of land on condition of holding the border against the enemy, and pushing it forward a league or two when possible, Christian men are set down in their places to be 'wardens of the marches,' citizen soldiers who hold their homesteads on a military tenure, and are to 'strive together for the faith of the gospel.'

There is no space here and now to go into details of the exposition of this part of our text. Enough to say in brief that we are here exhorted to 'stand fast'; that is, as it were, the defensive side of our warfare, maintaining our ground and repelling all assaults ; that this successful resistance is to be 'in one spirit,' inas-much as all resistance depends on our poor feeble spirits being ingrafted and rooted in God's Spirit, in vital union with whom we may be knit together into a unity which shall oppose a granite breakwater to the onrushing tide of opposition; that in addition to the unyielding resistance which will not yield an inch of the sacred soil to the enemy, we are to carry the war

with one mind to strive together for the faith of the
gospel. There is to be discipline, then, and compact
organisation, like that of the legions whom Paul, from
his prison among the Prætorian guards, had often seen
shining in steel, moving like a machine, grim, irre-
sistible. The cause for which we are to fight is the
faith of the gospel, an expression which almost seems
to justify the opinion that 'the faith' here means, as
it does in later usage, the sum and substance of that
which is believed. But even here the word may have
its usual meaning of the subjective act of trust in the
gospel, and the thought may be that we are unitedly
to fight for its growing power in our own hearts and in
the hearts of others. In any case, the idea is plainly
here that Christian men are set down in the world,
like the frontier guard, to push the conquests of the
empire, and to win more ground for their King.

Such work is ever needed, never more needed than
now. In this day when a wave of unbelief seems
passing over society, when material comfort and
worldly prosperity are so dazzlingly attractive to so
many, the solemn duty is laid upon us with even more
than usual emphasis, and we are called upon to feel
more than ever the oneness of all true Christians, and
to close up our ranks for the fight. All this can only
be done after we have obeyed the other injunctions of
this text. The degree in which we feel that we belong
to another order of things than this around us, and the
degree in which we live by the Imperial laws, will
determine the degree in which we can fight with vigour
for the growth of the dominion of the City. Be
ours to cherish the vivid consciousness that we are here
dwelling not in the cities of the Canaanites, but,
the father of the faithful, in tents pitched at t

gates, nomads in the midst of a civic life to which we
do not belong, in order that we may breathe a hallowing influence through it, and win hearts to the love of
Him whom to imitate is perfection, whom to serve is
freedom.

IV. The last exhortation to the colonists is, Be sure
of victory.

'In nothing terrified by your adversaries,' says Paul.
He uses a very vivid, and some people might think,
a very vulgar metaphor here.   The word rendered
terrified properly refers to a horse shying or plunging
at some object.   It is generally things half seen and
mistaken for something more dreadful than themselves
that make horses shy; and it is usually a half-look at
adversaries, and a mistaken estimate of their strength,
that make Christians afraid.   Go up to your fears and
speak to them, and as ghosts are said to do, they will
generally fade away.   So we may go into the battle,
as the rash French minister said he did into the Franco-
German war, 'with a light heart,' and that for good
reasons.   We have no reason to fear for ourselves.
We have no reason to fear for the ark of God.   We
have no reason to fear for the growth of Christianity
in the world.   Many good men in this time seem to be
getting half-ashamed of the gospel, and some preachers
are preaching it in words which sound like an apology
rather than a creed.   Do not let us allow the enemy to
overpower our imaginations in that fashion.   Do not
us fight as if we expected to be beaten, always
our eyes over our shoulders, even while we are
sure of our re   but let us t

Such courage is a prophecy of victory. Such courage is based upon a sure hope. 'Our citizenship is in heaven, from whence also we look for the Lord Jesus as Saviour.' The little outlying colony in this far-off edge of the empire is ringed about by wide-stretching hosts of dusky barbarians. Far as the eye can reach their myriads cover the land, and the watchers from the ramparts might well be dismayed if they had only their own resources to depend on. But they know that the Emperor in his progress will come to this sorely beset outpost, and their eyes are fixed on the pass in the hills where they expect to see the waving banners and the gleaming spears. Soon, like our countrymen in Lucknow, they will hear the music and the shouts that tell that He is at hand. Then when He comes, He will raise the siege and scatter all the enemies as the chaff of the threshing-floor, and the colonists who held the post will go with Him to the land which they have never seen, but which is their home, and will, with the Victor, sweep in triumph 'through the gates into the city.'

A PLEA FOR UNITY

'If there is therefore any comfort in Christ, if any consolation of love, if any fellowship of the Spirit, if any tender mercies and compassions, 2. Fulfil ye my joy, that ye be of the same mind, having the same love, being of one accord, of one mind ; 3. Doing nothing through faction or through vainglory, but in low-liness of mind each counting other better than himself ; 4. Not looking each of you to his own things, but each of you also to the things of others.'—PHIL. ii. 1-4 (R.V.).

THERE was much in the state of the Philippian church which filled Paul's heart with thankfulness, and nothing which drew forth his censures, but these verses, with their extraordinary energy of pleading, seem to b

that there was some defect in the unity of heart and
mind of members of the community. It did not
amount to discord, but the concord was not as full as
it might have been. There is another hint pointing
in the same direction in the appeal to Paul's true yoke-
fellow, in chapter iv., to help two good women who,
though they had laboured much in the gospel, had not
managed to keep ' of the same mind in the Lord,' and
there is perhaps a still further indication that Paul's
sensitive heart was conscious of the beginnings of
strife in the air, in the remarkable emphasis with
which, at the very outset of the letter, he over and
over again pours out his confidence and affection on
them ' all,' as if aware of some incipient rifts in their
brotherhood. There are always forces at work which
tend to part the most closely knit unities even when
these are consecrated by Christian faith. Where there
are no dogmatical grounds of discord, nor any open
alienation, there may still be the beginnings of separation, and a chill breeze may be felt even when the sun
is shining with summer warmth. Wasps are attracted
by the ripest fruit.

The words of our text present no special difficulty,
and bring before us a well-worn subject, but it has at
least this element of interest, that it grips very tightly
the deepest things in Christian life, and that none of
us can truly say that we do not need to listen to Paul's
pleading voice. We may notice the general division
⬛ thoughts in these words, in that he puts first the
⬛ching motives for listening to his appeal,
⬛th the ⬛ of ⬛

I. The motives and bonds of Christian unity.

It is not a pedantic dissection (and vivisection) of the Apostle's earnest words, if we point out that they fall into four clauses, of which the first and third ('any comfort in Christ, any fellowship of the Spirit') urge the objective facts of Christian revelation, and the second and fourth ('any consolation of love, any tender mercies and compassions') put emphasis on the subjective emotions of Christian experience. We may lay the warmth of all of these on our own hearts, and shall find that these hearts will be drawn into the blessedness of Christian unity in the precise measure in which they are affected by them.

As to the first of them, it may be suggested that here, as elsewhere in the New Testament, the true idea of the word rendered 'comfort' is rather 'exhortation.' The Apostle is probably not so much pointing to the consolations for trouble which come from Jesus, as to the stimulus to unity which flows from Him. It would rather weaken the force of Paul's appeal, if the two former grounds of it were so nearly identical as they are, if the one is based upon 'comfort' and the other on 'consolation.' The Apostle is true to his dominant belief, that in Jesus Christ there lies, and from Him flows, the sovereign exhortation that rouses men to 'whatsoever things are lovely and of good report.' In Him we shall find in the measure in which we are in Him, the most persuasive of all exhortations to unity, and the most omnipotent of all powers to enforce it. Shall we not be glad to be in the flock of the Good Shepherd, and to preserve the oneness which gave His life to establish? Can we live in Him, [...] love for His sheep? Surely thos[...] [...]diction of His breath on thei[...]

heads when He prayed 'that they may all be one;
even as Thou, Father, art in Me and I in Thee,' cannot
but do what is in them to fulfil that prayer, and to
bring a little nearer the realisation of their Lord's
purpose in it, 'that the world may believe that Thou
didst send Me.' Surely if we lay to heart, and enter
into sympathy with, the whole life and death of Jesus
Christ, we shall not fail to feel the dynamic power
fusing us together, nor fail to catch the exhortation to
unity which comes from the lips that said, 'I am the
vine, ye are the branches.'

The Apostle next bases his appeal for unity on the
experiences of the Philippian Christians, and on their
memories of the comfort which they have tasted in the
exercise of mutual love. Our hearts find it hard to
answer the question whether they are more blessed
when their love passes out from them in a warm
stream to others, or when the love of others pours
into them. To love and to be loved equally elevate
courage, and brace the weakest for calm endurance
and high deeds. The man who loves and knows that he
is loved will be a hero. It must always seem strange
and inexplicable that a heart which has known the
enlargement and joy of love given and received,
should ever fall so far beneath itself as to be narrowed
and troubled by nourishing feelings of separation and
alienation from those whom it might have gathered
i____ its embrace, and thereby communicated, and in
____ting acquired, courage and strength. We
____ the comfort of love; should it not impel

But Paul has still further heart-melting motives to urge. He turns the Philippians' thoughts to their fellowship in the Spirit. All believers have been made to drink into one spirit, and in that common participation in the same supernatural life they partake of a oneness, which renders any clefts or divisions unnatural, and contradictory of the deepest truths of their experience. The branch can no more shiver itself off from the tree, or keep the life sap enclosed within itself, than one possessor of the common gift of the Spirit can separate himself from the others who share it. We are one in Him; let us be one in heart and mind. The final appeal is connected with the preceding, inasmuch as it lays emphasis on the emotions which flow from the one life common to all believers. That participation in the Spirit naturally leads in each participant to 'tender mercies and compassions' directed to all sharers in it. The very mark of truly possessing the Spirit's life is a nature full of tenderness and swift to pity, and they who have experienced the heaven on earth of such emotions should need no other motive than the memory of its blessedness, to send them out among their brethren, and even into a hostile world, as the apostles of love, the bearers of tender mercies, and the messengers of pity.

II. The fair ideal which would complete the Apostle's joy.

We may gather from the rich abundance of moti... which the Apostle suggests before he comes to pr... his exhortation, that he suspected the existence... some tendencies in the opposite direction in Phi... a... ibly the same conclusion may be drawn...

the exuberance of the exhortation itself, and from its
preceding the dehortation which follows. He does
not scold, he scarcely even rebukes, but he begins by
trying to melt away any light frost that had crept
over the warmth of the Philippians' love; and having
made that preparation, he sets before them with a
fulness which would be tautological but for the
earnestness that throbs in it, the ideal of unity, and
presses it upon them still more meltingly, by telling
them that their realisation of it will be the completion
of his joy. The main injunction is 'that ye be of the
same mind,' and that is followed by three clauses which
are all but exactly synonymous with it, 'having the
same love, being of one accord, of one mind.' The
resemblance of the latter clause to the main exhortation is still more complete, if we read with Revised
Version (margin) ' of the same mind,' but in any case
the exhortations are all practically the same. The
unity which Paul would fain see, is far deeper and
more vital than mere unanimity of opinion, or identity
of polity, or co-operation in practice. The clauses
which expand it guard us against the mistake of
thinking that intellectual or practical oneness is all
that is meant by Christian unity. They are 'of the
same mind,' who have the same wishes, aims, outlooks,
the same hopes and fears, and who are one in the
depths of their being. They have 'the same love,' all
clearly loving and being loved, the same emotion filling the heart. They are united in soul, or ' with accor-
and being th

arc of the great circle which the Apostle drew, and none of us can read these fervid words without shame. His joy is not yet fulfilled.

That exhortation to be 'of the same mind,' not only points to a deep and vital unity, but suggests that the ground of the unity is to be found without us, in the common direction of our 'minds,' which means far more than popular phraseology means by it, to an external object. It is having our hearts directed to Christ that makes us one. He is the bond and centre of unity. We have just said that the object is external, but that has to be taken with a modification, for the true basis of unity is the common possession of 'Christ in us.' It is when we have this mind in us 'which was also in Christ Jesus,' that we have 'the same mind' one with another.

The very keynote of the letter is joy, as may be seen by a glance over it. He joys and rejoices with them all, but his cup is not quite full. One more precious drop is needed to make it run over. Probably the coldness which he had heard of between Euodias and Syntyche had troubled him, and if he could be sure of the Philippians' mutual love he would rejoice in his prison. We cannot tell whether that loving and careful heart is still aware of the fortunes of the Church, but we know of a more loving and careful heart which is, and we cannot but believe that the alienations and discords of His professed followers bring some shadow over the joy of Christ. Do we not hear His voice again asking, 'what was it that you disput among yourselves by the way?' and must we not, l th s, 'hold our peace' when that questio y we not hear a voice sweeter i more melting in its tendern

Paul's, saying to us 'Fulfil ye My joy that ye be of the same mind.'

III. The hindrances and helps to being of the same mind.

The original has no verb in front of 'nothing' in verse 3, and it seems better to supply the one which has been so frequently used in the preceding exhortation than 'doing,' which carries us too abruptly into the outer region of action. Paul indicates two main hindrances to being of the same mind, namely, faction and vainglory on the one hand, and self-absorption on the other, and opposed to each the tone of mind which is its best conqueror. Faction and vainglory are best defeated by humility and unselfishness. As to the former, the love of making or heading little cliques in religion or politics or society, has oftenest its roots in nothing loftier than vanity or pride. Many a man who poses as guided by staunch adherence to conviction is really impelled only by a wish to make himself notorious as a leader, and loves to talk of 'those with whom I act.' There is a strong admixture of a too lofty estimate of self in most of the disagreements of Christian people. They expect more deference than they get, or their judgment is not taken as law, or their place is not so high as they think is their due, or in a hundred different ways self-love is wounded, and self-esteem is inflamed. All this is true in reference to the smaller communities of congregations, and with the necessary modifications it is quite as true in to the larger aggregations which we call or denominations. If all in their work th to faction and vainglory were st

The cure for all these evils is lowliness of mind. That is a Christian word. Used by Greek thinkers, it meant abjectness; and it is one conspicuous instance of the change effected in morals by Christian teaching that it has become the name of a virtue. We are to dwell not on our gifts but on our imperfections, and if we judge ourselves with constant reference to the standard in Christ's life, we shall need little more to bring us to our knees in true lowliness of mind. The man who has been forgiven so many talents will not be in a hurry to take his brother by the throat and leave the marks of his fingers for tenpence.

Christian unity is further broken by selfishness. To be absorbed in self is of course to have the heart shut to others. Our own interests, inclinations, possessions, when they assert themselves in our lives, build up impassable barriers between us and our fellows. To live to self is the real root of every sin as it is of all loveless life. The Apostle uses careful language: he admits the necessity for attention to our 'own things,' and only requires that we should look 'also' on the things of others. His cure for the hindrances to Christian unity is very complete, very practical, and very simple. Each counting other better than himself, and each 'looking also to the things of others' seem very homely and pedestrian virtues, but homely as they are we shall find that they grip us tight, if we honestly try to practise them in our daily lives, and we shall find also that the ladder which has its foot on earth has its top in the heavens, and that the practice of humility and unselfishness leads straight to having 'the mind which was also in Christ Jesus.'

THE DESCENT OF THE WORD

'Have this mind in you which was also in Christ Jesus: 6. Who, being in the form of God, counted it not a prize to be on an equality with God, 7. But emptied Himself, taking the form of a servant, being made in the likeness of men ; 8. And being found in fashion as a man, He humbled Himself, becoming obedient even unto death, yea, the death of the cross.'—PHIL. ii. 5-8 (R. V.).

THE purpose of the Apostle in this great passage must ever be kept clearly in view. Our Lord's example is set forth as the pattern of that unselfish disregard of one's own things, and devotion to the things of others, which has just been urged on the Philippians, and the mind which was in Him is presented as the model on which they are to fashion their minds. This purpose in some measure explains some of the peculiarities of the language here, and may help to guide us through some of the intricacies and doubtful points in the interpretation of the words. It explains why Christ's death is looked at in them only in its bearing upon Himself, as an act of obedience and of condescension, and why even that death in which Jesus stands most inimitable and unique is presented as capable of being imitated by us. The general drift of these verses is clear, but there are few Scripture passages which have evoked more difference of opinion as to the precise meaning of nearly every phrase. To enter on the subtle discussions involved in the adequate exposition of the words would far exceed our limits, and we must be content ourselves with a slight treatment of chiefly at bringing out th

and self-sacrifice. To be born was His supreme act of
condescension. It was love which made Him assume
the vesture of human flesh. To die was the climax of
His voluntary obedience, and of His devotion to us.

I. The height from which Jesus descended.

The whole strange conception of birth as being the
voluntary act of the Person born, and as being the
most stupendous instance of condescension in the
world's history, necessarily reposes on the clear conviction that He had a prior existence so lofty that it
was an all but infinite descent to become man. Hence
Paul begins with the most emphatic assertion that he
who bore the name of Jesus lived a divine life before
He was born. He uses a very strong word which is
given in the margin of the Revised Version, and might
well have been in its text. 'Being originally' as the
word accurately means, carries our thoughts back not
only to a state which preceded Bethlehem and the
cradle, but to that same timeless eternity from which
the prologue of the Gospel of John partially draws
the veil when it says, 'In the beginning was the
Word,' and to which Jesus Himself more obscurely
pointed when He said, 'Before Abraham was I am.'

Equally emphatic in another direction is Paul's next
expression, 'In the form of God,' for 'form' means
much more than 'shape.' I would point out the
careful selection in this passage of three words to
express three ideas which are often by hasty thought
regarded as identical. We read of 'the *form* of God'
(verse 6), 'the *likeness* of men' (verse 7), and 'in *fashi*
as a man.' Careful investigation of these two wor
'form' and 'fashion' has established a broad distinct
them, the former being more fixed, the
t which is accidental and ou

which may be fleeting and unsubstantial. The possession of the form involves participation in the essence
also. Here it implies no corporeal idea as if God had
a material form, but it implies also much more than a
mere apparent resemblance. He who is in the form
of God possesses the essential divine attributes. Only
God can be 'in the form of God': man is made in the
likeness of God, but man is not 'in the form of God.'
Light is thrown on this lofty phrase by its antithesis
with the succeeding expression in the next verse,
'the form of a servant,' and as that is immediately
explained to refer to Christ's assumption of human
nature, there is no room for candid doubt that 'being
originally in the form of God' is a deliberately asserted
claim of the divinity of Christ in His pre-existent
state.

As we have already pointed out, Paul soars here to
the same lofty height to which the prologue of John's
Gospel rises, and he echoes our Lord's own words
about 'the glory which I had with Thee before the
foundation of the world.' Our thoughts are carried
back before creatures were, and we become dimly
aware of an eternal distinction in the divine nature
which only perfects its eternal oneness. Such an
eternal participation in the divine nature before all
ion and before time is the necessary pre-supposi-
of the worth of Christ's life as the pattern of
and self-sacrifice. That pre-s

Him as simply a man, like all the rest of us, beginning to be when He was born, takes away from His example its mightiest constraining force. Only when we with all our hearts believe 'that the Word became flesh,' do we discern the overwhelming depths of condescension manifested in the Birth. If it was not the incarnation of God, it has no claim on the hearts of men.

II. The wondrous act of descent.

The stages in that long descent are marked out with a precision and definiteness which would be intolerable presumption, if Paul were speaking only his own thoughts, or telling what he had seen with his own eyes. They begin with what was in the mind of the eternal Word before He began His descent, and whilst yet He is 'in the form of God.' He stands on the lofty level before the descent begins, and in spirit makes the surrender, which, stage by stage, is afterwards to be wrought out in act. Before any of these acts there must have been the disposition of mind and will which Paul describes as 'counting it not a thing to be grasped to be on an equality with God.' He did not regard the being equal to God as a prey or treasure to be clutched and retained at all hazards. That sweeps our thoughts into the dim regions far beyond Calvary or Bethlehem, and is a more overwhelming manifestation of love than are the acts of lowly gentleness and patient endurance which followed in time. It included and transcended them all.

It was the supreme example of not 'looking on one's own things.' And what made Him so count? What but infinite love. To rescue men, and win them to Him-self and goodness, and finally to lift them to the place from which He came down for them, seemed to Him be the temporary surrender of that glory

majesty. We can but bow and adore the perfect love.
We look more deeply into the depths of Deity than
unaided eyes could ever penetrate, and what we see is
the movement in that abyss of Godhead of purest
surrender which, by beholding, we are to assimilate.

Then comes the wonder of wonders, 'He emptied
Himself.' We cannot enter here on the questions which
gather round that phrase, and which give it a factitious
importance in regard to present controversies. All
that we would point out now is that while the Apostle
distinctly treats the Incarnation as being a laying
aside of what made the Word to be equal with God,
he says nothing, on which an exact determination can
be based, of the degree or particulars in which the
divine nature of our Lord was limited by His
humanity. The fact he asserts, and that is all. The
scene in the Upper Chamber was but a feeble picture
of what had already been done behind the veil. Unless He had laid aside His garments of divine glory
and majesty, He would have had no human flesh from
which to strip the robes. Unless He had willed to
take the 'form of a servant,' He would not have had a
body to gird with the slave's towel. The Incarnation,
which made all His acts of lowly love possible, was a
greater act of lowly love than those which flowed
from it. Looking at it from earth, men say, 'Jesus
was born.' Looking at it from heaven, Angels say,
'He emptied Himself.'

how did He empty Himself? By taking the
lave, that is to God. And how did He take
? By 'be

as 'emptying Himself' was His own act, also the taking the form of a slave by His being born was His own act, and was more truly described as a 'becoming.' We note, too, the strong contrast between that most remarkable word and the 'being originally' which is used to express the mystery of divine pre-existence.

Whilst His becoming in the likeness of men stands in strong contrast with 'being originally,' and energetically expresses the voluntariness of our Lord's birth, the 'likeness of men' does not cast any doubt on the reality of His manhood, but points to the fact that 'though certainly perfect man, He was by reason of the divine nature present in Him not simply and merely man.'

Here then the beginning of Christ's manhood is spoken of in terms which are only explicable, if it was a second form of being, preceded by a pre-existent form, and was assumed by His own act. The language, too, demands that that humanity should have been true essential manhood. It was in 'the form' of man and possessed of all essential attributes. It was in 'the likeness' of man possessed of all external characteristics, and yet was something more. It summed up human nature, and was its representative.

III. The obedience which attended the descent.

It was not merely an act of humiliation and condescension to become man, but all His life was one long act of lowliness. Just as He 'emptied Himself' in the act of becoming in the 'likeness of men,' so He 'humbled Himself,' and all along the course of His earthly life He chose constant lowliness and to be 'despised and rejected of men.' It was the result m   moment of His own will that to the o   d 'no form nor comeliness,' and will was moment by moment steadied in its unmoved humility, because He perpetually looked 'not on His own things, but on the things of others.' The guise He presented to the eyes of men was 'the *fashion* of a man.' That word corresponds exactly to Paul's carefully selected term, and makes emphatic both its superficial and its transitory character.

The lifelong humbling of Himself was further manifested in His becoming 'obedient.' That obedience was, of course, to God. And here we cannot but pause to ask the question, How comes it that to the man Jesus obedience to God was an act of humiliation? Surely there is but one explanation of such a statement. For all men but this one to be God's slaves is their highest honour, and to speak of obedience as humiliation is a sheer absurdity.

Not only was the life of Jesus so perfect an example of unbroken obedience that He could safely front His adversaries with the question, 'Which of you convinceth Me of sin?' and with the claim to 'do always the things that pleased Him,' but the obedience to the Father was perfected in His death. Consider the extraordinary fact that a man's death is the crowning instance of his humility, and ask yourselves the question, Who then is this who chose to be born, and stooped in the act of dying? His death was obedience to God, because by it He carried out the Father's will for the salvation of the world, His death is the greatest instance of unselfish self-sacrifice, and the loftiest example of looking on the 'things of others' that the world ever seen. It dwindles in significance, in

Sorrows, and the Cross. No theory of Christ's life and death but that He was born for us, and died for us, either explains the facts and the apostolic language concerning them, or leaves them invested with their full power to melt our hearts and mould our lives. There is a possibility of imitating Him in the most transcendent of His acts. The mind may be in us which was in Christ Jesus. That it may, His death must first be the ground of our hope, and then we must make it the pattern of our lives, and draw from it the power to shape them after His blessed Example.

THE ASCENT OF JESUS

'Wherefore also God highly exalted Him and gave unto Him the name which is above every name; 10. That in the name of Jesus every knee should bow, of things in heaven, and things on earth, and things under the earth; 11. And that every tongue should confess that Jesus Christ is Lord, to the glory of God the Father.'—PHIL. ii. 9-11 (R.V.).

'HE that humbleth himself shall be exalted,' said Jesus. He is Himself the great example of that law. The Apostle here goes on to complete his picture of the Lord Jesus as our pattern. In previous verses we had the solemn steps of His descent, and the lifelong humility and obedience of the incarnate Son, the man Christ Jesus. Here we have the wondrous ascent which reverses all the former process. Our text describes the reflex motion by which Jesus is borne back to the same level as that from which the descent began.

We have

I. ct of exaltation which forms the cont

to the descent.

d Him.' The Apostle

emphatic word which doubly expresses elevation, and in its grammatical form shows that it indicates a historical fact. That elevation was a thing once accomplished on this green earth; that is to say it came to pass in the fact of our Lord's ascension when from some fold of the Mount of Olives He was borne upwards and, with blessing hands, was received into the Shechinah cloud, the glory of which hid Him from the upward-gazing eyes.

It is plain that the 'Him' of whom this tremendous assertion is made, must be the same as the 'He' of whom the previous verses spoke, that is, the Incarnate Jesus. It is the manhood which is exalted. His humiliation consisted in His becoming man, but His exaltation does not consist in His laying aside His humanity. It is not a transient but an eternal union into which in the Incarnation it entered with divinity. Henceforward we have to think of Him in all the glory of His heavenly state as man, and as truly and completely in the 'likeness of men' as when He walked with bleeding feet on the flinty road of earthly life. He now bears for ever the 'form of God' and 'the fashion of a man.'

Here I would pause for a moment to point out that the calm tone of this reference to the ascension in- ﹒ ﹒tes that it was part of the recognised Christian ﹒﹒ and implies that it had been familiar long ﹒﹒ date of this Epistle, which itself d﹒﹒s from ﹒﹒ the most ﹒﹒ty y﹒﹒

truth required that the exaltation should be God's act.
'He humbled Himself,' but 'God exalted Him.' True,
He sometimes represented Himself as the Agent of
His own Resurrection and Ascension, and established a
complete parallel between His descent and His ascent,
as when He said, 'I came out from the Father, and am
come into the world: again, I leave the world, and go
unto the Father.' He was no less obedient to the
Father's will when He ascended up on high, than He
was when He came down to earth, and whilst, from
one point of view, His Resurrection and Ascension were
as truly His own acts as were His birth and His death,
from another, He had to pray, 'And now, O Father,
glorify Thou Me with Thine own self with the glory
which I had with Thee before the world was.' The
Titans presumptuously scaled the heavens, according
to the old legend, but the Incarnate Lord returned to
'His own calm home, His habitation from eternity,'
was exalted thither by God, in token to the universe
that the Father approved the Son's descent, and that
the work which the Son had done was indeed, as He
declared it to be, 'finished.' By exalting Him, the
Father not merely reinstated the divine Word in its
eternal union with God, but received into the cloud of
glory the manhood which the Word had assumed.

II. The glory of the name of Jesus.

What is the name 'which is above every name'? It is
the name Jesus. It is to be noted that Paul scarcely
ever uses that simple appellative. There are, rough
speaking, about two hundred instances in which
names our Lord in his Epistles, and there are only f
places, besides this, in which he uses this as his own,
hich he, as it were, puts it into the me
y. Probably then, some special reason

its occurrence here, and it is not difficult, I think, to see what that reason is. The simple personal name was given indeed with reference to His work, but had been borne by many a Jewish child before Mary called her child Jesus, and the fact that it is this common name which is exalted above every name, brings out still more strongly the thought already dwelt upon, that what is thus exalted is the manhood of our Lord. The name which expressed His true humanity, which showed His full identification with us, which was written over His Cross, which perhaps shaped the taunt 'He *saved* others, Himself He cannot save,'—that name God has lifted high above all names of council and valour, of wisdom and might, of authority and rule. It is shrined in the hearts of millions who render to it perfect trust, unconditional obedience, absolute loyalty. Its growing power, and the warmth of personal love which it evokes, in centuries and lands so far removed from the theatre of His life, is a unique thing in the world's history. It reigns in heaven.

But Paul is not content with simply asserting the sovereign glory of the name of Jesus. He goes on to set it forth as being what no other name borne by man can be, the ground and object of worship, when he declares, that 'in the name of Jesus every knee shall bow.' The words are quoted from the second Isaiah, occur in one of the most solemn and majestic of the monotheism of the Old Testament. takes these words, undeterred by the declara-de them, 'I Am am God and there is

unmistakably set forth, as not only being that He has
declared God to men, who through Him are drawn to
worship the Father, but that their emotions of love,
reverence, worship, are turned to *Him*, though as the
Apostle is careful immediately to note, they are not
thereby intercepted from, but directed to, the glory of
God the Father. In the eternities before His descent,
there was equality with God, and when He returns, it
is to the Father, who in Him has become the object of
adoration, and round whose throne gather with bended
knees all those who in Jesus see the Father.

The Apostle still further dwells on the glory of the
name as that of the acknowledged Lord. And here we
have with significant variation in strong contrast to
the previous name of Jesus, the full title 'Jesus Christ
Lord.' That is almost as unusual in its completeness
as the other in its simplicity, and it comes in here with
tremendous energy, reminding us of the great act to
which we owe our redemption, and of all the prophecies
and hopes which, from of old, had gathered round the
persistent hope of the coming Messiah, while the name
of Lord proclaims His absolute dominion. The knee is
bowed in reverence, the tongue is vocal in confession.
That confession is incomplete if either of these three
names is falteringly uttered, and still more so, if
either of them is wanting. The Jesus whom Christians
confess is not merely the man who was born in
Bethlehem and known among men as 'Jesus the
carpenter.' In these modern days, His manhood has
been so emphasised as to obscure His Messiahship and
to obliterate His dominion, and alas! there are many
who exalt Him by the name that Mary gave Him,
turn away from the name of Jesus as 'Hebrew
and from the name of Lord as anti

superstition. But in all the lowliness and gentleness of Jesus there were not wanting lofty claims to be the Christ of whom prophets and righteous men of old spake, and whose coming many a generation desired to see and died without the sight, and still loftier and more absolute claims to be invested with 'all power in heaven and earth,' and to sit down with the Father on His throne. It is dangerous work to venture to toss aside two of these three names, and to hope that if we pronounce the third of them, Jesus, with appreciation, it will not matter if we do not name Him either Christ or Lord.

If it is true that the manhood of Jesus is thus exalted, how wondrous must be the kindred between the human and the divine, that it should be capable of this, that it should dwell in the everlasting burnings of the Divine Glory and not be consumed! How blessed for us the belief that our Brother wields all the forces of the universe, that the human love which Jesus had when He bent over the sick and comforted the sorrowful, is at the centre. Jesus is Lord, the Lord is Jesus!

The Psalmist was moved to a rapture of thanksgiving when he thought of man as 'made a little lower than the angels, and crowned with glory and honour,' but when we think of the Man Jesus 'sitting at the right hand of God,' the Psalmist's words seem pale and and we can repeat them with a deeper meaning emphasis, 'Thou madest Him to have of y things under the earth,' he simply intends to declare, that Jesus is the object of all worship, and the words are not to be pressed as containing dogmatic assertions as to the different classes mentioned. But guided by other words of Scripture, we may permissibly think that the 'things in heaven' tell us that the angels who do not need His mediation learn more of God by His work and bow before His throne. We cannot be wrong in believing that the glory of His work stretches far beyond the limits of humanity, and that His kingdom numbers other subjects than those who draw human breath. Other lips than ours say with a great voice, 'Worthy is the Lamb that hath been slain to receive power and riches and wisdom and might and honour and glory and blessing.'

The things on earth are of course men, and the words encourage us to dim hopes about which we cannot dogmatise of a time when all the wayward self-seeking and self-tormenting children of men shall have learned to know and love their best friend, and 'there shall be one flock and one shepherd.'

'Things under the earth' seems to point to the old thought of 'Sheol' or 'Hades' or a separate state of the dead. The words certainly suggest that those who have gone from us are not unconscious nor cut off from the true life, but are capable of adoration and confession. We cannot but remember the old belief that Jesus in His death 'descended into Hell,' and some of us will not forget Fra Angelico's picture of t open doorway with a demon crushed beneath the fal portal, and the crowd of eager faces and outstretc hands swarming up the dark passage, to welcome Christ. Whatever we may think of ation, we may at least be sure wherever they are, the dead in Christ praise and reverence and love.

IV. The glory of the Father in the glory of the name of Jesus.

Knees bent and tongues confessing the absolute dominion of Jesus Christ could only be offence and sin if He were not one with the Father. But the experience of all the thousands since Paul wrote, whose hearts have been drawn in reverent and worshipping trust to the Son, has verified the assertion, that to confess that Jesus Christ is Lord diverts no worship from God, but swells and deepens the ocean of praise that breaks round the throne. If it is true, and only if it is true, that in the life and death of Jesus all previous revelations of the Father's heart are surpassed, if it is true and only if it is true, as He Himself said, that 'I and the Father are one,' can Paul's words here be anything but an incredible paradox. But unless these great words close and crown the Apostle's glowing vision, it is maimed and imperfect, and Jesus interposes between loving hearts and God. One could almost venture to believe that at the back of Paul's mind, when he wrote these words, was some remembrance of the great prayer, 'I glorified Thee on the earth, having accomplished the work which Thou gavest Me to do.' When the Son is glorified we glorify the Father, and the words of our text may well be remembered and laid to heart by any who will not own the deity of the Son, because it seems to dishonour the Father. Their honour is inseparably one.

is for us the pattern for earthly life, though the deeds
in which that mind was expressed, and especially His
'obedience to the death of the Cross,' are so far beyond
any self-sacrifice of ours, and are inimitable, unique,
and needing no repetition while the world lasts. And
as we can imitate His unexampled sacrifice, so we may
share His divine glory, and, resting on His own faithful
word, may follow the calm motion of His Ascension,
assured that where He is there we shall be also, and
that the manhood which is exalted in Him is the
prophecy that all who love Him will share His glory.
The question for us all is, have we in us 'the mind that
was in Christ'? and the other question is, what is that
name to us? Can we say, 'Thy mighty name salvation
is'? If in our deepest hearts we grasp that name, and
with unfaltering lips can say that 'there is none other
name under heaven given amongst men whereby we
must be saved but the name of Jesus,' then we shall
know that

> 'To us with Thy dear name are given,
> Pardon, and holiness, and heaven.'

WORK OUT YOUR OWN SALVATION

'Work out your own salvation with fear and trembling, 13. For it is God which
worketh in you both to will and to do of His good pleasure.'—PHIL. ii. 12, 13.

'WHAT God hath joined together, let no man put
asunder!' Here are, joined together, in the comp[ass]
of one practical exhortation, the truths which, p[ut]
asunder, have been the war-cries and shibboleths [of]
sects ever since. *Faith* in a finished
[w]ork; God working all *in* me,

I able and bound to work likewise; God upholding and sustaining His child to the very end; 'perfecting that which concerns him,' making his salvation certain and sure, and yet the Christian working 'with fear and trembling,' lest he should be a castaway and come short of the grace of God;—who does not recognise in these phrases the mottoes that have been written on the opposing banners in many a fierce theological battle, waged with much harm to both sides, and ending in no clear victory for either? Yet here they are blended in the words of one who was no less profound a thinker than any that have come after, and who had the gift of a divine inspiration to boot.

Not less remarkable than the fusion here of apparent antagonisms, the harmonising of apparent opposites, is the intensely practical character of the purpose for which they are adduced at all. Paul has no idea of giving his disciples a lesson in abstract theology, or laying for them a foundation of a philosophy of free will and divine sovereignty; he is not merely communicating to these Philippians truths for their creed, but precepts for their deeds. The Bible knows nothing of an unpractical theology, but, on the other hand, the Bible knows still less of an untheological morality. It digs deep, bottoming the simplest right action upon right thinking, and going down to the mountain bases on which the very pillars of the universe rest, in order to lay there, firm and immoveable, the courses of the temple of a holy life. Just as little as Scripture gives countenance to the error that makes religion theology rather than life, just so little does it give countenance to the far more common and shallower error common in our day *means,* 'Therefore, it does not matter what theology you have, you can work a good life out with any creed!' The Bible never teaches unpractical speculations, and the Bible never gives precepts which do not rest on the profoundest truths. Would God, brethren, that we all had souls as wide as would take in the whole of the many-sided scriptural representation of the truths of the Gospel, and so avoid the narrowness of petty, partial views of God's infinite counsel; and that we had as close, direct, and as free communication between head, and heart, and hand, as the Scripture has between precept and practice!

But in reference more especially to my text. Keeping in view these two points I have already suggested, namely,—that it is the reconciling of apparent opposites, and that it is intensely practical, I find in it these three thoughts;—First, a Christian has his whole salvation accomplished for him, and yet he is to work it out. Secondly, a Christian has everything done in him by God, and yet he is to work. Lastly, a Christian has his salvation certainly secured, and yet he is to fear and tremble.

I. In the first place, A Christian man has his whole salvation already accomplished for him in Christ, and yet he is to work it out.

There are two points absolutely necessary to be kept in view in order to a right understanding of the words before us, for the want of noticing which it has become the occasion of terrible mistakes. These are—the persons to whom it is addressed, and the force of the scriptural expression 'salvation.' As to the first, the exhortation has been misapplied by being addressed the to have no claim to be Christians, and by having deduced from it as, You do your part

God will do His; You work, and God will certainly
help you; You co-operate in the great work of
your salvation, and you will get grace and pardon
through Jesus Christ. Now let us remember the very
simple thing, but very important to the right understanding of these words, that none but Christian
people have anything to do with them. To all others,
to all who are not already resting on the finished
salvation of Jesus Christ, this injunction is utterly
inapplicable. It is addressed to the 'beloved, who
have always obeyed'; to the 'saints in Christ Jesus,
which are at Philippi.' The whole Epistle is addressed,
and this injunction with the rest, to Christian men.
That is the first thing to be remembered. If there be
any of you, who have thought that these words of
Paul's to those who had believed on Christ contained a
rule of action for you, though you have not rested
your souls on Him, and exhorted you to try to win
salvation by your own doings, let me remind you of
what Christ said when the Jews came to Him in a
similar spirit and asked Him, 'What shall we do that
we may work the works of God?' His answer to
them was, and His answer to you, my brother, is, '*This*
is the work of God, that ye should *believe* in Him whom
He hath sent.' That is the first lesson: Not *work*, but
faith; unless there be faith, no work. Unless you are
a Christian, the passage has nothing to do with you.

But now, if this injunction be addressed to those
re looking for their salvation only to the perfect
ist, how can they be exhorted to work it
? Is not the oft-recurring bur of

peated assertions that Christ has done all for us, and
that we have nothing to do, and can do nothing? To
answer this question, we have to remember that that
scriptural expression, 'salvation,' is used with considerable width and complexity of signification. It sometimes means the whole of the process, from the beginning to the end, by which we are delivered from
sin in all its aspects, and are set safe and stable at
the right hand of God. It sometimes means one or
other of three different parts of that process—either
deliverance from the guilt, punishment, condemnation
of sin; or secondly, the gradual process of deliverance
from its power in our own hearts; or thirdly, the
completion of that process by the final and perfect
deliverance from sin and sorrow, from death and the
body, from earth and all its weariness and troubles,
which is achieved when we are landed on the other
side of the river. Salvation, in one aspect, is a thing
past to the Christian; in another, it is a thing *present*;
in a third, it is a thing *future*. But all these three are
one; all are elements of the one deliverance—the one
mighty and perfect act which includes them all.

These three all come equally from Christ Himself.
These three all depend equally on His work and His
power. These three are all given to a Christian man
in the first act of faith. But the attitude in which he
stands in reference to that *accomplished* salvation
which means deliverance from sin as a penalty and a
curse, and that in which he stands to the continuing
and progressive salvation which means deliverance
from the power of evil in his own heart, are somewhat
different. In regard to the one, he has only to take
the finished blessing. He has to exercise faith and
hope. He has nothing to do, nothing to

in order to fit himself for it, but simply to receive the gift of God, and to believe on Him whom He hath sent.   But then, though that reception involves what shall come after it, and though every one who has and holds the first thing, the pardon of his transgres· sion, has and holds thereby and therein his growing sanctifying and his final glory, yet the salvation which means our being delivered from the evil that is in our hearts, and having our souls made like unto Christ, is one which—free gift though it be—is not ours on the sole condition of an initial act of faith, but is ours on the condition of continuous faithful reception and daily effort, not in our own strength, but in God's strength, to become like Him, and to make our own that which God has given us, and which Christ is continually bestowing upon us.

The two things, then, are not inconsistent—an accomplished salvation, a full, free, perfect redemption, with which a man has nothing to do at all, but to take it;—and, on the other hand, the injunction to them who have received this divine gift: 'Work out your own salvation.' Work, as well as believe, and in the daily practice of faithful obedience, in the daily subjugation of your own spirits to His divine power, in the daily crucifixion of your flesh with its affections and lusts, in the daily straining after loftier heights of godliness and purer atmospheres of devotion and love make more thoroughly your own that which you Work into the substance of your souls that have. Apprehend that for which you are Christ. 'Give all ce to m and yet yours, is the 'holding fast the beginning of your confidence firm unto the end.'

II. In the second place, God works all in us, and yet we have to work.

There can be no mistake about the good faith and firm emphasis—as of a man who knows his own mind, and *knows* that his word is true—with which the Apostle holds up here the two sides of what I venture to call the one truth; 'Work out your own salvation—for God works in you.' Command implies power. Command and power involve duty. The freedom of the Christian's action, the responsibility of the believer for his Christian growth in grace, the committal to the Christian man's own hands of the means of sanctifying, lie in that injunction, 'Work out your own salvation.' Is there any faltering, any paring down or cautious guarding of the words, in order that they may not seem to clash with the other side of the truth? No: Paul does not say, 'Work it out; *yet* it is God that worketh in you'; not 'Work it out *although* it is God that worketh in you'; not 'Work it out, but then it must always be remembered and taken as a caution that it is God that worketh in you!' He blends the two things together in an altogether different connection, and sees—strangely to some people, no contradiction, nor limitation, nor puzzle, but a ground of encouragement to cheerful obedience. Do you work, '*for* it is God that worke[th] in you both to will and to do of His good pleasu[re.] And does the Apostle limit the divine operati[on] No[t so;] how his words seem picked out on purp[ose] e[xpr]es[s] m[o]st emphatically its all-pervading [...] seem picked out on pur[pose] e emp[ty]

which a good man is, and does, is its fruit. It is God
that *worketh in* you. That expresses more than bringing outward means to bear upon heart and will. It
speaks of an inward, real, and efficacious operation of
the Indwelling Spirit of all energy on the spirit in
which He dwells. 'Worketh in you *to will*'; this
expresses more than the presentation of motives from
without, it points to a direct action on the will, by
which impulses are originated within. God puts in
you the first faint motions of a better will. 'Worketh
in you, doing as well as willing'; this points to all
practical obedience, to all external acts as flowing
from His grace in us, no less than all inward good
thoughts and holy desires.

It is not that God gives men the power, and then
leaves them to make the use of it. It is not that the
desire and purpose come forth from Him, and that
then we are left to ourselves to be faithful or unfaithful stewards in carrying it out. The whole process,
from the first sowing of the seed until its last blossom-
ing and fruiting, in the shape of an accomplished act,
of which God shall bless the springing—it is all God's
together! There is a thorough-going, absolute attri-
bution of every power, every action, all the thoughts,
words, and deeds of a Christian soul, to God. No words
could be selected which would more thoroughly cut
away the ground from every half-and-half system
which attempts to deal them out in two portions, part
God's and part mine. With all emphasis Paul attributes all to God.

And none the less strongly does he teach, by the
implication contained in his earnest injunction, that
h——— ———ibility, that human control over the
b——— — re——y of human a———cy ——

are often thought to be annihilated by these broad
views of God as originating all good in the soul and life.
The Apostle thought that this doctrine did not absorb
all our individuality in one great divine Cause which
made men mere tools and puppets. He did not believe
that the inference from it was, 'Therefore do you sit
still, and feel yourselves the cyphers that you are.'
His practical conclusion is the very opposite. It is—
God does all, therefore do you work. His belief in
the power of God's grace was the foundation of the
most intense conviction of the reality and indispens-
ableness of his own power, and was the motive which
stimulated him to vigorous action. Work, for God
works in you.

Each of these truths rests firmly on its own appropriate evidence. My own consciousness tells me that
I am free, that I have power, that I am therefore
responsible and exposed to punishment for neglect of
duty. I know what I mean when I speak of the will
of God, because I myself am conscious of a will. The
power of God is an object of intelligent thought to
me, because I myself am conscious of power. And on
the other hand, that belief in a God which is one of
the deep and universal beliefs of men contains in it,
when it comes to be thought about, the belief in Him
as the source of all power, as the great cause of all.
If I believe in a God at all, I must believe that He
whom I so call, worketh all things after the counsel of
His own will. These two convictions are both given
to us in the primitive beliefs which belong to us
The one rests on consciousness, and underlies all
moral judgments. The other rests on an orig
belief which belongs to man as such. These
s on which all morality and all re

repose have their foundations down deep in our nature, and tower up beyond our sight. They seem to stand opposite to each other, but it is only as the strong piers of some tall arch are opposed. Beneath they repose on one foundation, above they join together in the completing keystone and bear the whole steady structure.

Wise and good men have toiled to harmonise them, in vain. The task transcends the limits of human faculties, as exercised here, at all events. Perhaps the time may come when we shall be lifted high enough to see the binding arch, but here on earth we can only behold the shafts on either side. The history of controversy on the matter surely proves abundantly what a hopeless task they undertake who attempt to reconcile these truths. The attempt has usually consisted in speaking the one loudly and the other in a whisper, and then the opposite side has thundered what had been whispered, and has whispered very softly what had been shouted very loudly. One party lays hold of the one pole of the ark, and the other lays hold of that on the other side. The fancied reconciliation consists in paring down one half of the full-orbed truth to nothing, or in admitting it in words while every principle of the reconciler's system demands its denial. Each antagonist is strong in his assertions, and weak in his denials, victorious when he establishes his half of the whole, easily defeated when he tries to throw his opponent's.

apparent incompatibility is no reason for re-
ch commended to our acceptance on
grounds. It may be a reason for n
may

limited understandings have no firm footing, but it is no ground for suspecting the evidence which certifies the truths. The Bible admits and enforces them both. It never tones down the emphasis of its statement of the one for fear of clashing against the other, but points to us the true path for thought, in a firm grasp of both, in the abandonment of all attempts to reconcile them, and for practical conduct, in the peaceful trust in God who hath wrought all our works in us, and in strenuous working out of our own salvation. Let us, as we look back on that battlefield where much wiser men than we have fought in vain, doing little but raising up 'a little dust that is lightly laid again,' and building trophies that are soon struck down, learn the lesson it teaches, and be contented to say, The short cord of my plummet does not quite go down to the bottom of the bottomless, and I do not profess either to understand God or to understand man, both of which I should want to do before I understood the mystery of their conjoint action. Enough for me to believe that,

'If any force we have, it is to ill,
And all the power is God's, to do and eke to will.'

Enough for me to know that I have solemn duties laid upon me, a life's task to be done, my deliverance from mine own evil to work out, and that I shall only accomplish that work when I can say with the Apostle, 'I live, yet not I, but Christ liveth in me.'

God is all, but *thou* canst work! My brother, ta this belief, that God worketh all in you, for ground of your confidence, and feel that unless He all you can do nothing. Take this conviction, th k, for the spur and stimulus life, and think, These desires in my soul come from a far deeper source than the little cistern of my own individual life. They are God's gift. Let me cherish them with the awful carefulness which their origin requires, lest I should seem to have received the grace of God in vain. These two streams of truth are like the rain-shower that falls upon the watershed of a country. The one half flows down the one side of the everlasting hills, and the other down the other. Falling into rivers that water different continents, they at length find the sea, separated by the distance of half the globe. But the sea into which they fall is one, in every creek and channel. And so, the truth into which these two apparent opposites converge, is 'the depth of the wisdom and the knowledge of God,' whose ways are past finding out—the Author of all goodness, who, if we have any holy thought, has given it us; if we have any true desire, has implanted it; has given us the strength to do the right and to live in His fear; and who yet, doing all the willing and the doing, says to us, 'Because I do everything, therefore let not *thy* will be paralysed, or *thy* hand palsied; but because I do everything, therefore will *thou* according to My will, and do *thou* according to My commandments!'

III. Lastly: The Christian has his salvation secured, and yet he is to fear and tremble.

ar and trembling.' 'But,' you may say, 'perfect out fear.' So it does. The fear which has ts out. But there is another fear

us it is certain since he believes. And your faith
can be worth nothing unless it have, bedded deep
in it, that trembling distrust of your own power
which is the pre-requisite and the companion of all
thankful and faithful reception of God's infinite
mercy. Your horizon ought to be full of fear, if your
gaze be limited to yourself; but oh! above our earthly
horizon with its fogs, God's infinite blue stretches
untroubled by the mist and cloud which are earth-
born. I, as working, have need to tremble and to
fear, but I, as wrought upon, have a right to confidence
and hope, a hope that is full of immortality, and an
assurance which is the pledge of its own fulfilment.
The worker is nothing, the Worker in him is all.
Fear and trembling, when the thoughts turn to mine
own sins and weaknesses, hope and confidence when
they turn to the happier vision of God! 'Not I'—
there is the tremulous self-distrust; 'the grace of God
in me'—there is the calm assurance of victory. Forasmuch, then, as God worketh all things, be *you*
diligent, faithful, prayerful, confident. Forasmuch as
Christ has perfected the work for you, do *you* ' go on
unto perfection.' Let all fear and trembling be yours,
as a man; let all confidence and calm trust be yours
as a child of God. Turn your confidence and your
fears alike into prayer. ' Perfect, O Lord, that which
concerneth me; forsake not the work of Thine own
hands!'—and the prayer will evoke the merciful
answer, 'I will never leave thee, nor forsake th
God is faithful, who hath called you unto the Go
of His Son; and *will* keep you unto His everla
k   n of glory.'

COPIES OF JESUS

'Do all things without murmurings and disputings; 15. That ye may be blameless and harmless, children of God without blemish in the midst of a crooked and perverse generation, among whom ye are seen as lights in the world, 16. Holding forth the word of life.'—PHIL. ii. 14-16 (R.V.).

WE are told by some superfine modern moralists, that to regard one's own salvation as the great work of our lives is a kind of selfishness, and no doubt there may be a colour of truth in the charge. At least the meaning of the injunction to work out our own salvation may have been sometimes so misunderstood, and there have been types of Christian character, such as the ascetic and monastic, which have made the representation plausible. I do not think that there is much danger of anybody so misunderstanding the precept now. But it is worthy of notice that there stand here side by side two paragraphs, in the former of which the effort to work out one's own salvation is urged in the strongest terms, and in the other of which the regard for others is predominant. We shall see that the connection between these two is not accidental, but that one great reason for working out our salvation is here set forth as being the good we may thereby do to others.

I. We note the one great duty of cheerful yielding to God's will.

clear, I think, that the precept to do 'all things murmurings and disputings' stands in the n with what goes before. It is, in us on our parts do with ready submission all the things which He so inspires to will and to do.

The 'murmurings' are not against men but against God. The 'disputings' are not wrangling with others but the division of mind in one's self-questionings, hesitations, and the like. So the one are more moral, the other more intellectual, and together they represent the ways in which Christian men may resist the action on their spirits of God's Spirit, 'willing,' or the action of God's providence on their circumstances, 'doing.' Have we never known what it was to have some course manifestly prescribed to us as right, from which we have shrunk with reluctance of will? If some course has all at once struck us as wrong which we had been long accustomed to do without hesitation, has there been no 'murmuring' before we yielded? A voice has said to us, ' Give up such and such a habit,' or 'such and such a pursuit is becoming too engrossing': do we not all know what it is not only to feel obedience an effort, but even to cherish reluctance, and to let it stifle the voice?

There are often 'disputings' which do not get the length of 'murmurings.' The old word which tried to weaken the plain imperative of the first command by the subtle suggestion, 'Yea, hath God said?' still is whispered into our ears. We know what it is to answer God's commands with a ' But, Lord.' A reluctant will is clever to drape itself with more or less honest excuses, and the only safety is in cheerful obedience and glad submission. The will of God ought not only to recei obedience, but prompt obedience, and such inst taneous and whole-souled submission is indispensabl e ar to ' ork out our own salvation,' and to pr f true, receptive correspondence to t

God, who 'works in us both to will and to do of His
own good pleasure.' Our surrender of ourselves into
the hands of God, in respect both to inward and outward things, should be complete. As has been profoundly said, that surrender consists 'in a continual
forsaking and losing all self in the will of God, willing
only what God from eternity has willed, forgetting
what is past, giving up the time present to God, and
leaving to His providence that which is to come,
making ourselves content in the actual moment seeing
it brings along with it the eternal order of God concerning us' (Madame Guyon).

II. The conscious aim in all our activity

What God works in us for is that for which we too
are to yield ourselves to His working, 'without murmurings and disputings,' and to co-operate with glad submission and cheerful obedience. We are to have as
our distinct aim the building up of a character 'blameless and harmless, children of God without rebuke.'
The blamelessness is probably in reference to men's
judgment rather than to God's, and the difficulty of
coming untarnished from contact with the actions and
criticisms of a crooked and perverse generation is
emphasised by the very fact that such blamelessness is
the first requirement for Christian conduct. It was a
ther in Daniel's cap that the president and princes
foiled in their attempt to pick holes in his con-
had to confess that they would not 'find any
him, concerning the

reasonable, but on the whole it would not be a bad rule
for Christian people, 'Do what irreligious men expect
you to do.' The worst man knows more than the best
man practises, and his conscience is quick to decide the
course for other people. Our weaknesses and com-
promises, and love of the world, might receive a salutary
rebuke if we would try to meet the expectations which
'the man in the street' forms of us.

'Harmless' is more correctly pure, all of a piece,
homogeneous and entire. It expresses what the
Christian life should be in itself, whilst the former
designation describes it more as it appears. The piece
of cloth is to be so evenly and carefully woven that if
held up against the light it will show no flaws nor
knots. Many a professing Christian life has a veneer of
godliness nailed thinly over a solid bulk of selfishness.
There are many goods in the market finely dressed so
as to hide that the warp is cotton and only the weft
silk. No Christian man who has memory and self-
knowledge can for a moment claim to have reached
the height of his ideal; the best of us, at the best, are
like Nebuchadnezzar's image, whose feet were iron and
clay, but we ought to strain after it and to remember
that a stain shows most on the whitest robe. What
made David's sin glaring and memorable was its contradiction of his habitual nobler self. One spot more
matters little on a robe already covered with many.
The world is fully warranted in pointing gleefully or
contemptuously at Christians' inconsistencies, and we
have no right to find fault with their most pointed
sarcasms, or their severest judgments. It is the
'that bear the vessels of the Lord' whose bur
im   on them the duty 'be ye clean,' and makes
                more foul in them than in any other.

The Apostle sets forth the place and function of Christians in the world, by bringing together in the sharpest contrast the 'children of God' and a 'crooked and perverse generation.' He is thinking of the old description in Deuteronomy, where the ancient Israel is charged with forgetting 'Thy Father that hath bought thee,' and as showing by their corruption that they are a 'perverse and crooked generation.' The ancient Israel had been the Son of God, and yet had corrupted itself; the Christian Israel are 'sons of God' set among a world all deformed, twisted, perverted. 'Perverse' is a stronger word than 'crooked,' which latter may be a metaphor for moral obliquity, like our own right and wrong, or perhaps points to personal deformity. Be that as it may, the position which the Apostle takes is plain enough. He regards the two classes as broadly separated in antagonism in the very roots of their being. Because the 'sons of God' are set in the midst of that 'crooked and perverse generation' constant watchfulness is needed lest they should conform, constant resort to their Father lest they should lose the sense of sonship, and constant effort that they may witness of Him.

III. The solemn reason for this aim.

That is drawn from a consideration of the office and function of Christian men. Their position in the midst a 'crooked and perverse generation' devolves on a duty in relation to that generation. They are lights in the world.' The relation be merely of cont but on th lighten the darkness with their myriad lucid points, so in the divine ideal Christian men are to be as twinkling lights in the abyss of darkness. Their light rays forth without effort, being an involuntary efflux. Possibly the old paradox of the Psalmist was in the Apostle's mind, which speaks of the eloquent silence, in which 'there is no speech nor language, and their voice is not heard,' but yet 'their line has gone out through all the earth, and their words unto the end of the world.'

Christian men appear as lights by 'holding forth the word of life.' In themselves they have no brightness but that which comes from raying out the light that is in them. The word of life must live, giving life in us, if we are ever to be seen as 'lights in the world.' As surely as the electric light dies out of a lamp when the current is switched off, so surely shall we be light only when we are 'in the Lord.' There are many so-called Christians in this day who stand tragically unaware that their 'lamps are gone out.' When the sun rises and smites the mountain tops they burn, when its light falls on Memnon's stony lips they breathe out music, ' Arise, shine, for thy light has come.'

Undoubtedly one way of 'holding forth the word of life' must be to speak the word, but silent living 'blameless and harmless' and leaving the secret of the life very much to tell itself is perhaps the best way for most Christian people to bear witness. Such a witness is constant, diffused wherever the witness-bearer is seen, and free from the difficulties that beset speech, and especially from the assumption of superiority which often gives offence. It was the sight of 'your good deeds' to which Jesus pointed as the strong reason for men's 'glorifying your Father.' If we lived such lives there would be less need for preachers.

any will not hear the word they may without the word be won.' And reasonably so, for Christianity is a life and cannot be all told in words, and the Gospel is the proclamation of freedom from sin, and is best preached and proved by showing that we are free. The Gospel was lived as well as spoken. Christ's life was Christ's mightiest preaching.

> 'The word was flesh and wrought
> With human hands the creed of creeds.'

If we keep near to Him we too shall witness, and if our faces shine like Moses' as he came down from the mountain, or like Stephen's in the council chamber, men will 'take knowledge of us that we have been with Jesus.'

A WILLING SACRIFICE

'That I may have whereof to glory in the day of Christ, that I did not run in vain neither labour in vain. 17. Yea, and if I am offered upon the sacrifice and service of your faith, I joy, and rejoice with you all. 18. And in the same manner do ye also joy, and rejoice with me.'—PHIL. ii. 16-18 (R.V.).

WE come here to another of the passages in which the Apostle pours out all his heart to his beloved Church. Perhaps there never was a Christian teacher (always excepting Christ) who spoke more about himself than Paul. His own experience was always at hand for illustration. His preaching was but the generalisation ...life. He had felt it all first, before he threw it ...rm of doctrine. It is very hard to keep such ...coming egotism.

...rem...le, ...ly if we con-

deep love between Paul and the Philippians to make
such words as these true and appropriate. They open
the very depths of his heart in a way from which a less
noble and fervid nature would have shrunk, and express
his absolute consecration in his work, and his eager
desire for their spiritual good, with such force as would
have been exaggeration in most men.

We have here a wonderful picture of the relation
between him and the church at Philippi which may well
stand as a pattern for us all. I do not mean to parallel
our relations with that between him and them, but it
is sufficiently analogous to make these words very
weighty and solemn for us.

I. The Philippians' faithfulness Paul's glory in the
day of Christ.

The Apostle strikes a solemn note, which was always
sounding through his life, when he points to that great
Day of Christ as the time when his work was to be
tested. The thought of that gave earnestness to all
his service, and in conjunction with the joyful thought
that, however his work might be marred by failures
and flaws, he himself was 'accepted in the beloved,'
was the impulse which carried him on through a life
than which none of Christ's servants have dared, and
done, and suffered more for Him. Paul believed that,
according to the results of that test, his position would
in some sort be determined. Of course he does not
here contradict the foundation principle of his whole
Gospel, that salvation is not the result of our own
works, or virtues, but is the free unmerited gift of
Christ's grace. But while that is true, it is none the
less true, that the degree in which believers receive
that gift depends on their Christian character, both
their life on earth and in the day of Christ.

element in that character is faithful work for Jesus. Faithful work indeed is not necessarily successful work, and many who are welcomed by Jesus, the judge, will have the memory of many disappointments and few harvested grains. It was not a reaper, 'bringing his sheaves with him,' who stayed himself against the experience of failure, by the assurance, 'Though Israel be not gathered yet shall I be glorious in the eyes of the Lord.' If our want of success, and others' lapse, and apostasy or coldness has not been occasioned by any fault of ours, there will be no diminution of our reward. But we can so seldom be sure of that, and even then there will be an absence of what might have added to gladness.

We need not do more than note that the text plainly implies, that at that testing time men's knowledge of all that they did, and the results of it, will be complete. Marvellous as it seems to us, with our fragmentary memories, and the great tracts of our lives through which we have passed mechanically, and which seem to have left no trace on the mirror of our consciousness, we still, all of us, have experiences which make that all-recovering memory credible. Some passing association, a look, a touch, an odour, a sun-set sky, a chord of music will bring before us some trivial long-forgotten incident or emotion, as the chance thrust of a boat-hook will draw to the surface by its a long-drowned corpse. If we are, as assuredly writing with invisible ink our whole life's es of our own minds, and if we

But there is another way of looking at Paul's words as being an indication of his warm love for the Philippians. Even among the glories, he would feel his heart filled with new gladness when he found them there. The hunger for the good of others which cannot bear to think even of heaven without their presence has been a master note of all true Christian teachers, and without it there will be little of the toil, of which Paul speaks in the context, 'running and labouring.' He that would win men's hearts for any great cause must give his heart to them.

That Paul should have felt warranted in using such a motive with the Philippians tells how surely he reckoned on their true and deep love. He believes that they care enough for him to feel the power as a motive with them, that their faithfulness will make Paul more blessed amidst the blessings of heaven. Oh! if such love knit together all Christian teachers and their hearers in this time, and if the 'Day of Christ' burned before them, as it did before him, and if the vision stirred to such running and labouring as his, teachers and taught would oftener have to say, 'We are your rejoicing, even as ye are also ours in the Day of our Lord Jesus.' The voice of the man who is in the true 'Apostolic Succession' will dare to make the appeal, knowing that it will call forth an abundant answer, 'Look to yourselves that we lose not the things which we have wrought, but that we receive a full reward.'

II. Paul's death an aid to the Philippians' faith.

The general meaning of the Apostle's words is, 'I have not only to run and labour, but to die in di_____ __ __ Apostolic Mission, I joy and a_____ __ice with me.' We need on

that the Apostle here casts his language into the forms
consecrated for sacrifice. He will not speak of death
by its own ugly and threadbare name, but thinks of
himself as a devoted victim, and of his death as making
the sacrifice complete. In the figure there is a solemn
scorn of death, and at the same time a joyful recognition that it is the means of bringing him more nearly
to God, with whom he would fain be. It is interesting,
as showing the persistence of these thoughts in the
Apostle's mind, that the word rendered in our text
'offered,' which fully means 'poured out as a drink
offering,' occurs again in the same connection in the
great words of the swan song in II. Timothy, 'I am
already being offered, and the time of my departure is
come.' Death looked to him, when he looked it in the
eyes, and the block was close by him, as it had done
when he spoke of it to his Philippian friends.

It is to be noted, in order to bring out more vividly
the force of the figure, that Paul here speaks of
the libation being poured '*on*' the sacrifice, as was the
practice in heathen ritual. The sacrifice is the victim,
'service' is the technical word for priestly ministration, and the general meaning is, 'If my blood is
poured out as a drink offering on the sacrifice ministered by you, which is your faith, I joy with you all.'
This man had no fear of death, and no shrinking from
ing the warm precincts of the cheerful day.' He
ually ready to live or to die as might best serve
Jesus, for to him 'to live was Christ,' and
could othi   ain' t

the contrast between his mood of mind here and that
in the previous chapter (i. 25) where the 'desire to
depart and to be with Christ' is deliberately suppressed,
because his continuous life is regarded as essential for
the Philippians' 'progress and joy in faith.' Here he
discerns that perhaps his death would do more for their
faith than would his life, and being ready for either alternative he welcomes the possibility. May we not see
in the calm heart, which is at leisure to think of death
in such a fashion, a pattern for us all? Remember how
near and real his danger was. Nero was not in the
habit of letting a man, whose head had been in the
mouth of the lion, take it out unhurt. Paul is no
eloquent writer or poet playing with the idea of death,
and trying to say pretty things about it, but a man
who did not know when the blow would come, but *did*
know that it would come before long.

We may point here to the two great thoughts in
Paul's words, and notice the priesthood and sacrifice
of life, and the sacrifice and libation of death. The
Philippians offered as their sacrifice their faith, and all
the works which flow therefrom. Is that our idea of
life? Is it our idea of faith? We have no gifts to
bring, we come empty-handed unless we carry in our
hands the offering of our faith, which includes the
surrender of our will, and the giving away of our
hearts, and is essentially laying hold of Christ's sacrifice.
When we come empty, needy, sinful, but cleaving
wholly to that perfect sacrifice of the Great Priest,
too become priests and our poor gift is accepted.

But another possibility than that of a life of run
and labour presented itself to Paul, and it is a reve
of t   nquillity of his heart in the midst of i
in   r, all the more pathetic because it is e

unconscious, that he should be free to cast his anticipations into that calm metaphor of being, 'offered
upon the sacrifice and service of your faith.' His heart
beats no faster, nor does the faintest shadow of reluctance cross his will, when he thinks of his death. All
the repulsive accompaniments of a Roman execution
fade away from his imagination. These are but
negligible accidents; the substantial reality which
obscures them all is that his blood will be poured out
as a libation, and that by it his brethren's faith will be
strengthened. To this man death had finally and
completely ceased to be a terror, and had become what
it should be to all Christians, a voluntary surrender
to God, an offering to Him, an act of worship, of trust,
and of thankful praise. Seneca, in his death, poured
out a libation to Jupiter the Liberator, and if we could
only know beforehand what death delivers us from,
and admits us to, we should not be so prone to call it
'the last enemy.' What Paul's death was for himself
in the process of his perfecting called forth, and
warranted, the 'joy' with which he anticipated it. It
did no more for him than it will do for each of us, and
if our vision were as clear, and our faith as firm as his,
we should be more ready than, alas! we too often are,
to catch up the exulting note with which he hails the
possibility of its coming.

But it is not the personal bearing only of his death
gives him joy. He thinks of it mainly as contri-

rejoice' with him in his shedding of his martyr's blood.

The Philippians might well have thought, as we all are tempted to think, that the withdrawal of those round whom our hearts desperately cling, and who seem to us to bring love and trust nearer to us, can only be loss, but surely the example in our text may well speak to our hearts of the way in which we should look at death for ourselves, and for our dearest. Their very withdrawal may send us nearer to Christ. The holy memories which linger in the sky, like the radiance of a sunken sun, may clothe familiar truths with unfamiliar power and loveliness. The thought of where the departed have gone may lift our thoughts wistfully thither with a new feeling of home. The path that they have trodden may become less strange to us, and the victory that they have won may prophesy that we too shall be 'more than conquerors through Him that loveth us.' So the mirror broken may turn us to the sun, and the passing of the dearest that can die may draw us to the Dearer who lives.

Paul, living, rejoiced in the prospect of death. We may be sure that he rejoiced in it no less dead than living. And we may permissibly think of this text as suggesting how

> 'The saints on earth and all the dead
> But one communion make,'

and are to be united in one joy. They rejoice for their own sakes, but their joy is not self-absorbed, and putting them farther away from us. They look ba upon earth, the runnings and labourings of the fo   n life here; and are glad to bear in their h the i   table token that they have 'not run in

neither laboured in vain.' But surely the depth of
their own repose will not make them indifferent to
those who are still in the midst of struggle and toil,
nor the fulness of their own felicity make them forget
those whom they loved of old, and love now with the
perfect love of Heaven. It is hard for us to rise to
complete sympathy with these serenely blessed spirits,
but yet we too should rejoice. Not indeed to the ex-
clusion of sorrow, nor to the neglect of the great
purpose to be effected in us by the withdrawal, as by
the presence of dear ones, the furtherance of our faith,
but having made sure that that purpose has been
effected in us, we should then give solemn thanksgivings if it has. It is sad and strange to think of how
opposite are the feelings about their departure, of those
who have gone and of those who are left. Would it
not be better that we should try to share theirs and
so bring about a true union? We may be sure that
their deepest desire is that we should. If some lips
that we shall never hear any more, till we come where
they are, could speak, would not they bring to us as
their message from Heaven, Do 'ye also joy and rejoice
with me'?

PAUL AND TIMOTHY

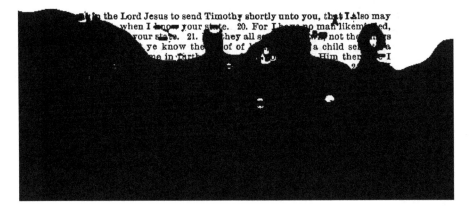

planet draws in small aerolites which catch fire as
they pass through its atmosphere. There is no more
beautiful page in the history of the early Church than
the story of Paul and his companions. They gathered
round him with such devotion, and followed him with
such love. They were not small men. Luke and
Aquila were among them, and they would have been
prominent in most companies, but gladly took a place
second to Paul. He impressed his own personality and
his type of teaching on his followers as Luther did on
his, and as many another great teacher has done.

Among all these Timothy seems to have held a
special place. Paul first found him on his second
journey either at Derbe or Lystra. His mother, Eunice,
was already a believer, his father a Greek. Timothy
seems to have been converted on Paul's first visit, for
on his second he was already a disciple well reported
of, and Paul more than once calls him his 'son in the
faith.' He seems to have come in to take John Mark's
place as the Apostle's 'minister,' and from that time to
have been usually Paul's trusted attendant. We hear
of him as with the Apostle on his first visit to Philippi,
and to have gone with him to Thessalonica and Berœa,
but then to have been parted until Corinth. Thence
Paul went quickly up to Jerusalem and back to
Antioch, from which he set out again to visit the
churches, and made a special stay in Ephesus. While
there he planned a visit to Macedonia and Achaia, in
preparation for one to Jerusalem, and finally to Ron
So he sent Timothy and Erastus on ahead to Macedo
which would of course include Philippi. After
visit to Macedonia and Greece Paul returne
Ph   i   which he sailed with Timothy
co   He was probably with him all the

Rome, and we find him mentioned as sharer in the imprisonment both here and in Colossians.

The references made to him point to a very sweet, good, pure and gracious character without much strength, needing to be stayed and stiffened by the stronger character, but full of sympathy, unselfish disregard of self, and consecrated love to Christ. He had been surrounded with a hallowed atmosphere from his youth, and 'from a child had known the holy Scriptures,' and 'prophecies' like fluttering doves had gone before on him. He had 'often infirmities,' and 'tears.' He needed to be roused to 'stir up the gift that was in him,' and braced up 'not to be ashamed,' but to fight against the disabling 'spirit of fear,' and to be 'strong in the grace that is in Christ Jesus.'

The bond between these two was evidently very close, and the Apostle felt something of a paternal interest in the very weakness of character which was in such contrast to his own strength, and which obviously dreaded the discouragement which was likely to be produced by his own martyrdom. This favourite companion he will now send to his favourite church. The verses of our text express that intention, and give us a glimpse into the Apostle's thoughts and feelings in his imprisonment.

I. The prisoner's longing and hope.

The first point which strikes us in this self-revelation l's is his conscious uncertainty as to his future. us chapter (ver. 25) he is confident that e verses immediately preceding our he r hoping and sometimes doubting. He had a tyrant's caprice to depend on, and knew how a moment's whim might end all. Surely his way of bearing that suspense was very noteworthy and noble. It is difficult to keep a calm heart, and still more difficult to keep on steadily at work, when any moment might bring the victor's axe. Suspense almost enforces idleness, but Paul crowded these moments of his prison time with letters, and Ephesians, Philippians, Colossians, and Philemon are the fruits for which we are indebted to a period which would have been to many men a reason for throwing aside all work.

How calmly too he speaks of the uncertain issue! Surely never was the possibility of death more quietly spoken of than in 'so soon as I shall see how it will go with me.' That means—'as soon as my fate is decided, be it what it may, I will send Timothy to tell you.' What a calm pulse he must have had! There is no attitudinising here, all is perfectly simple and natural. Can we look, do we habitually look, into the uncertain future with such a temper—accepting all that may be in its grey mists, and feeling that our task is to fill the present with strenuous loving service, leaving to-morrow with all its alternatives, even that tremendous one of life and death, to Him who will shape it to a perfect end?

We note, further, the purpose of Paul's love. It is beautiful to see how he yearns over these Philippians and feels that his joy will be increased when he hears from them. He is sure, as he believes, to hear good and news which will be a comfort. Among the so whom he bore on his heart were many in the Macedonian city, and a word from them would be like 'water to a thirsty soul.'

What a noble suppression of self; how deep and
strong the tie that bound him to them must have been !
Is there not a lesson here for all Christian workers, for
all teachers, preachers, parents, that no good is to be
done without loving sympathy? Unless our hearts go
out to people we shall never reach their hearts. We may
talk to them for ever, but unless we have this loving
sympathy we might as well be silent. It is possible to
pelt people with the Gospel, and to produce the effect
of flinging stones at them. Much Christian work comes
to nothing mainly for that reason.

And how deep a love does he show in his depriving
himself of Timothy for their sakes, and in his reason
for sending him ! Those reasons would have been for
most of us the strongest reason for keeping him. It is
not everybody who will denude himself of the help of
one who serves him 'as a child serveth a father,' and
will part with the only like-minded friend he has,
because his loving eye will clearly see the state of
others.

Paul's expression of his purpose to send Timothy is
very much more than a piece of emotional piety. He
'hopes in the Lord' to accomplish his design, and that
hope so rooted and conditioned is but one instance of
the all-comprehending law of his life, that, to him, to
'live is Christ.' His whole being was so interpenetrated
with Christ's that all his thoughts and feelings were
'in the Lord Jesus.' So should our purposes be. Our
hopes should be derived from union with Him. They
should not be the play of our own fancy or imagination.
They should be held in submission to him, and ever with
'Not as I will, but as Thou wilt.'

tempting us away from Him by delusive brightnesses. There is a religious use of hope not only when it is directed to heavenly certainties, and 'enters within the veil,' but even when occupied about earthly things. Spenser twice paints for us the figure of Hope, one has always something of dread in her blue eyes, the other, and the other only, leans on the anchor, and 'maketh not ashamed'; and her name is 'Hope in the Lord.'

II. The prisoner solitary among self-seeking men.

With wonderful self-surrender the Apostle thinks of his lack of like-minded companions as being a reason for depriving himself of the only like-minded one who was left with him. He felt that Timothy's sympathetic soul would truly care for the Philippians' condition, and would minister to it lovingly. He could rely that Timothy would have no selfish by-ends to serve, but would seek the things of Jesus Christ. We know too little of the circumstances of Paul's imprisonment to know how he came to be thus lonely. In the other Epistles of the Captivity we have mention of a considerable group of friends, many of whom would certainly have been included in a list of the 'like-minded.' We hear, for example, of Tychicus, Onesimus, Aristarchus, John Mark, Epaphras, and Luke. What had become of them all we do not know. They were evidently away on Christian service, somewhere or other, or some of them perhaps had not yet arrived. At all events for some reason Paul was for the time left alone but for Timothy. Not that there were no Christian men in Rome, but of those who could have been sent on such an errand there were none in whom love to Christ and care for His cause and flock wer strong enough to mark them as fit for it.

So the e have to take account of Paul's loneli

in addition to his other sorrows, and we may well mark
how calmly and uncomplainingly he bears it. We are
perpetually hearing complaints of isolation and the
difficulty of finding sympathy, or 'people who understand me.' That is often the complaint of a morbid
nature, or of one which has never given itself the
trouble of trying to 'understand' others, or of showing
the sympathy for which it says that it thirsts.   And
many of these complaining spirits might take a lesson
from the lonely Apostle.   There never was a man,
except Paul's Master and ours, who cared more for
human sympathy, had his own heart fuller of it, and
received less of it from others than Paul.   But he had
discovered what it would be blessedness for us all to
lay to heart, that a man who has Christ for his companion can do without others, and that a heart in
which there whispers, 'Lo, I am with you always,' can
never be utterly solitary.

May we not take the further lesson that the sympathy
which we should chiefly desire is sympathy and fellow-
service in Christian work? Paul did not want like-
minded people in order that he might have the luxury
of enjoying their sympathy, but what he wanted was
allies in his work for Christ. It was sympathy in his
care for the Philippians that he sought for in his
messenger.   And that is the noblest form of like-
mindedness that we can desire—some one to hold the
ropes for us.

Note, too, that Paul does not weakly complain because
he had no helpers. Good and earnest men are very
about the half-hearted way in which
they

learn a lesson from him who had 'no man like-minded,' and yet never dreamt of whimpering because of it, or of flinging down his tools because of the indolence of his fellow-workers?

There is another point to be observed in the Apostle's words here. He felt that their attitude to Christ determined his affinities with men. He could have no deep and true fellowship with others, whatever their name to live, who were daily 'seeking their own,' and at the same time leaving unsought 'the things of Jesus Christ.' They who are not alike in their deepest aims can have no real kindred. Must we not say that hosts of so-called Christian people do not seem to feel, if one can judge by the company they affect, that the deepest bond uniting men is that which binds them to Jesus Christ? I would press the question, Do we feel that nothing draws us so close to men as common love to Jesus, and that if we are not alike on that cardinal point there is a deep gulf of separation beneath a deceptive surface of union, an unfathomable gorge marked by a quaking film of earth?

It is a solemn estimate of some professing Christians which the Apostle gives here, if he is including the members of the Roman Church in his judgment that they are not 'like-minded' with him, and are 'seeking their own, not the things of Jesus Christ.' We may rather hope that he is speaking of others around him, and that for some reason unknown to us he was at the time secluded from the Roman Christians. He brings out with unflinching precision the choice which deter mines a life. There is always that terrible 'either—o To live for Christ is the antagonist, and only antago of life for self. To live for self is death. To for Jesus is the only life. There are two ce

heliocentric and geocentric as the scientists say. We
can choose round which we shall draw our orbit, and
everything depends on the choice which we make. To
seek 'the things of Jesus Christ' is sure to lead to, and
is the only basis of, care for men. Religion is the parent
of compassion, and if we are looking for a man who
will care truly for the state of others, we must do as
Paul did, look for him among those who 'seek the
things of Jesus Christ.'

III. The prisoner's joy in loving co-operation.

The Apostle's eulogium on Timothy points to his
long and intimate association with Paul and to the
Philippians' knowledge of him as well as to the
Apostle's clinging to him. There is a piece of delicate
beauty in the words which we may pause for a moment
to point out. Paul writes as 'a child serveth a father,'
and the natural sequence would have been 'so he served
me,' but he remembers that the service was not to him,
Paul, but to another, and so he changes the words and
says he 'served *with* me in furtherance of the Gospel.'
We are both servants alike—Christ's servants for the
Gospel.

Paul's joy in Timothy's loving co-operation was so
deep because Paul's whole heart was set on 'the furtherance of the Gospel.' Help towards that end was help
indeed. We may measure the ardour and intensity of
 ul's devotion to his apostolic work by the warmth
      itude which he shows to his helper. They who
        to our reaching our chief   wi   ur
          d the cat   ue

have been held out to the Apostle and not been thought worth stooping to take, nor would the offerer have been thanked, but any proffered service that had the smallest bearing on that great work to which Paul's life was given, and which his conscience told him there would be a curse on himself if he did not fulfil, was welcomed as a priceless gift. Do we arrange the lists of our helpers on the same fashion, and count that they serve us best who help us to serve Christ? It should be as much the purpose of every Christian life as it was that of Paul to spread the salvation and glory of the 'name that is above every name.' If we lived as continually under the influence of that truth as he did, we should construe the circumstances of our lives, whether helpful or hindering, very differently, and we could shake the world.

Christian unity is very good and infinitely to be desired, but the true field on which it should display itself is that of united work for the common Lord. The men who have marched side by side through a campaign are knit together as nothing else would bind them. Even two horses drawing one carriage will have ways and feelings and a common understanding, which they would never have attained in any other way. There is nothing like common work for clearing away mists. Much so-called Christian sympathy and like-mindedness are something like the penal cranks that used to be in jails, which generated immense power on this side of the wall but ground out nothing on the other.

Let us not forget that in the field of Christian service there is room for all manner of workers, and that they are associated, however different their work. Pa often o   Timothy his 'fellow-labourer,' and o gives him the eulogium, 'he worketh the work of the Lord as I also do.' Think of the difference between the two men in age, endowment, and sphere! Apparently Timothy at first had very subordinate work taking John Mark's place, and is described as being one of those who 'ministered' to Paul. It is the cup of cold water over again. All work done for the same Lord, and with the same motive is the same; 'he that receiveth a prophet in the name of a prophet shall receive a prophet's reward.' When Paul associates Timothy with himself he is copying from afar off his Lord, who lets us think of even our poor deeds as done by those whom He does not disdain to call His fellow-workers. It would be worth living for if, at the last, He should acknowledge us, and say even of us, 'he hath served with Me in the Gospel.'

PAUL AND EPAPHRODITUS

'But I counted it necessary to send to you Epaphroditus, my brother and fellow-worker and fellow-soldier, and your messenger and minister to my need. 26. Since he longed after you all, and was sore troubled, because ye had heard that he was sick. 27. For indeed he was sick nigh unto death: but God had mercy on him; and not on him only, but on me also, that I might not have sorrow upon sorrow. 28. I have sent him therefore the more diligently, that, when ye see him again, ye may rejoice, and that I may be the less sorrowful. 29. Receive him therefore in the Lord with all joy; and hold such in honour: 30. Because for the work of Christ he came nigh unto death, hazarding his life to supply that which was lacking in your service toward me.'—PHIL. ii. 25-30 (R.V.).

EPAPHRODITUS is one of the less known of Paul's friends. All our information about him is contained in this context, and in a brief reference in Chapter iv.

the moonlight, and then vanishes ghost-like into darkness. Of all the inhabitants of Philippi at that time we know the names of but three, Euodias, Syntiche, and Epaphroditus, and we owe them all to Paul. The context gives us an interesting miniature of the last, and pathetic glimpses into the private life of the Apostle in his imprisonment, and it is worth our while to try to bring our historic imagination to bear on Epaphroditus, and to make him a living man.

The first fact about him is, that he was one of the Philippian Christians, and sent by them to Rome, with some pecuniary or material help, such as comforts for Paul's prison-house, food, clothing, or money. There was no reliable way of getting these to Paul but to take them, and so Epaphroditus faced the long journey across Greece to Brindisi and Rome, and when arrived there threw himself with ardour into serving Paul. The Apostle's heartfelt eulogium upon him shows two phases of his work. He was in the first place Paul's helper in the Gospel, and his faithfulness there is set forth in a glowing climax, 'My brother and fellow-worker and fellow-soldier.' He was in the second place the minister to Paul's needs. There would be many ways of serving the captive, looking after his comfort, doing his errands, procuring daily necessaries, managing affairs, perhaps writing his letters, easing his chain, chafing his aching wrists, and ministering in a thousand ways which we cannot and need not specify. At all events he gladly undertook even servile work for love of Paul.

He had an illness which was probably the consequence of his toil. Perhaps over-exertion in travel, or perhaps his Macedonian constitution could not bear the enervating air of Rome, or perhaps Paul's pris was unhealthy. At any rate he worked till he made himself ill. The news reached Philippi in some round-about way, and, as it appears, the news of his illness only, not of his recovery. The difficulty of communication would sufficiently account for the partial intelligence. Then the report found its way back to Rome, and Epaphroditus got home-sick and was restless, uneasy, 'sore troubled,' as the Apostle says, because they had heard he had been sick. In his low, nervous state, barely convalescent, the thought of home and of his brethren's anxiety about him was too much for him. It is a pathetic little picture of the Macedonian stranger in the great city—pallid looks, recent illness, and pining for home and a breath of pure mountain air, and for the friends he had left. So Paul with rare abnegation sent him away at once, though Timothy was to follow shortly, and accompanied him with this outpouring of love and praise in his long homeward journey. Let us hope he got safe back to his friends, and as Paul bade them, they received him in the Lord with all joy, the echoes of which we almost hear as he passes out of our knowledge.

In the remainder of this sermon we shall simply deal with the two figures which the text sets before us, and we may look first at the glimpses of Paul's character which we get here.

e may note the generous heartiness of his praise in ciating Epaphroditus with himself as on full t as worker and soldier, and the warm recognition of all that he had done the last words of the context, where he says that the Philippian messenger had 'hazarded' his life, or, as we might put it with equal accuracy and more force, had 'gambled' his life, or 'staked it on the die' for Paul's sake. No wonder that men were eager to risk their lives for a leader who lavished such praise and such love upon them. A man who never opens his lips but to censure or criticise, who fastens on faults as wasps do on blemished fruit, will never be surrounded by loyal love. Faithful service is most surely bought by hearty praise. A caressing hand on a horse's neck is better than a whip.

We may further note the intensity of Paul's sympathy. He speaks of Epaphroditus' recovery as a mercy to himself 'lest he should have the sorrow of imprisonment increased by the sorrow of his friend's death.' That attitude of mind stands in striking contrast to the heroism which said, 'To me, to live is Christ and to die is gain,' but the two are perfectly consistent, and it was a great soul which had room for them both.

We must not leave unnoticed the beautiful self-abnegation which sends off Epaphroditus as soon as he was well enough to travel, as a gift of the Apostle's love, in order to repay them for what they had done for him. He says nothing of his own loss or of how much more lonely he would be when the brother whom he had praised so warmly had left him alone. But he suns himself in the thought of the Philippians' jo and in the hope that some reflection of it will tra across the seas to him, and make him, if not wh glad, at any rate 'the less sorrowful.'

We have also to notice Paul's delicate recogniti help. He says that Epaphroditus

his life to 'supply that which was lacking in your
service toward me.' That implies that all which the
Philippians' ministration lacked was their personal
presence, and that Epaphroditus, in supplying that,
made his work in a real sense theirs. All the loving
thoughts, and all the material expressions of them
which Epaphroditus brought to Paul were fragrant
with the perfume of the Philippians' love, 'an odour of
a sweet smell, acceptable' to Paul as to Paul's Lord.

We briefly note some general lessons which may be
suggested by the picture of Epaphroditus as he stands
by the side of Paul.

The first one suggested is the very familiar one of
the great uniting principle which a common faith in
Christ brought into action. Think of the profound clefts
of separation between the Macedonian and the Jew,
the antipathies of race, the differences of language,
the dissimilarities of manner, and then think of what
an unheard-of new thing it must have been that a
Macedonian should 'serve' a Jew! We but feebly
echo Paul's rapture when he thought that there was
'neither Barbarian or Scythian, bond or free, but all
were one in Christ Jesus,' and for all our talk about
the unity of humanity and the like, we permit the old
gulfs of separation to gape as deeply as ever. Dread-
noughts are a peculiar expression of the brotherhood of men after nineteen centuries of so-called
Christianity.

terms in which the work of Epaphroditus is
Paul are very significant. He has no
ibing the work done for hi

Paul was done for Jesus, and that, not because of any
special apostolic closeness of relation of Paul to Jesus,
but because, like all other Christians, he was one with
his Lord. 'The cup of cold water' given 'in the name
of a disciple' is grateful to the lips of the Master. We
have no reason to suppose that Epaphroditus took part
with Paul in his more properly apostolic work, and
the fact that the purely material help, and pecuniary
service which most probably comprised all his 'ministering,' is honoured by Paul with these lofty designa-
tions, carries with it large lessons as to the sanctity of
common life. All deeds done from the same motive
are the same, however different they may be in regard
to the material on which they are wrought. If our
hearts are set to 'hallow all we find,' the most secular
duties will be acts of worship. It is possible for us in
the ordering of our own lives to fulfil the great
prophecy with which Zechariah crowned his vision of
the Future, 'In that day shall there be on the bells of
the horses Holiness unto the Lord'; and the 'pots in
the Lord's house shall be like the bowls before the
altar.'

May we not further draw from Paul's words here a
lesson as to the honour due to Christian workers? It
was his brethren who were exhorted to receive their
own messenger back again 'in the Lord with all joy,
and to hold him in honour.' Possibly there were in
Philippi some sharp tongues and envious spirits, who
needed the exhortation. Whether there were so or no
the exhortation itself traces lightly but surely t
lines on which Christians should render, and th
fellow-Christians can rightly receive, even praise f
m n. phroditus were 'received in the
t be no foolish and hurtful adulat

him, nor prostration before him, but he would be recognised as but the instrument through which the true Helper worked, and not he, but the Grace of Christ in him would finally receive the praise.   There are very many Christian workers who never get their due of recognition and welcome from their brethren, and there are many who get far more of both than belongs to them, and both they and the crowds who bring them adulation would be freed from dangers, which can scarcely be over-stated, if the spirit of Paul's warm-hearted praise of Epaphroditus were kept in view.

Epaphroditus but passes across the illuminated disc of the lantern for a moment, and we have scarcely time to catch a glimpse of his face before it is lost to us.   He and all his brethren are gone, but his name lives for ever, and Paul's praise of him and of his work outshines all else remembered of the city, where conquerors once reigned, and outside whose walls was fought a battle that decided for a time the fate of the world.

PREPARING TO END

'Finally, my brethren, rejoice in the Lord. To write the same things to you, to me indeed is not irksome, but for you it is safe. 2. Beware of the dogs, beware of the evil workers, beware of the concision : 3. For we are the circumcision, worship by the Spirit of God, and glory in Christ Jesus, and have no confidence in the flesh.'—PHIL. iii. 1-3 (R.V.).

first words of the text show that Paul was beginning the work of winding up his letter, and the also suggests that.

also most fitting there, for it is really the key-note of the letter. How then does he come to desert his purpose? The answer is to be found in his next advice, the warning against the Judaising teachers who were his great antagonists all his life. A reference to them always roused him, and here the vehement exhortation to mark them well and avoid them opens the flood-gates. Forgetting all about his purpose to come to an end, he pours out his soul in the long and precious passage which follows. Not till the next chapter does he get back to his theme in the reiterated exhortation (iv. 4), 'Rejoice in the Lord alway; again I will say, rejoice.' This outburst is very remarkable, for its vehemence is so unlike the tone of the rest of the letter. That is calm, joyous, bright, but this is stormy and impassioned, full of flashing and scathing words, the sudden thunder-storm breaks in on a mellow, autumn day, but it hurtles past and the sun shines out again, and the air is clearer.

Another question suggested is the reference of the second half of verse 1. What are 'the same things' to write which is 'safe' for the Philippians? Are they the injunctions preceding to 'rejoice in the Lord,' or that following, the warning against the Judaisers? The former explanation may be recommended by the fact that 'Rejoice' is in a sense the key-note of the Epistle, but on the other hand, the things where repetition would be 'safe' would most probably be warnings against some evil that threatened the Philippians' Christian standing.

There is no attempt at unity in the words before u and I shall not try to force them into apparent o ness, but follow the Apostle's thoughts as they We note—

I. The crowning injunction as to the duty of Christian gladness.

A very slight glance over the Epistle will show how continually the note of gladness is struck in it.   Whatever in Paul's circumstances was 'at enmity with joy' could not darken his sunny outlook.   This bird could sing in a darkened cage.   If we brought together the expressions of his joy in this letter, they would yield us some precious lessons as to what were the sources of his, and what may be the sources of ours.   There runs through all the instances in the Epistle the implication which comes out most emphatically in his earnest exhortation, 'Rejoice in the Lord always, and again I say rejoice.'   The true source of true joy lies in our union with Jesus.   To be in Him is the condition of every good, and, just as in the former verses 'trust *in the Lord*' is set forth, so the joy which comes from trust is traced to the same source.   The joy that is worthy, real, permanent, and the ally of lofty endeavour and noble thoughts has its root in union with Jesus, is realised in communion with Him, has Him for its reason or motive, and Him for its safeguard or measure.   As the passages in question in this Epistle show, such joy does not shut out but hallows other sources of satisfaction.   In our weakness creatural love and kindness but too often draw us away from our joy in Him.   But with Paul the sources which we too often find antagonistic were ously blended, and flowed side by side in the so that he could express them both

Christian joy, some of us even take mortified countenances and voices in a minor key as marks of grace,
and there is but little in any of us of 'the joy in the
Lord' which a saint of the Old Testament had learned
was our 'strength.' There is plenty of gladness amongst
professing Christians, but a good many of them would
resent the question, is your gladness 'in the Lord'?
No doubt any deep experience in the Christian life
makes us aware of much in ourselves that saddens,
and may depress, and our joy in Him must always be
shaded by penitent sorrow for ourselves.   But that
necessary element of sadness in the Christian life
is not the cause why so many Christian lives have
little of the buoyancy and hope and spontaneity
which should mark them.   The reason rather lies in
the lack of true union with Christ, and habitual
keeping of ourselves 'in the love of God.'

II. Paul's apology for reiteration.

He is going to give once more old and well-worn precepts which are often very tedious to the hearer, and
not much less so to the speaker.   He can only say that
to him the repetition of familiar injunctions is not
'irksome,' and that to them it is 'safe.'   The diseased
craving for 'originality' in the present day tempts us
all, hearers and speakers alike, and we ever need to
be reminded that the staple of Christian teaching
must be old truths reiterated, and that it is not time
to stop proclaiming them until all men have begun
to practise them.   But a speaker must try to make
the thousandth repetition of a truth fresh to himself
and not a wearisome form, or a dead commonplace
by freshening it to his own mind and by living on
in his own practice, and the hearers must remem
that it is only the completeness of their obe

that antiquates the commandment. The most threadbare commonplace becomes a novelty when occasions
for its application arise in our own lives, just as a
prescription may lie long unnoticed in a drawer, but
when a fever attacks its possessor it will be quickly
drawn out and worth its weight in gold.

III. Paul's warning against teachers of a ceremonial
religion.

It scarcely seems congruous with the tone of the
rest of this letter that the preachers whom Paul so
scathingly points out here had obtained any firm
footing in the Philippian Church, but no doubt there,
as everywhere, they had dogged Paul's footsteps, and
had tried as they always did to mar his work. They
had not missionary fervour or Christian energy
enough to initiate efforts amongst the Gentiles so as
to make them proselytes, but when Paul and his companions had made them Christians, they did their
best, or their worst, to insist that they could not be
truly Christians, unless they submitted to the outward sign of being Jews. Paul points a scathing
finger at them when he bids the Philippians 'beware,'
and he permits himself a bitter retort when he lays
hold of the Jewish contemptuous word for Gentiles
which stigmatised them as 'dogs,' that is profane and
unclean, and hurls it back at the givers. But he is
not indulging in mere bitter retorts when he brings
against these teachers the definite charge that they
are 'evil workers.' People who believed that an outward observance was the condition of salvation would

sticklers for circumcision had themselves been circumcised. 'I will not call them the circumcision,
they have not been circumcised, they have only been
gashed and mutilated, it has been a mere fleshly
maiming.' His reason for denying the name to them
is his profound belief that it belonged to true
Christians. His contemptuous reference puts in a
word, the principle which he definitely states in
another place, 'He is not a Jew who is one out-
wardly; neither is that circumcision which is outward
in the flesh.'

The Apostle here is not only telling us who are
the truly circumcised, but at the same time he is
telling us what makes a Christian, and he states three
points in which, as I take it, he begins at the end and
works backwards to the beginning. 'We are the
circumcision who worship in the Spirit of God'—that
is the final result—'and glory in Christ Jesus'—'and
have no confidence in the flesh'—that is the starting-
point. The beginning of all true Christianity is distrust of self. What does Paul mean by 'flesh'?
Body? Certainly not. Animal nature, or the passions
rooted in it? Not only these, as may be seen by noting
the catalogue which follows of the things in the flesh,
in which he might have trusted. What are these?
'Circumcised the eighth day, of the tribe of Israel,
of the tribe of Benjamin, a Hebrew of the Hebrews'
—these belong to ritual and race; 'as touching the
law a Pharisee'—that belongs to ecclesiastical
standing; 'concerning zeal persecuting the church'—
that has nothing to do with the animal nature: 'tou
ing the righteousness which is in the law blamel
—that concerns the moral nature. All these
un   ory of the 'flesh,' which, the

plainly includes all that belongs to humanity apart
from God. Paul's old-fashioned language translated
into modern English just comes to this—it is vain to
trust in external connection with the sacred community of the Church, or in participation in any of its
ordinances and rites. To Paul, Christian rites and
Jewish rites were equally rites and equally insufficient
as bases of confidence. Do not let us fancy that
dependence on these is peculiar to certain forms of
Christian belief. It is a very subtle all-pervasive
tendency, and there is no need to lift up Noncon-
formist hands in holy horror at the corruptions of
Romanism and the like. Their origin is not solely
priestly ambition, but also the desires of the so-called
laity. Demand creates a supply, and if there were
not people to think, 'Now it shall be well with me
because I have a Levite for my priest,' there would be
no Levites to meet their wishes.

Notice that Paul includes amongst the things belonging to the flesh this 'touching the righteousness
which is in the law blameless.' Many of us can say
the same. We do our duties so far as we know them,
and are respectable law-abiding people, but if we are
trusting to that, we are of the 'flesh.' Have we estimated what God is, and what the real worth of our
conduct is? Have we looked not at our actions but at
our motives, and seen them as they are seen from
above or from the inside? How many 'blameless'
are like the scenes in a theatre, effective and
when seen with the artificial glory of the
behind the and what d

The beginning of our Christianity is the consciousness that we are 'naked and poor, and blind, and in
need of all things.' Men come to Jesus Christ by many
ways, thank God, and I care little by what road they
come so long as they get there, nor do I insist upon
any stereotyped order of religious experience. But
of this I am very sure: that unless we abandon confidence in ourselves, because we have seen ourselves in
the light of God's law, we have not learned all that
we need nor laid hold of all that Christ gives. Let
us measure ourselves in the light of God, and we shall
learn that we have to take our places beside Job,
when the vision of God silenced his protestations of
innocence. 'I have heard of Thee by the hearing of
the ear, but now mine eye seeth Thee; wherefore I
abhor myself and repent in dust and ashes.'

That self-distrust should pass into glorying in Christ
Jesus. If a man has learned his emptiness he will
look about for something to fill it. Unless I know
myself to be under condemnation because of my sin,
and fevered, disturbed, and made wretched, by
its inward consequences which forbid repose, the
sweetest words of Gospel invitation will pass by me
like wind whistling through an archway. But if once
I have been driven from self-confidence, then like
music from heaven will come the word, 'Trust in
Jesus.' The seed dropped into the ground puts out a
downward-going shoot, which is the root, and an
upward-growing one, which is the stalk. The downward-going shoot is 'no confidence in the flesh,' t
upward-going is 'glorying in Christ Jesus.'

But that word suggests the blessed experience
triu   the possession of the Person know
f to   and to give all that life n

true Christian should ever be triumphant in a felt experience, in a Name proved to be sufficient, in a power which infuses strength into his weakness, and enables him to do the will of God. It is for want of utter self-distrust and absolute faith in Christ that 'glorying' in Him is so far beyond the ordinary mood of the average Christian. You say, 'I hope, sometimes I doubt, sometimes I fear, sometimes I tremblingly trust.' Is that the kind of experience that these words shadow? Why do we continue amidst the mist when we might rise into the clear blue above the obscuring pall? Only because we are still in some measure clinging to self, and still in some measure distrusting our Lord. If our faith were firm and full our 'glorying' would be constant. Do not be contented with the prevailing sombre type of Christian life which is always endeavouring, and always foiled, which is often doubting and often indifferent, but seek to live in the sunshine, and expatiate in the light, and 'rejoice in the Lord always.'

'Glorying' not only describes an attitude of mind, but an activity of life. Many things to-day tempt Christian people to speak of their religion and of their Lord in an apologetic tone, in the face of strong and educated unbelief; but if we have within us, as we all may have, and ought to have, the triumphant a__rance of His sufficiency, nearness, and power, it __ be with bated breath that we shall speak of __ or apologise for our Christianity, but we __ commandment, 'Lift up thy voice wi__

have the experience, if you are a Christian, which more
than answers all that they can say.

We have said that the final result set forth here
by Paul is, 'We worship by the Spirit of God.' The
expression translated worship is the technical word for
rendering priestly service. Just as Paul has asserted
that uncircumcised Christians, not circumcised Jews,
are the true circumcision, so he asserts that they are the
true priests, and that these officials in the outward
temple at Jerusalem have forfeited the title, and that
it has passed over to the despised followers of the
despised Nazarene. If we have 'no confidence in
the flesh,' and are 'glorying in Christ Jesus,' we are
all priests of the most high God. 'Worship in the
Spirit' is our function and privilege. The externals
of ceremonial worship dwindle into insignificance.
They may be means of helping, or they may be means
of hindering, the 'worship in the Spirit,' which I
venture to think all experience shows is the more
likely to be pure and real, the less it invokes the aid of
flesh and sense. To make the senses the ladder for
the soul by which to climb to God is quite as likely to
end in the soul's going down the ladder as up it.
Aesthetic aids to worship are crutches which keep a
lame soul lame all its days.

Such worship is the obligation as well as the prerogative of the Christian. We have no right to say
that we have truly forsaken confidence in ourselves,
and are truly 'glorying' in Christ Jesus, unless ou
daily life is communion with God, and all your wo
'worshipping by the Spirit of God.' Such communi
and worship are possible for those, and for those
who have 'no confidence in the flesh' and who '
C

THE LOSS OF ALL

'Though I myself might have confidence even in the flesh: if any other man thinketh to have confidence in the flesh, I yet more: circumcised the eighth day of the stock of Israel, of the tribe of Benjamin, a Hebrew of Hebrews; as touching the law, a Pharisee; as touching zeal, persecuting the church; as touching the righteousness which is in the law, found blameless. Howbeit what things were gain to me, these have I counted loss for Christ. Yea verily, and I count all things to be loss for the excellency of the knowledge of Christ Jesus my Lord: for whom I suffered the loss of all things, and do count them but dung.'—PHIL. iii. 4-8 (R.V.).

WE have already noted that in the previous verses the Apostle is beginning to prepare for closing his letter, but is carried away into the long digression of which our text forms the beginning. The last words of the former verse open a thought of which his mind is always full. It is as when an excavator strikes his pickaxe unwittingly into a hidden reservoir and the blow is followed by a rush of water, which carries away workmen and tools. Paul has struck into the very deepest thoughts which he has of the Gospel and out they pour. That one antithesis, 'the loss of all, the gain of Christ,' carried in it to him the whole truth of the Christian message. We may well ask ourselves what are the subjects which lie so near our hearts, and so fill our thoughts, that a chance word sets us off on them, and we cannot help talking of them when once we begin.

The text exemplifies another characteristic of Paul's, his constant habit of quoting his own experience as the truth. His theology is the generalisa- experience, and yet that conti ference is no for th

himself with the Gospel. It was to him no mere body of
principles or thoughts, it was the very food and life
of his life. And so this characteristic reveals not only
his natural fervour of character, but the profound and
penetrating hold which the Gospel had on his whole
being.

In our text he presents his own experience as the
type to which ours must on the whole be conformed.
He had gone through an earthquake which had
shattered the very foundations of his life. He had
come to despise all that he had counted most precious,
and to clasp as the only true treasures all that he had
despised. With him the revolution had turned his
whole life upside down. Though the change cannot be
so subversive and violent with us, the forsaking of
self-confidence must be as real, and the clinging to
Jesus must be as close, if our Christianity is to be
fervid and dominant in our lives.

I. The treasures that were discovered to be worthless.

We have already had occasion in the previous sermon
to refer to Paul's catalogue of 'things that were gain'
to him, but we must consider it a little more closely
here. We may repeat that it is important for understanding Paul's point of view to note that by 'flesh'
he means the whole self considered as independent of
God. The antithesis to it is 'spirit,' that is humanity
regenerated and vitalised by Divine influence. 'Flesh,'
then, is humanity not so vitalised. That is to say, it is
'self,' including both body and emotions, affectio
thoughts, and will.

As to the points enumerated, they are those whi
made the ideal to a Jew, including purity of
punctilious orthodoxy, flaming zeal, pugnacious

tagonism, and blameless morality. With reference
to race, the Jewish pride was in 'circumcision on the
eighth day,' which was the exclusive privilege of one
of pure blood. Proselytes might be circumcised in
later life, but one of the 'stock of Israel' only on
the 'eighth day.' Saul of Tarsus had in earlier
days been proud of his tribal genealogy, which had
apparently been carefully preserved in the Gentile
home, and had shared ancestral pride in belonging to
the once royal tribe, and perhaps in thinking that the
blood of the king after whom he was named flowed in
his veins. He was a 'Hebrew of the Hebrews,' which
does not mean, as it is usually taken to do, intensely,
superlatively Hebrew, but simply is equivalent to 'myself a Hebrew, and come from pure Hebrew ancestors
on both sides.' Possibly also the phrase may have
reference to purity of language and customs as well
as blood. These four items make the first group.
Paul still remembers the time when, in the blindness
which he shared with his race, he believed that these
wholly irrelevant points had to do with a man's
acceptance before God. He had once agreed with
the Judaisers that 'circumcision' admitted Gentiles
into the Jewish community, and so gave them a right
to participate in the blessings of the Covenant.

Then follow the items of his more properly religious
character, which seem in their three clauses to make a
climax. 'As touching the law a Pharisee,' he was of
the 'straitest sect,' the champions and representatives
of the law. 'As touching zeal persecuting the Church,'
in Judaism that the mark of zeal for
its opponents. We

of the clothes trusted to his care by the witnesses who
stoned Stephen, and how he had 'breathed threatening
and slaughter' against the disciples. 'As touching the
righteousness which is in the law found blameless,' he
is evidently speaking of the obedience of outward
actions and of blamelessness in the judgment of men.

So we get a living picture of Paul and of his confidence before he was a Christian. All these grounds
for pride and self-satisfaction were like triple armour
round the heart of the young Pharisee, who rode out
of Jerusalem on the road to Damascus. How little he
thought that they would all have been pierced and
have dropped from him before he got there! The
grounds of his confidence are antiquated in form, but
in substance are modern. At bottom the things in
which Paul's 'flesh' trusted are exactly the same as
those in which many of us trust. Even his pride of
race continues to influence some of us. We have got
the length of separating between our nationality and
our acceptance with God, but we have still a kind of
feeling that 'God's Englishmen,' as Milton called them,
have a place of their own, which is, if not a ground of
confidence before God, at any rate a ground for carrying ourselves with very considerable complacency
before men. It is not unheard of that people should
rely, if not on 'circumcision on the eighth day,' on
an outward rite which seems to connect them with a
visible Church. Strict orthodoxy takes the place
among us which Pharisaism held in Paul's mind before
he was a Christian, and it is easier to prove our zeal
by pugnacity against heretics, than by fervour of
devotion. The modern analogue of Paul's, 'touching
the righteousness which is in the law blameless,' is 'I
have done my best, I have lived a decent life. My

religion is to do good to other people.' All such talk,
which used to be a vague sentiment or excuse, is now
put forward in definite theoretical substitution for
the Christian Truth, and finds numerous teachers and
acceptors.   But how short a way all such grounds of
confidence go to satisfy a soul that has once seen the
vision that blazed in on Paul's mind on the road to
Damascus !

II. The discovery of their worthlessness.

'These have I counted loss for Christ.' There is a
possibility of exaggeration in interpreting Paul's
words. The things that were 'gain' to him were in
themselves better than their opposites.   It is better to
to be 'blameless' than to have a life all stained with
foulness and reeking with sins.   But these 'gains'
were 'losses,' disadvantages, in so far as they led him
to build upon them, and trust in them as solid wealth.
The earthquake that shattered his life had two shocks:
the first turned upside down his estimate of the value
of his gains, the second robbed him of them.   He first
saw them to be worthless, and then, so far as others'
judgment went, he was stripped of them.   Actively he
'counted them loss,' passively he 'suffered the loss of
all things.' His estimate came, and was followed by
the practical outcome of his brethren's excommuni-
cation.

What changed his estimate?   In our text he answers
the question in two forms: first he gives the simple,
all-sufficient monosyllabic reason for his whole life
— or C----t,' and then he enlarges that motive into
---- f the knowledge of Christ Jesus
---- ies us ---- ght t

had abhorred. The latter dwells a little more upon the subjective process which followed on the vision, but the two are substantially the same, and we need only note the solemn fulness of the name of 'Jesus Christ,' and the intense motion of submission and of personal appropriation contained in the designation, ' my Lord.' It was not when he found his way blinded into Damascus that he had learned that knowledge, or could apprehend its 'excellency.' The words are enriched and enlarged by later experiences. The sacrifice of his earlier 'gains' had been made before the 'excellency of the knowledge' had been discerned. It was no mere intellectual perception which could be imparted in words, or by eyesight, but here as always Paul by 'knowledge' means experience which comes from possession and acquaintance, and which there-fore gleams ever before us as we move, and is capable of endless increase, in the measure in which we are true to the estimate of 'gains' and 'losses' to which our initial vision of Him has led us. At first we may not know that that knowledge excels all others, but as we grow in acquaintance with Jesus, and in experience of Him, we shall be sure that it transcends all others, because He does and we possess Him.

The revolutionising motive may be conceived of in two ways. We have to abandon the lower 'gains' in order to gain Christ, or to abandon these because we have gained Him. Both are true. The discernment of Christ as the one ground of confidence is eve followed by the casting away of all others. Self-di trust is a part of faith. When we feel our feet up the rock, the crumbling sands on which we stood left to be broken up by the sea. They who have the Apollo Belvedere will set little store by p

of Paris casts.   In all our lives there come times
when the glimpse of some loftier ideal shows up our
ordinary as hollow and poor and low.   And when
once Christ is seen, as Scripture shows Him, our former
self appears poor and crumbles away.

We are not to suppose that the act of renunciation
must be completed before a second act of possession
is begun.   That is the error of many ascetic books.
The two go together, and abandonment in order to
win merges into abandonment because we have won.
The strongest power to make renunciation possible is
'the expulsive power of a new affection.'   When the
heart is filled with love to Christ there is no sense of
'loss,' but only of 'exceeding gain,' in casting away all
things for Him.

III. The continuous repetition of the discovery.

Paul compares his present self with his former
Christian self, and with a vehement 'Yea, verily,'
affirms his former judgment, and reiterates it in still
more emphatic terms.   It is often easy to depreciate
the treasures which we possess.   They sometimes grow
in value as they slip from our hands.   It is not usual
for a man who has 'suffered the loss of all things' to
follow their disappearance by counting them 'but
dung.'   The constant repetition through the whole
Christian course of the depreciatory estimate of
grounds of confidence is plainly necessary.   There are
subtle temptations to the opposite course.   It is hard
to keep perfectly clear of all building on our own
blamelessness or on our connection with the Christian
Church, and we have need ever to renew the estimate
which was once so epoch-making, and which 'cast
down all our imaginations and high things.'   If we do
not carefully watch ourselves, the whispering tempter

that was silenced will recover his breath again, and be
once more ready to drop into our ears his poisonous
suggestions. We have to take pains and 'give earnest
heed' to the initial, revolutionary estimate, and to see
that it is worked out habitually in our daily lives. It
is a good exchange when we count 'all but loss for
the excellency of the knowledge of Christ Jesus our
Lord.'

THE GAIN OF CHRIST

'That I may gain Christ, and be found in Him, not having a righteousness of my
own, even that which is of the law, but that which is through faith in Christ, the
righteousness which is of God by faith.'—PHIL. iii. 8, 9 (R.V.).

IT is not everybody who *can* say what is his aim in life.
Many of us have never thought enough about it to
have one beyond keeping alive. We lose life in seeking
for the means of living. Many of us have such a multitude of aims, each in its turn drawing us, that no one
of them is predominant and rules the crowd. There is
no strong hand at the tiller, and so the ship washes
about in the trough of the waves.

It is not everybody who *dares* to say what is his aim
in life. We are ashamed to acknowledge even to ourselves what we are not at all ashamed to do. Paul
knew his aim, and was not afraid to speak it. It was
high and noble, and was passionately and persistently
pursued. He tells us it here, and we can see his soul
kindling as he speaks. We may note how there is here
the same double reference as we found in the previous
verses, gaining Christ corresponding to the previous
loss for Christ, and the later words of our text being
an expansion of the 'excellency of the knowledge of
Christ Jesus.' No man will ever succeed in any

purpose, unless like Paul he is enthusiastic about it. If his aim does not rouse his fervour when he speaks of it, he will never accomplish it. We may just remark that Paul does not suppose his aim to be wholly un-attained, even although he does not count himself to 'have apprehended.' He knows that he has gained Christ, and is 'found in Him,' but he knows also that there stretch before him the possibilities of infinite increase.

I. His life's aim was to have the closest possession of, and incorporation in, Christ.

His two expressions, 'that I may gain Christ and be found in Him,' are substantially identical in meaning, though they put the same truth from different sides, and with some variety of metaphor. We may deal with them separately.

The 'gain' is of course the opposite of the 'loss.' His balance-sheet has on one side 'all things lost,' on the other 'Christ gained,' and that is profitable trading. But we have to go deeper than such a metaphor, and to give full scope to the Scriptural truth, that Christ really imparts Himself to the believing soul. There is a real communication of His own life to us, and thereby we live, as He Himself declared, 'He that hath the Son hath life.' The true deep sense in which we possess Christ is not to be weakened down, as it, alas! so often is in our shallow Christianity, which is but the echo of a shallow experience, and a feeble hold of that posses-sion of the Son to which Jesus called us, as the condi-tion of our possession of life. Christ is thus Himself possessed by all our faculties, each after its kind; head and heart

nobler life, restraining and controlling, gradually transforming and ultimately conforming them to His own
likeness.   Till that Divine Indweller enters in, the
shrine is empty, and unclean things lurk in its hidden
corners.   To be a man full summed in all his powers,
each of us must 'gain Christ.'

The other expression in the text, 'be found in Him,'
presents the same truth from the completing point of
view.   We gain Christ in us when we are 'found in Him.'
We are to be incorporated as members are in the body,
or imbedded as a stone in the foundation, or to go
back to the sweetest words, which are the source of all
these representations, included as 'a branch in the
vine.'   We are to be in Him for safety and shelter, as
fugitives take refuge in a strong tower when an enemy
swarms over the land.

> 'And lo ! from sin and grief and shame,
>   I hide me, Jesus, in Thy name.'

We are to be in Him that the life sap may freely flow
through us.   We are to be in Him that the Divine
Love may fall on us, and that in Jesus we may receive
our portion of all which is His heritage.

This mutual possession and indwelling is possible if
Jesus be the Son of God, but the language is absurd in
any other interpretation of His person.   It is clearly in
its very nature capable of indefinite increase, and as
containing in itself the supply of all which we need for
life and blessedness, is fitted to be what nothing else
can pretend to be, without wrecking the lives that a
unwise enough to pursue it—the sovereign aim o
human life.   In following it, and only in followin
the highest wisdom says Amen to the aspiration
lo   .   'This one thing I do.'

II. Paul's life's aim was righteousness to be received.

He goes on to present some of the consequences which follow on his gaining Christ and being 'found in Him,' and before all others he names as his aim the possession of 'righteousness.' We must remember that Paul believed that righteousness in the sense of 'justification' had been his from the moment when Ananias came to where he was sitting in darkness, and bid him be baptized and wash away his sins. The word here must be taken in its full sense of moral perfectness; even if we included only this in our thoughts of his life's aim, how high above most men would he tower! But his statement carries him still higher above, and farther away from, the common ideas of moral perfection, and what he means by righteousness is widely separated from the world's conception, not only in regard to its elements, but still more in regard to its source.

It is possible to lose oneself in a dreamy mysticism which has had much to say of 'gaining Christ and being found in Him,' and has had too little to say about 'having righteousness,' and so has turned out to be an ally of indifference and sometimes of unrighteousness. Buddhism and some forms of mystical Christianity have fallen into a pit of immorality from which Paul's sane combination here would have saved them. There is no danger in the most mystical interpretation of the former statement of his aim, when it is as closely connected as it is here with the second form in which he states it. I have just said that Paul differed from

a gift, and not as the result of his own efforts. To him
the only righteousness which availed was one which
was not 'my own,' but had its source in, and was
imparted by, God. The world thought of righteousness
as the general designation under which were summed
up a man's specific acts of conformity to law, the sum
total reached by the addition of many specific instances
of conformity to a standard of duty. Paul had learned
to think of it as preceding and producing the specific
acts. The world therefore said, and says, Do the deeds
and win the character; Paul says, Receive the character
and do the deeds. The result of the one conception of
righteousness is in the average man spasmodic efforts
after isolated achievements, with long periods between
in which effort subsides into torpor. The result in
Paul's case was what we know: a continuous effort to
keep his mind and heart open for the influx of the
power which, entering into him, would make him able
to do the specific acts which constitute righteousness.
The one road is a weary path, hard to tread, and, as a
matter of fact, not often trodden. To pile up a righteousness by the accumulation of individual righteous acts
is an endeavour less hopeful than that of the coral
polypes slowly building up their reef out of the depths
of the Pacific, till it rises above the waves. He who
assumes to be righteous on the strength of a succession
of righteous acts, not only needs a profounder idea of
what makes his acts righteous, but should also make a
catalogue of his unrighteous ones and call himself
wicked. The other course is the final deliverance of a
man from dependence upon his own struggles, and substitutes for the dreary alternations of effort and torpor
and for the imperfect harvest of imperfectly righteous
acts, the attitude of receiving, which supersedes pai

strife and weary endeavour. To seek after a righteousness which is 'my own,' is to seek what we shall never
find, and what, if found, would crumble beneath us.
To seek the righteousness which is from God, is to seek
what He is waiting to bestow, and what the blessed
receivers blessedly know is more than they dreamed of.

But Paul looked for this great gift as a gift in Christ.
It was when he was 'found in Him' that it became his,
and he was found 'blameless.' That gift of an imparted
life, which has a bias towards all goodness, and the
natural operation of which is to incline all our faculties
towards conformity with the will of God, is bestowed
when we 'win Christ.' Possessing Him, we possess it.
It is not only 'imputed,' as our fathers delighted to say,
but it is 'imparted.' And because it is the gift of God
in Christ, it was in Paul's view received by faith. He
expresses that conviction in a double form in our text.
It is 'through faith' as the channel by which it passes
into our happy hands. It is 'by faith,' or, more
accurately, 'upon faith,' as the foundation on which
it rests, or the condition on which it depends. Our
trust in Christ does bring His life to us to sanctify us,
and the plain English of all this blessed teaching is—
if we wish to be better let us trust Christ and get Him
into the depths of our lives, and righteousness will be
ours. That transforming Presence laid up in 'the hidden
man of the heart,' will be like some pungent scent in
a wardrobe which keeps away moths, and gives out a
f___ ___t perfumes all that hangs near it.

___ have been ___ying ___t to be u___

grace given. The righteousness is bestowed whenever faith is exercised. The hand is never stretched out and the gift not lodged in it. But it is a life's aim to possess the 'righteousness which is of God by faith,' because that gift is capable of indefinite increase, and will reward the most strenuous efforts of a believing soul as long as life continues.

III. Paul's life's aim stretches beyond this life.

Shall we be chargeable with crowding too much meaning into his words, if we fix on his remarkable expression, 'be found in Him,' as containing a clear reference to that great day of final judgment? We recall other instances of the use of the same expression in connections which unmistakably point to that time. Such as 'being clothed we shall not be found naked,' or 'the proof of your faith . . . might be found unto praise and glory and honour at the revelation of Jesus Christ,' or 'found of Him in peace without spot, blameless.' In the light of these and similar passages, it does not seem unreasonable to suppose that this 'being found' does include a reference to the Apostle's place after death, though it is not confined to that. He thinks of the searching eye of the Judge taking keen account, piercing through all disguises, and wistfully as well as penetratingly scrutinising characters, till it finds that for which it seeks. They who are 'found in Him' in that day, are there and thus for ever. There is no further fear of falling out of union with Him, or of being, by either gradual and unco scious stages, or by sudden and overmastering assau carried out of the sacred enclosure of the City Refuge, in which they dwell henceforth for ever danger ous presumptuousness has sometimes led t assertion, 'Once in Christ al

Christ.' But Paul teaches us that that security of permanent dwelling in Him is to be for ever in this life the aim of our efforts, rather than an accomplished fact. So long as we are here, the possibility of falling away cannot be shut out, and there must always rise before us the question, Am I in Christ? Hence there is need for continual watchfulness, self-control, and self-distrust, and the life's aim has to be perpetual, not only because it is capable of indefinite expansion, but because our weakness is capable of deserting it. It is only when at the last we are found by Him, in Him, that we are there for ever, with all dangers of departure from Him at an end. In that City of Refuge, and there only, 'the gates shall not be shut at all,' not solely because no enemies shall attempt to come in, but also because no citizens shall desire to go out.

We should ever have before us that hour, and our life's aim should ever definitely include the final scrutiny in which many a hidden thing will come to light, many a long-lost thing be found, and each man's ultimate place in relation to Jesus Christ will be freed from uncertainties, ambiguities, hypocrisies, and disguises, and made plain to all beholders. In that great day of 'finding,' some of us will have to ask with sinking hearts, 'Hast thou found me, O mine enemy?' and others will break forth into the glad acclaim, 'I have found Him,' or rather 'been found of Him.'

have before us the one reasonable aim for a Christ, to be found in to

SAVING KNOWLEDGE

'That I may know Him, and the power of His resurrection, and the fellowship of His sufferings, becoming conformed unto His death; if by any means I may attain unto the resurrection from the dead.'—PHIL. iii. 10-11 (R.V.).

WE have seen how the Apostle was prepared to close his letter at the beginning of this chapter, and how that intention was swept away by the rush of new thoughts. His fervid faith caught fire when he turned to think of what he had lost, and how infinitely more he had gained in Christ. His wealth is so great that it cannot be crowded into the narrow space of one brief sentence, and after all the glowing words which precede our text, he feels that he has not yet adequately set forth either his present possessions or his ultimate aims. So here he continues the theme which might have seemed most fully dealt with in the great thoughts that occupied us in the former sermon, but which still wait to be completed here. They are most closely connected with the former, and the unity of the sentence is but a parallel to the oneness of the idea. The elements of our present text constitute a part of the Apostle's aim in life, and may be dealt with as such.

I. Paul's life's aim was the knowledge of Christ.

That sounds an anti-climax after 'Gain' and 'Be in Him.' These phrases seem to express a much more intimate relation than this, but we must note that it is no mere theoretical or intellectual knowledge whi is intended. Such knowledge would need no surre or suffering 'the loss of all things.' We can only the know of Christ at such a rate, but we ca k ut Him very much cheaper.

knowledge would not be worth the price; it lies on the surface of the soul, and does nothing. Many a man amongst us has it, and it is of no use to him. If Paul had undergone all that he had undergone and sacrificed all that he had given up, and for his reward had only gained accurate knowledge about Christ, he had certainly wasted his life and made a bad bargain. But as always, so here, to know means knowledge based upon experience. Did Christ mean that a correct creed was eternal life when He said, 'This is life eternal to know Thee, the only true God and Jesus Christ whom Thou has sent?' Did Paul mean the dry light of the understanding when he prayed that the Ephesians might know the love of Christ which passeth knowledge, in order to be filled with all the fulness of God? Clearly we have to go much deeper down than that superficial interpretation in order to reach the reality of the New Testament conception of knowledge. It is co-extensive with life, and is built upon inward experience. In a word, it is one aspect of winning Jesus. It is consciousness contemplating its riches, counting its gains. As a man knows the bliss of parental or wedded love only by having it, or as he knows the taste of wine only by drinking it, or the glory of music only by hearing it, and the brightness of the day only by seeing it, so we know Christ only by winning Him. There must first be the perception and possession by sense or emotion, and then the reflection on the possession by understanding. This applies to all religious truth. It must be possessed ere it be fully known. Like the new name written upon the Apocalyptic stone, 'No one knoweth but he that receiveth it.'

The k... w... ch was Paul's life's aim

knowledge of a Person: the object determines the nature of the knowledge. The mental act of knowing a proposition or a science or even of knowing about a person by hearing of him is different from that of knowing people when we have lived beside them. We need not be afraid of attaching too familiar a meaning to this word of our text, if we say that it implies personal acquaintance with the Christ whom we know. Of course we come to know Him in the first instance through the medium of statements about Him, and we cannot too strongly insist, in these days of destructive criticism, on the absolute necessity of accepting the Gospel statements as to the life of Jesus as the only possible method of knowing Him. But then, beyond that acceptance of the record must come the application and appropriation of it, and the transmutation of a historical fact into a personal experience. We may take an illustration from any of the Scriptural truths about Jesus:—For instance, Scripture declares Him to be our Redeemer. One man believes Him to be so, welcomes Him into his life as such, and finds Him to be such. Another man believes Him to be so, but never puts His redeeming power to the proof. Is the knowledge of these two rightly called by the same name? That which comes after experience is surely not rightly designated by the same title as that which has no vivification nor verification of such a sort to build on, and is the mere product of the understanding. There is nothing which the great mass of so-called Christians need more than to have forced into their thoughts the difference between these two kinds of knowledge of Christ. There are thousands of them who, if asked, are ready to profess that they know Jesus, but to whom He has never been anything than a partially understood article of an uncared for creed, and has never been in living contact with their needs, nor known for their strength in weakness, their comforter in sorrow, 'their life in death,' their all in all.

To deepen that experimental knowledge of Jesus is a worthy aim for the whole life, and is a process that may go on indefinitely through it all. To know Him more and more is to have more of heaven in us. To be penetrating ever deeper into His fulness, and finding every day new depths to penetrate is to have a fountain of freshness in our dusty days that will never fail or run dry. There is only one inexhaustible person, and that is Jesus Christ. We have all fulness in our Lord: we have already received all when we received Him. Are we advancing in the experience that is the parent of knowing Him? Do new discoveries meet us every day as if we were explorers in a virgin land? To have this for our aim is enough for satisfaction, for blessedness, and for growth. To know Him is a liberal education.

II. That knowledge involves knowing the power of His Resurrection.

The power of His Resurrection is an expression which covers a wide ground. There are several distinct and well-marked powers ascribed to it in Paul's writings. It has a demonstrative force in reference to our Lord's person and work. For He is by it 'declared to be the Son of God with power.' That rising again from the dead, taken in conjunction with the fact that He dieth no more, but is ascended up on high, and in conjunction with His own words concerning Himself and His Resurrection, sets Him forth before the world as the Son of God, the solemn and approval of

It has a revealing power in regard to the condition of humanity in death. It is the one fact which establishes immortality, and which not only establishes it, but casts some light on the manner of it. The possibility of personal life after, and therefore, in death, the unbroken continuity of being, the possibility of a resurrection, and a glorifying of this corporeal frame, with all the far-reaching consequences of these truths in the triumph they give over death, in the support and substance they afford to the else-shadowy idea of immortality, in the lofty place which they assign to the bodily frame, and the conception which they give of man's perfection as consisting of body, soul, and spirit—these thoughts have flashed light into all the darkness of the grave, have narrowed to a mere strip of coast-line the boundaries of the kingdom of death, have proclaimed love as the victor in her contest with that shrouded horror. The basis of them all is Christ's Resurrection; its power in this respect is the power to illuminate, to console, to certify, to wrench the sceptre from the hands of death, and to put it in the pierced hands of the Living One that was dead, and is Lord both of the dead and the living.

Further, the Resurrection is treated by Paul as having a power for our justification, in so far as the risen Lord bestows upon us by His risen life the blessings of His righteousness. Paul also represents the Resurrection of Christ as having the power of quickening ou Spiritual life. I need not spend time in quoting t many passages where His rising from the dead, a His life after the Resurrection, are treated as the t and pattern of our lives: and are not only reg but are also regarded as the po life of ours is brought about.

the power of raising us from **the death** of sin, and bringing us into a new life of **the Spirit**. And finally, the Resurrection of Christ is regarded as having the power of raising His servants from the grave to the full possession of His own glorious life, and so it is the power of our final victory over death.

Now I do not know that we are entitled to exclude any of these powers from view. The broad words of the text include them all, but perhaps the two last are mainly meant, and of these chiefly the former.

The risen life of Christ quickens and raises us, and that not merely as a pattern, but as a power. It is only if we are in Him that there is so real a unity of life between Him and us that there enters into us some breath of His own life.

That risen life of the Saviour which we share if we have Him, enters into our nature as leaven into the three measures of meal; transforming and quickening it, gives new directions, tastes, motives, impulses, and power. It bids and inclines us to seek the things that are above, and its great exhortation to the hearts in which it dwells, to fix themselves there, and to forsake the things that are on the earth, is based upon the fact that they have died, and 'their life is hid with Christ in God.' Without that leaven the life that we live is a death, because it is lived in the 'lusts of the flesh,' doing the desires of the flesh and of the mind. There is no real union with Jesus Christ, of which the direct is not a living experience of the power of His rrec in bringing us to the likeness of its in m from the to si need to press upon our consciences, that the only infallible sign that we have been in any measure quickened together with Christ and raised up with Him is that we have ceased to live in the lusts of our flesh, doing the desires of the flesh and of the mind. The risen life of Jesus may indefinitely increase, and will do so in the measure in which we honestly make it our life's aim to know Him and the power of His Resurrection.

III. The experience of the power of Christ's Resurrection is inseparable from the fellowship of His sufferings.

We must not suppose that Paul's solemn and awful words here trench in the smallest degree on the solitary unapproachableness of Christ's death. He would have answered, as in fact he does answer, the appeal of the prophetic sufferer, 'Behold and see if there be any sorrow like unto my sorrow' with the strongest negative. No other human lips have ever tasted, or can ever taste, a cup of such bitterness as He drained for us all, and no other human lips have ever been so exquisitely sensitive to the bitterness which they have drunk. The identification of Himself with a sinful world, the depth and closeness of His community of feeling with all sorrow, the consciousness of the glory which He had left, and the perpetual sense of the hostility into which He had come, set Christ's sufferings by themselves as surely as the effects that flow from them declare that they need no repetition, and cannot be degraded by any parallel whilst the world lasts.

But yet His Death, like His Resurrection, is set f
i   being a type and power of ou
world by the power of the C

we truly trust in His sacrifice there will operate upon us motives which separate and detach us from our old selves and the old world. A fundamental, ethical, and spiritual change is effected on us through faith. We were dead in sin, we are dead to sin. We have to blend the two thoughts of the Christian life as being a daily dying and a continual resurrection in order to get the whole truth of the double aspect of it.

It may be a question whether the Apostle is here referring to outward or inward and ethical sorrows, but perhaps we should not do justice to the thought unless we extend it to cover both of these. Certainly if his theology was but the generalising of his experience, he had ample material in his daily life for knowing the fellowship of Christ's sufferings. One of his most frequently recurring and most cherished thoughts is, that to suffer for Christ is to suffer with Christ, and in it he found and teaches us to find strength to endure, and patience to outlast any sorrows that may swoop upon us like birds of prey because we are Christians. Happy shall we be if Christ's sufferings are ours, because it is our union with Him and our likeness to Him, not to ourselves, our sins, or our worldliness, that is their occasion. There is an old legend that Peter was crucified head downwards, because he felt himself unworthy to be as his Master. We may well feel that nothing which we can ever bear for Him is worthy to be compared with what He has be for us, and be the more overwhelmed with the

But there is another sense in which it is a worthy aim of our lives that our sufferings may be felt to be fellowship with His. That is a blessed sorrow which brings us closer to our Lord. That is a wholesome sorrow of which the issue is an intenser faith in Him, a fuller experience of His sufficiency. The storm blows us well when it blows us to His breast, and sorrow enriches us, whatever it may take away, which gives us fuller and more assured possession of Jesus.

But when we are living in fellowship with Jesus, that union works in two directions, and while on the one hand we may then humbly venture to feel that our sufferings for Him are sufferings with Him, we may thankfully feel, too, that in all our affliction He is afflicted. If His sufferings are ours we may be sure that ours are His. And how different they all become when we are certain of His sympathy! It is possible that we may have a kind of common consciousness with our Lord, if our whole hearts and wills are kept in close touch with Him, so that in our experience there may be a repetition in a higher form of that strange experience alleged to be familiar in hypnotism, where the bitter in one mouth is tasted in another.

So, what we ought to make our aim is that in our lives our growing knowledge of Christ should lead to the two results, so inexorably intertwined, of daily death and daily resurrection, and that we may be kept faithful to Him so that our outward sufferings may caused by our union with Him, and not by our o faithlessness, and may be discerned by us to be fell ship with His. Then we shall also feel that He b ours with us, and sorrow itself will be calmed be tified into a silent bliss, as the chill peaks wh me strikes them glow with tender pink, a

soft and warm, though they are grim rock and ice-
cold snow. Then some faint echo of His history
'who was acquainted with grief' may be audible in our
outward lives and we, too, may have our Gethsemane
and our Calvary. It may not be presumption in us to
say 'We are able' when He asks 'Can ye drink of the
cup that I drink of'? nor terror to hear Him prophesy
'Ye shall indeed drink of the cup that I drink of,' for
we shall remember 'joint-heirs in Christ, if so be that
we suffer with Him, that we may be also glorified
together.'

IV. The end attained.

The Christian life as here manifested is even in its
highest forms manifestly incomplete. It is a reflected
light, and like the reflected light in the heavens,
advances by imperceptible degrees to fill the whole
silver round. It may be 'e'en in its imperfections
beautiful,' but it assuredly has 'a ragged edge.' The
hypothetical form of the last words of our text does
not so much imply a doubt of the possibility of attaining the result as the recognition of the indispensable
condition of effort on the part of him who attains it.
That effort forthcoming, the attainment is certain.

The Revised Version makes a slight correction which
involves a great matter, in reading 'the resurrection
from the dead.' It is necessary to insist on this change
in rendering, not because it implies that only saints
are raised, but because Paul is thinking of that first
resurrection of which the New Testament habitually
speaks. 'The dead in Christ shall rise first' as he
himself declared in his earliest epistle, and the seer in
the Apocalypse shed a benediction on 'him that hath
part in the first resurrection.' Our knowledge of that
solemn future is so fragmentary that we cannot

ture to draw dogmatic inferences from the little that has been declared to us, but we cannot forget the distinct words of Jesus in which He not only plainly declares a universal resurrection, but as plainly proclaims that it falls into two parts, one a 'resurrection of life,' and one a 'resurrection of judgment.' The former may well be the final aim of a Christian life: the latter is a fate which one would think no sane man would deliberately provoke. Each carries in its name its dominant characteristic, the one full of attractiveness, the other partially unveiling depths of shame and punitive retributions which might appal the stoutest heart.

This resurrection of life is the last result of the power of Christ's Resurrection received into and working on the human spirit. It is plain enough that if the Spirit of Him that raised up Jesus from the dead dwell in us there is no term to its operations until our mortal bodies also are quickened by His Spirit that dwelleth in us. The ethical and spiritual resurrection in the present life finds its completion in the bodily resurrection in the future. It cannot be that the transformation wrought in a human life shall be complete until it has flowed outwards into and permeated the whole of manhood, body, soul, and spirit. The three measures of meal have each to be influenced before 'the whole is leavened.' If we duly consider the elements necessary to a perfect realisation of the divine ideal of humanity, we shall discern that redemption must have a gospel to bring to the body as well as to the spirit. Whatever has been devastated by sin must be healed by Jesus. It is not necessary suppose that the body which dies is the body which rises again, rather the Apostle's far-reaching seri

antitheses between that which is sown and that which
is raised leads us to think that the natural body, which
has passed through corruption, and the particles of
which have been gathered into many different combina-
tions, does not become the spiritual body. The person
who dies is the person who lives through death, and
who assumes the body of the resurrection, and it is the
person, not the elements which make up the personality,
who is spoken of as risen from the dead. The vesture
may be different, but the wearer is the same.

So that resurrection from the dead is the end of a
supernatural life begun here and destined to culminate
hereafter. It is the last step in the manifestation of
our being in Christ, and so is being prepared for here
by every step in advance in gaining Jesus. It should
ever be before every Christian soul that participation
in Christ hereafter is conditioned by its progress in
likeness to Him here. The Resurrection from the dead
is not a gift which can be bestowed apart from a man's
moral state. If he dies having had no knowledge by
experience of the power of Christ's Resurrection, there
is nothing in the fact of death to give him that knowledge, and it is impossible to bring 'any means' to bear
on him by which he will attain unto the 'resurrection
from the dead.' If God could give that gift irrespec-
tive of a man's relations to Jesus, He would give it to
all. Let us ask ourselves, then, is it not worth making
the dominant aim of our lives the same as that of
Paul's? How stands our account then? Are we not
wise traders presenting a good balance-sheet when we
s   on the one side the lo   of all things,
             gaining of C   the at

of the perfect Lord? Does the other balance-sheet show the man as equally solvent who enters on one side the gain of a world, and on the other a Christless life, to be followed by a resurrection in which is no joy, no advance, no life, but which is a resurrection of judgment? May we all be found in Him, and attain to the resurrection from the dead!

LAID HOLD OF AND LAYING HOLD

'I follow after if that I may apprehend that for which also I was apprehended of Christ Jesus.'—PHIL. iii. 12.

'I WAS laid hold of by Jesus Christ.' That is how Paul thinks of what we call his conversion. He would never have 'turned' unless a hand had been laid upon him. A strong loving grasp had gripped him in the midst of his career of persecution, and all that he had done was to yield to the grip, and not to wriggle out of it. The strong expression suggests, as it seems to me, the suddenness of the incident. Possibly impressions may have been working underground, ever since the martyrdom of Stephen, which were undermining his convictions, and the very insanity of his zeal may have been due to an uneasy consciousness that the ground was yielding beneath his feet. That may have been so, but, whether it were so or not, the crisis came like a bolt out of the blue, and he was checked in full career, as if a voice had spoken to the sea in its wildest storm, and frozen its waves into immobility.

There is suggested in the word, too, distinctly, Lord's own action in the matter. No doubt,

fact of His supernatural appearance gives emphasis
to the phrase here. But every Christian man and
woman has been, as truly as ever Paul was, laid hold
of by the personal action of Jesus Christ. He is
present in His Word, and, by multitudes of inward
impulses and outward providences, He is putting out a
gentle and a firm hand, and laying it upon the
shoulders of all of us. Have we yielded? Have we
resisted, when we were laid hold of? Did we try to
get away? Did we plant our feet and say, 'I will not
be drawn,' or did we simply neglect the pressure? If
we have yielded, my text tells us what we have to do
next. For that hand is laid upon a man for a purpose,
and that purpose is not secured by the hand being laid
upon him, unless he, in his turn, will put out a hand
and grasp. Our activity is needed; that activity will
not be put forth without very distinct effort, and that
effort has to be life-long, because our grasp at the best
is incomplete. So then, we have here, first of all, to
consider—

I. What Christ has laid His grip on us for.

Now, the immediate result of that grasp, when it is
yielded to, is the sense of the removal of guilt, forgiveness of sins, acceptance with God. But these, the
immediate results, are by no means the whole results,
although a great many of us live as if we thought that
the only thing that Christianity is meant to do to us
is that it bars the gates of some future hell, and brings
to us the message of forgiveness. We cannot think
too nobly or too loftily of that gift of forgiveness, the
initial gift that is laid in every Christian man's hands,
but we think too exclusively of it, and a great

off a door, or a wall, before he lays on the new. The
initial gift that comes from being laid hold of by Jesus
Christ is the burning off of the old coat of paint. But
that is only the preliminary to the laying on of the
new. A man away in the backwoods will spend a
couple of years after he has got his bit of land in felling
and burning the trees, and rooting out and destroying the weeds. But is that what he got the clearing
for? That is only a preliminary to sowing the seed.
My friend! If Jesus Christ has laid hold of you, and
you have let Him keep hold of you, it is not only that
you may be forgiven, not only that you may sun yourself in the light of God's countenance, and feel that a
new blessed relation is set up between you and Him,
but there are great purposes lying at the back of that,
of which all that is only the preliminary and the
preparation.

Conversion. Yes; but what is the good of turning
a man round unless he goes in the direction in which
his face is turned? And so here the Apostle having
for years lived in the light of that great thought, that
God was reconciled in Jesus Christ, and that he was
God's friend, discerns far beyond that, in dim per-
spective, towering high above the land in the front,
the snowy sunlit summits of a great range to which
he has yet to climb, and says, 'I press on to lay hold
of that for which I was laid hold of by Jesus
Christ.'

And what was that? On the road to Damascus
Paul was only told one thing, that Christ had grasp
him and drawn him to Himself in order that
might make him a chosen vessel to bear the Word
hence amongst the Gentiles. The bearing of His
version upon Paul himself was never mentioned.

bearing of His conversion on the world was the only
subject that Jesus spoke of at first. But here Paul
has nothing to say about his world-wide mission. He
does not think of himself as being called to be an
Apostle, but as being summoned to be a Christian.
And so, forgetting for the time all the glorious and
yet burdensome obligations which were laid upon him,
and the discharge of which was the very life of his
life, he thinks only of what affects his own character,
the perfecting of which he regards as being the one
thing for which he was 'laid hold of by Christ Jesus.'
The purpose is twofold. No Christian man is made a
Christian only in order that he may secure his own
salvation; there is the world to think of. No Christian man is made a Christian only in order that he
may be Christ's instrument for carrying the Word to
other people; there is himself to think of. And these
two phases of the purpose for which Jesus Christ lays
hold upon us are very hard to unite in practice, giving
to each its due place and prominence, and they are
often separated, to the detriment of both the one that
is attended to, and the one that is neglected. The
monastic life has not produced the noblest Christians;
and there are pitfalls lying in the path of every man
who, like me, has for his profession to preach the
Gospel, which, if they are fallen into, the inward life is
utterly wrecked.

The two sides of Christ's purpose have, in our
practice, to be held together, but for the present I only
w   o say   ord or two about that which, as I have
        e hemisphere of the completed

fully in a previous verse. Here is his conception of the purpose, 'that I may know Him, and the power of His resurrection, and the fellowship of His sufferings, being made conformable unto His death, if by any means I might attain unto the resurrection of the dead.' That is what you were forgiven for; that is what you have 'passed from death unto life' for; that is what you have come into the sweet fellowship of God, and can think of Him as your Friend and Helper for.

Let us take the clauses *seriatim*, and say a word about each of them. 'That I may know Him.' Ah! there is a great deal more in Jesus Christ than a man sees when he first sees Him through his tears and his fears, and apprehends Him as the Saviour of his soul, and the sacrifice on whom the burden and the guilt of his sins were laid. We must begin there, as I believe. But woe to us if we stop there. There is far more in Christ than that; although all that is in Him is included in that, yet you have to dig deep before you find all that is included in it. You have to live with Him day by day, and year by year, and to learn to know Him as we learn to know husbands and wives, by continual intercourse, by continual experience of a sweet and unfailing love, by many a sacred hour of interchange of affection and reception of gifts and counsels. It is only thus that we learn to know what Jesus Christ is. When He lays hold of us, He comes like the angel that came to Peter in the prison in the dark and awoke him out of his sleep and said 'Rise! and follow me.' It is only when we get out into the street, and have been with Him for awhile, and the daylight begins to stream in, that we see clearly the face of our Deliverer, and know Him for all that He is. This knowledge is not the sort of knowledge t you can get by thinking, or out of a book. It is the knowledge of experience. It is the knowledge of love, it is the knowledge of union, and it is in order that we may know Christ that He lays his hand upon us.

'The power of His Resurrection.' Now, by that I understand a similar knowledge, by experience, of the risen life of Jesus Christ flowing into us, and filling our hearts and minds with its own power. The risen life of Jesus is the nourishment and strengthening and blessing and life of a Christian. Our daily experience ought to be that there comes, wavelet by wavelet, that silent, gentle, and yet omnipotent influx into our empty hearts, the very life of Christ Himself.

I know that this generation says that that is mysticism. I do not know whether it is mysticism or not. I am sure it is truth; and I do not understand Christianity at all, unless there is that kind of mysticism, perfectly wholesome and good, in it. You will never know Jesus Christ until you know Him as pouring into your hearts the power of an endless life, His own life. Christ for us by all means,—Christ's death the basis of our hope, but Christ in us, and Christ's life as the true gift to His Church. Have you got that? Do you know the power of His Resurrection?

'The fellowship of His sufferings.' Has Paul made a mistake, and deserted the chronological order? Why does he put the 'fellowship of the sufferings' after the 'power of the Resurrection'? For this plain reason, that if we get Christ's life into our hearts, in the measure in which we get it we shall bear a similar

that 'if they hate Me they will hate you also.'
Brethren, the test of us who have the life of Christ in
our hearts is that we shall, in some measure, suffer
with Him, because 'as He is, so are we, in this world,'
and because we must in that case look upon the world,
its sins and its sorrows, with something of the sad
gaze with which He looked across the valley to the
Temple sparkling in the morning light, and wept over
it. So if we know the power of His Resurrection we
shall know the fellowship of His sufferings.

And then Paul goes on, in his definition of the purpose for which Christ lays hold upon men, apparently
to say the same thing over again, only in the opposite
order, 'that I may be conformable to His death, if by
any means I might attain unto the resurrection of the
dead.' Both of these clauses, I think, refer to the
future, to the actual dying of the body, and the actual
future resurrection of the same. And the thought is
this, that if here, through our earthly lives, we have
been recipients of the risen life of Jesus Christ, and
so have stood to the world in our degree as He stood
to it, then when the moment of death comes to us,
we shall, in so far, have our departure shaped after
His as that we shall be able to say, 'Into Thy hands I
commit my spirit,' and die willingly, and at last shall
be partakers of that blessed Resurrection unto life
eternal which closes the vista of our earthly history.
Stephen's death was conformed to Christ's in outward
fashion, in so far as it echoed the Master's prayer,
'Father forgive them, for they know not what they
do,' and in so far as it echoed the Master's last words
with the significant alteration that, whilst Jesus c[om]-
mended His spirit to the Father, the first mart[yr]
commended his to Jesus Christ.

These, then, are the purposes for which Christ laid His hand upon us, that we might know Him, the power of His Resurrection, the fellowship of His sufferings, being made conformable to His death yet by attaining the resurrection of the dead.

II. Notice, again, our laying hold because we have been laid hold of.

Christ's laying hold of me, blessed and powerful as it is, does not of itself secure that I shall reach the end which He had in view in His arresting of me. What more is wanted? My effort. 'I follow after if I may apprehend that for which also I am apprehended.' Now, notice, in the one case, the Apostle speaks of himself, not as passive, but certainly not as active. 'I was laid hold of.' What did he do? As I have said, he simply yielded to the grasp. But 'I may lay hold of' conveys the idea of personal effort; and so these two expressions, 'I was apprehended,' and 'I apprehend,' suggest this consideration, that, for the initial blessings of the Christian life, forgiveness, acceptance, the sense of God's favour, and of reconciliation with him, nothing is needed but the simple faith that yields itself altogether to the grasp of Christ's hand, but that for my possessing what Christ means that I should possess when He lays His hand on me, there is needed not only faith but effort. I have to put out *my* hand and tighten my fingers round the thing, if I would make it my own, and keep it.

So—faith, to begin with, and work based on faith,

stimulus in the thought, I was laid hold of by Him
for a purpose. There is all the difference between
striving, however eagerly, however nobly, however
strenuously, however constantly, after self-improvement, by one's own effort only, and striving after it
because one knows that he is therein fulfilling the
purpose for which Jesus Christ drew him to Himself.

And if that be so, then the nature of the thing to
be laid hold of determines what we are to do to lay
hold of it. And since to know Christ, and the power
of His Resurrection, and the fellowship of His sufferings, is the aim and end of our conversion, the way to
secure it must be keeping in continual touch with
Jesus by meditating upon Him, by holding many a
moment of still, sacred, sweet communion with Him,
by carefully avoiding whatever might come between
us and our knowledge of Him, and the influx of His
life into us, and by yielding ourselves, day by day, to
the continual influence of His divine grace upon us,
and by the discipline which shall make our inward
natures more and more capable of receiving more and
more of that dear Lord. These being the things to
do, in regard to the inward life, there must be effort
too, in regard to the outward; for we must, if we are
to lay hold of that for which we are laid hold of by
Jesus Christ, bring all the outward life under the
dominion of this inward impulse, and when the flood
pours into our hearts we must, by many a sluice and
trench, guide it into every corner of the field, that a
may be irrigated. The first thing they do when th
are going to sow rice in an Eastern field is to floo
and then they cast in the seed, and it germin
Flood your lives with Christ, and then sow the
and you will get a crop.

III. Lastly, the text suggests the incompleteness of our grasp.

'I follow that,' says Paul, 'if that I may apprehend.' This letter was written far on in his career, in the time of his imprisonment in Rome, which all but ended his ministerial activity; and was many years after that day on the road to Damascus. And yet, matured Christian and exercised Apostle as he was, with all that past behind him, he says, 'I follow after, that I may apprehend.' Ah, brother, our experience must be incomplete, for we have an infinite aim set before us, and there is no end to the possibilities of plunging deeper and deeper and deeper into the knowledge of Christ, and having larger and larger and larger draughts of the fulness of His life. We have only been like goldseekers, who have contented themselves as yet with washing the precious grains out of the gravel of the river. There are great reefs filled with the ore that we have not touched. Thank God for the necessary incompleteness of our 'apprehend-ing.' It is the very salt of life. To have realised our aims, to have fulfilled our ideals, to have sucked dry the cluster of the grapes is the death of aspiration, of hope, of blessedness; and to have the distance beck-oning, and all experience 'an arch, wherethro' gleams the untravelled world to which we move,' is the secret of perpetual youth and energy.

incomplete, our experience should be pro-

churches have many grown babies, and cases of
arrested development—people that ought to be living
on strong meat, and are unable to masticate or digest
it, and by their own fault have still need of the milk
of infancy. There is an old fable about a strange
animal that fastened itself to the keel of sailing ships,
and by some uncanny power was able to arrest them
in mid-ocean, though the winds were filling all their
sails. There is a remora, as they called it, of that sort
adhering to a great many Christian people, and keeping them fixed on one spot, instead of 'following after,
if that they may apprehend.'

Dear friends—and especially you younger Christians
—Christ has laid hold of you. Well and good! that is
the beginning. He has laid hold of you for an end.
That end will not be reached without your effort, and
that effort must be perpetual. It is a life-long task.
Ay! and even up yonder the apprehending will be
incomplete. Like those mathematical lines that ever
approximate to a point which they never reach, we
shall through Eternity be, as it were, rising, in ascend-
ing and ever-closer drawing spirals, to that great
Throne, and to Him that sits upon it. So that, striking
out the humble 'may' from our text, the rest of it
describes the progressive blessedness of the endless
life in the heavens, as truly as it does the progressive
duty of the Christian life here, and the glorified fl
that follows the Lamb in the heavenly pastures m
each say: I follow after in order to apprehend t
'for which,' long ago and down amidst the
shadows of earth, 'I was apprehended of C
Je   '

THE RACE AND THE GOAL

'This one thing I do, forgetting those things which are behind, and reaching forth unto those things which are before, I press toward the mark for the prize.'—PHIL. iii. 13, 14.

THIS buoyant energy and onward looking are marvellous in 'Paul the aged, and now also a prisoner of Jesus Christ.' Forgetfulness of the past and eager anticipation for the future are, we sometimes think, the child's prerogatives. They may be ignoble and puerile, or they may be worthy and great. All depends on the future to which we look. If it be the creation of our fancies, we are babies for trusting it. If it be, as Paul's was, the revelation of God's purposes, we cannot do a wiser thing than look.

The Apostle here is letting us see the secret of his own life, and telling us what made him the sort of Christian that he was. He counsels wise obliviousness, wise anticipation, strenuous concentration, and these are the things that contribute to success in any field of life. Christianity is the perfection of common sense. Men become mature Christians by no other means than those by which they become good artisans, ripe scholars, or the like. But the misery is that, though people know well enough that they cannot be good carpenters, or doctors, or fiddlers without certain habits and practices, they seem to fancy that they can be good Christians without them.

The words of my text may suggest appropriate

'prize.' He aims at the one for the sake of the other. The one is the object of effort; the other is the sure result of successful effort. If I may so say, the crown hangs on the winning post; and he who touches the goal clutches the garland.

Then, mark that he regards the aim towards which he strains as being the aim which Christ had in view in his conversion. For he says in the preceding context, 'I labour if that I may lay hold of that for which also I have been laid hold of by Jesus Christ.' In the words that follow the text he speaks of the prize as being the result and purpose of the high calling of God 'in Christ Jesus.' So then he took God's purpose in calling, and Christ's purpose in redeeming him, as being his great object in life. God's aims and Paul's were identical.

What, then, is the aim of God in all that He has done for us? The production in us of God-like and God-pleasing character. For this suns rise and set; for this seasons and times come and go; for this sorrows and joys are experienced; for this hopes and fears and loves are kindled. For this all the discipline of life is set in motion. For this we were created; for this we have been redeemed. For this Jesus Christ lived and suffered and died. For this God's Spirit is poured out upon the world. All else is scaffolding; this is the building which it contemplates, and when the building is reared the scaffolding may be cleared away. God means to make us like Himself, and so pleasing Himself, and has no other end in all the varieties His gifts and bestowments but only this, the product of character.

Such is the aim that we should set before us. and that aim as ours will give nob lives nothing else different all our estimates of the meaning and true nature of events would be, if we kept clearly before us that their intention was not merely to make us blessed and glad, or to make us sorrowful, but that, through the blessedness, through the sorrow, through the gift, through the withdrawal, through all the variety of dealings, the intention was one and the same, to mould us to the likeness of our Lord and Saviour! There would be fewer mysteries in our lives, we should seldomer have to stand in astonishment, in vain regret, in miserable and weakening looking back upon vanished gifts, and saying to ourselves, 'Why has this darkness stooped upon my path?' if we looked beyond the darkness and the light to that for which both were sent. Some plants require frost to bring out their savour, and men need sorrow to test and to produce their highest qualities. There would be fewer knots in the thread of our lives, and fewer mysteries in our experience, if we made God's aim ours, and strove through all variations of condition to realise it.

How different all our estimate of nearer objects and aims would be, if once we clearly recognised what we are here for! The prostitution of powers to obviously unworthy aims and ends is the saddest thing in humanity. It is like elephants being set to pick up s; it is like the lightning being harnessed to carry he gossip and filth of one capital of the world to ent readers in another. Men take these great God has given them, and use t

There is nothing that needs more careful examination by us than our accepted schemes of life for ourselves; the roots of our errors mostly lie in these things that we take to be axioms, and that we never examine into. Let us begin this new year by an honest dealing with ourselves, asking ourselves this question, 'What am I living for?' And if the answer, first of all, be, as, of course, it will be, the accomplishment of the nearer and necessary aims, such as the conduct of our business, the cultivating of our understandings, the love and peace of our homes, then let us press the investigation a little further, and say, What then? Suppose I make a fortune, what then? Suppose I get the position I am striving for, what then? Suppose I cultivate my understanding and win the knowledge that I am nobly striving after, what then? Let us not cease to ask the question until we can say, 'Thy aim, O Lord, is my aim, and I press toward the mark,' the only mark which will make life noble, elastic, stable, and blessed, that I 'may be found in Christ, not having mine own righteousness, but that which is of God by faith.' For this we have all been made, guided, redeemed. If we carry this treasure out of life we shall carry all that is worth carrying. If we fail in this we fail altogether, whatever be our so-called success. There is one mark, one only, and every arrow that does not hit that target is wasted and spent in vain.

II. Secondly, let me say, concentrate all effort on this one aim.

'This one thing I do,' says the Apostle, 'I pr
toward the mark.' That aim is the one which God
in view in all circumstances and arrangements. T
fore, obviously, it is one which may be pursued i

Item 17.

AUTHOR   Maclaren, Alexander, 1826-1910.
TITLE   Expositions of Holy Scripture.
PUBLICATION Grand Rapids, Mich. : W. B. Eerdmans, 1959.

LOCATION   Main Collection
CALL NUMBER BS491 .M16 1959
LOCATION HAS c.1:v.1, c.1:v.2, c.1:v.3, c.1:v.4, c.1:v.5, c.1:v.6,
            c.1:v.7, c.1:v.8, c.1:v.9, c.1:v.10, c.1:v.11

Item 18.

AUTHOR   Maclaren, Alexander, 1826-1910.
TITLE   Philippians, Colossians I. and II. Thessalonians and I.
            Timothy / by Alexander Maclaren.
PUBLICATION New York : A. C. Armstrong, 1910.

LOCATION   Main Collection
CALL NUMBER BS491 .M16 59 RES.STORAGE
LOCATION HAS c.1

of these, and may be sought whatsoever we are doing.
All occupations of life except only sin are consistent
with this highest aim. It needs not that we should
seek any remote or cloistered form of life, nor sheer off
any legitimate and common interests and occupations,
but in them all we may be seeking for the one thing,
the moulding of our characters into the shapes that are
pleasing to Him. 'One thing have I desired of the
Lord, that will I seek after, that I may dwell in the
house of the Lord all the days of my life'; wheresoever
the outward days of my life may be passed. Whatsoever we are doing in business, in shop, at a study
table, in the kitchen, in the nursery, by the road, in the
house, we may still have the supreme aim in view,
that from all occupations there may come growth in
character and in likeness to Jesus Christ.

Only, to keep this supreme aim clear there will
require far more frequent and resolute effort of what
the old mystics used to call 'recollection' than we are
accustomed to put forth. It is hard, amidst the din of
business, and whilst yielding to other lower, legitimate
impulses and motives, to set this supreme one high
above them all. But it is possible if only we will do
two things: keep ourselves close to God, and be prepared
to surrender much, laying our own wills, our own
fancies, purposes, eager hopes and plans in His hands,
and asking Him to help us, that we may never lose
  of   our light because of any tossing waves
        en us and it, nor may ever be
        ds, which are only means

point; you can do nothing with a blunt one. Every
flight of wild ducks in the sky will tell you the form
that is most likely to secure the maximum of motion
with the minimum of effort. The wedge is that which
pierces through all the loosely-compacted textures
against which it is pressed. The Roman strategy
forced the way of the legion through the loose-ordered
ranks of barbarian foes by arraying it in that wedge-
like form. So we, if we are to advance, must gather
ourselves together and put a point upon our lives by
compaction and concentration of effort and energy on
the one purpose. The conquering word is, 'This one
thing I do.' The difference between the amateur and
the artist is that the one pursues an art at intervals by
spurts, as a *parergon*—a thing that is done in the
intervals of other occupations—and that the other
makes it his life's business. There are a great many
amateur Christians amongst us, who pursue the Christian life by spurts and starts. If you want to be a
Christian after God's pattern—and unless you are you
are scarcely a Christian at all—you have to make it your
business, to give the same attention, the same concentration, the same unwavering energy to it which
you do to your trade. The man of one book, the man
of one idea, the man of one aim is the formidable and
the successful man. People will call you a fanatic;
never mind. Better be a fanatic and get what you aim
at, which is the highest thing, than be so broad th
like a stream spreading itself out over miles of m
there is no scour in it anywhere, no current, and th
fore stagnation and death. Gather yourselves toget
and a   st all the side issues and nearer aim
           the aim to which all are b
                    I   r drink, or

I do, I may do all to the glory of God.' Let sorrow and
joy, and trade and profession, and study and business,
and house and wife and children, and all home joys, be
the means by which you may become like the Master
who has died for this end, that we may become
partakers of His holiness.

III. Pursue this end with a wise forgetfulness.

'Forgetting the things that are behind.' The art of
forgetting has much to do with the blessedness and
power of every life. Of course, when the Apostle says
'Forgetting the things that are behind,' he is thinking
of the runner, who has no time to cast his eye over his
shoulder to mark the steps already trod. He does not
mean, of course, either, to tell us that we are so to
cultivate obliviousness as to let God's mercies to us
'lie forgotten in unthankfulness, or without praises
die.' Nor does he mean to tell us that we are to deny
ourselves the solace of remembering the mercies which
may, perhaps, have gone from us. Memory may be
like the calm radiance that fills the western sky from
a sun that has set, sad and yet sweet, melancholy and
lovely. But he means that we should so forget as, by
the oblivion, to strengthen our concentration.

So I would say, let us remember, and yet forget, our
past failures and faults. Let us remember them in
order that the remembrance may cultivate in us a wise
chastening of our self-confidence. Let us remember
where we were foiled, in order that we may be the
of that place hereafter. If we know that
we fell into ambushes, 'not once

avoidance of places where he is weak, is an incurable fool.

But let us forget our failures in so far as these might paralyse our hopes, or make us fancy that future success is impossible where past failures frown. Ebenezer was a field of defeat before it rang with the hymns of victory. And there is no place in your past life where you have been shamefully baffled and beaten, but there, and in that, you may yet be victorious. Never let the past limit your hopes of the possibilities and your confidence in the certainties and victories of the future. And if ever you are tempted to say to yourselves, 'I have tried it so often, and so often failed, that it is no use trying it any more. I am beaten and I throw up the sponge,' remember Paul's wise exhortation, and 'forgetting the things that are behind . . . press toward the mark.'

In like manner I would say, remember and yet forget past successes and achievements. Remember them for thankfulness, remember them for hope, remember them for counsel and instruction, but forget them when they tend, as all that we accomplish does tend, to make us fancy that little more remains to be done; and forget them when they tend, as all that we accomplish ever does tend, to make us think that such and such things are our line, and of other virtues and graces and achievements of culture and of character, that these are not our line, and not to be won by us.

'Our line!' Astronomers take a thin thread from spider's web and stretch it across their object gla to measure stellar magnitudes. Just as is the sp line in comparison with the whole shining surf the sun acr which it is stretched, so is what alr av d to the boundless might and that to which we may come. Nothing short of the full measure of the likeness of Jesus Christ is the measure of our possibilities.

There is a mannerism in Christian life, as there is in everything else, which is to be avoided if we would grow into perfection. There was a great artist in the last century who never could paint a picture without sticking a brown tree in the foreground. We have all got our 'brown trees,' which we think we can do well, and these limit our ambition to secure other gifts which God is ready to bestow upon us. So 'forget the things that are behind.' Cultivate a wise obliviousness of past sorrows, past joys, past failures, past gifts, past achievements, in so far as these might limit the audacity of our hopes and the energy of our efforts.

IV. So, lastly, pursue the aim with a wise, eager reaching forward.

The Apostle employs a very graphic word here, which is only very partially expressed by that 'reaching forth.' It contains a condensed picture which it is scarcely possible to put into any one expression. 'Reaching out over' is the full though clumsy rendering of the word, and it gives us the picture of the runner with his whole body thrown forward, his hand extended, and his eye reaching even further than his hand, in eager anticipation of the mark and the prize. So we ... to live, with continual reaching out of confidence, ... r recognition, and eager desire to make our own

... which gives an element of nobleness to

their eyes. And so life is saved from commonplace, is happily stung into fresh effort, is redeemed from flagging, monotony, and weariness.

The measure of our attainments may be fairly estimated by the extent to which the unattained is clear in our sight. A man down in the valley sees the nearer shoulder of the hill, and he thinks it the top. The man up on the shoulder sees all the heights that lie beyond rising above him. Endeavour is better than success. It is more to see the Alpine heights unscaled than it is to have risen so far as we have done. They who thus have a boundless future before them have an endless source of inspiration, of energy, of buoyancy granted to them.

No man has such an absolutely boundless vision of the future which may be his as we have, if we are Christian people, as we ought to be. We only can thus look forward. For all others a blank wall stretches at the end of life, against which hopes, when they strike, fall back stunned and dead. But for us the wall may be overleaped, and, living by the energy of a boundless hope, we, and only we, can lay ourselves down to die, and say then, 'Reaching forth unto the things that are before.'

So, dear friends, make God's aim your aim; concentrate your life's efforts upon it; pursue it with a wise forgetfulness; pursue it with an eager confidence of anticipation that shall not be put to shame. Remember that God reaches His aim for you by giving to you Jesus Christ, and that you can only reach it by accepting the Christ who is given and being found in Him. Then the years will take away nothing from us which it is not well to lose. They will neither weaken our hope, nor dim our co and, at the last we shall reach the mark, and, as we touch it, we shall find dropping on our surprised and humble heads the crown of life which they receive who have so run, not as uncertainly, but doing this one thing, pressing towards the mark for the prize.

THE SOUL'S PERFECTION

Let us therefore, as many as be perfect, be thus minded : and if in anything ye be otherwise minded, God shall reveal even this unto you.'—PHIL. iii. 15.

'As many as be perfect'; and how many may they be? Surely a very short bede-roll would contain their names; or would there be any other but the Name which is above every name upon it? Part of the answer to such a question may be found in observing that the New Testament very frequently uses the word to express not so much the idea of moral completeness as that of physical maturity. For instance, when Paul says that he would have his converts to be '*men* in understanding,' and when the Epistle to the Hebrews speaks of 'them that are of full age,' the same word is used as this 'perfect' in our text. Clearly in such cases it means 'full grown,' as in contrast with 'babes,' and ⟨expre⟩sses not absolute completeness, but what we ⟨may⟩ term a relative perfection, a certain maturity of ⟨charact⟩er and advanced stage of Christian attain-⟨ment distinguish⟩ed from the infantile epoch of the to unattained heights, so that a sense of imperfection and a continual effort after higher life are parts of Paul's 'perfect man.' And it is to be still further noticed that on the same testimony 'perfect' people may probably be 'otherwise minded'; by which we understand not divergently minded from one another, but 'otherwise' than the true norm or law of life would prescribe, and so may stand in need of the hope that God will by degrees bring them into conformity with His will, and show them 'this,' namely, their divergence from His Pattern for them.

It is worth our while to look at these large thoughts thus involved in the words before us.

I. Then there are people whom without exaggeration the judgment of truth calls *perfect*.

The language of the New Testament has no scruple in calling men 'saints' who had many sins, and none in calling men perfect who had many imperfections; and it does so, not because it has any fantastic theory about religious emotions being the measure of moral purity, but partly for the reasons already referred to, and partly because it wisely considers the main thing about a character to be not the degree to which it has attained completeness in its ideal, but what that ideal is. The distance a man has got on his journey is of less consequence than the direction in which his face is turned. The arrow may fall short, but to what mark was it shot? In all regions of life a wise classification of men arranges them according to their aims rather tha their achievements. The visionary who attempts so thing high and accomplishes scarcely anything o is often a far nobler man, and his poor, broken, f resultless life far more perfect than his who a m on the low levels and hits them full. Su

as these, full of yearning and aspiration, though it be
for the most part vain, are

> 'Like the young moon with a ragged edge
> E'en in its imperfection beautiful.'

If then it be wise to rank men and their pursuits
according to their aims rather than their accomplish-
ments, is there one class of aims so absolutely corresponding to man's nature and relations that to take
them for one's own, and to reach some measure of
approximation to them, may fairly be called the perfection of human nature? Is there one way of living
concerning which we may say that whosoever adopts
it has, in so far as he does adopt it, discerned and
attained the purpose of his being? The literal force
of the word in our text gives pertinence to that
question, for it distinctly means 'having reached the
end.' And if that be taken as the meaning, there need
be no doubt about the answer. Grand old words have
taught us long ago 'Man's chief end is to glorify God
and to enjoy Him for ever.' Yes, he who lives for God
has taken that for his aim which all his nature and all
his relations prescribe, he is doing what he was made
and meant to do; and however incomplete may be its
attainments, the lowest form of a God-fearing, God-
obeying life is higher and more nearly 'perfect' than
the fairest career or character against which, as a
blight on all its beauty, the damning accusation may
be brought, 'The God in whose hand thy breath is, and
all thy ways, thou hast not glorified.'

at 'saints' and point at their fa

a morality of its own different from that of the world (except as being higher), nor because 'saints' make up for adultery and murder by making or singing psalms, but because the main set and current of the life was evidently towards God and goodness, and these hideous sins were glaring contradictions, eddies and backwaters, as it were, wept over with bitter self-abasement and conquered by strenuous effort. Better a life of God-ward aspiration and straining after purity, even if broken by such a fall, so recovered, than one of habitual earthward grubbing, undisturbed by gross sin.

And another reason warrants the application of the word to men whose present is full of incompleteness, namely, the fact that such men have in them the germ of a life which has no natural end but absolute completeness. The small seed may grow very slowly in the climate and soil which it finds here, and be only a poor little bit of ragged green, very shabby and in-conspicuous by the side of the native flowers of earth flaunting around it, but it has a divine germinant virtue within, and waits but being carried to its own clime and 'planted in the house of the Lord' above, to 'flourish in the courts of our God,' when these others with their glorious beauty have faded away and are flung out to rot.

II. We have set forth here very distinctly two of the characteristics of this perfection.

The Apostle in our text exhorts the perfect to be '*thus* minded.' How is that? Evidently the word points back to the previous clauses, in which he has been describing his own temper and feeling in the Christian race. He sets that before the Philippians as a pattern, or rather invites them to fellowship with him in the state of themselves and in their effort

higher attainments. 'Be thus minded' means, Think
as I do of yourselves, and do as I do in your daily life.

How did he think of himself? He tells us in the
sentence before, 'Not as though I were already perfect.
I count not myself to have apprehended.' So then a
leading characteristic of this true Christian perfection
is a constant consciousness of imperfection. In all fields
of effort, whether intellectual, moral, or mechanical, as
faculty grows, consciousness of insufficiency grows with
it. The farther we get up the hill, the more we see how
far it is to the horizon. The more we know, the more
we know our ignorance. The better we can do, the
more we discern how much we cannot do. Only people
who never have done and never will do anything, or
else raw apprentices with the mercifully granted self-
confidence of youth, which gets beaten out of most of
us soon enough, think that they can do everything.

In morals and in Christian life the same thing is true.
The measure of our perfection will be the consciousness
of our imperfection—a paradox, but a great truth. It
is plain enough that it will be so. Conscience becomes
more sensitive as we get nearer right. The worse a man
is the less it speaks to him, and the less he hears it.
When it ought to thunder it whispers; when we need it
most it is least active. The thick skin of a savage will
not be disturbed by lying on sharp stones, while a
crumpled rose-leaf robs the Sybarite of his sleep. So
the practice of evil hardens the cuticle of conscience, and
the practice of goodness restores tenderness and sensi-
bility; and many a man laden with crime knows less of
its tingling than some fair soul that looks almost spotless
to all eyes but its own. One little stain of rust
ightly polish but i

difference. As men grow better they become like that glycerine barometer recently introduced, on which a fall or a rise that would have been invisible with mercury to record it takes up inches, and is glaringly conspicuous. Good people sometimes wonder, and sometimes are made doubtful and sad about themselves, by this abiding and even increased consciousness of sin. There is no need to be so. The higher the temperature the more chilling would it be to pass into an ice-house, and the more our lives are brought into fellowship with the perfect life, the more shall we feel our own shortcomings. Let us be thankful if our consciences speak to us more loudly than they used to do. It is a sign of growing holiness, as the tingling in a frost-bitten limb is of returning life. Let us seek to cultivate and increase the sense of our own imperfection, and be sure that the diminution of a consciousness of sin means not diminished power of sin, but lessened horror of it, lessened perception of right, lessened love of goodness, and is an omen of death, not a symptom of life. Painter, scholar, craftsman all know that the condition of advance is the recognition of an ideal not attained. Whoever has not before him a standard to which he has not reached will grow no more. If we see no faults in our work we shall never do any better. The condition of all Christian, as of all other progress, is to be drawn by that fair vision before us, and to be stung into renewed effort to reach it, by the consciousness of present imperfection.

Another characteristic to which these perfect are exhorted is a constant striving after a fu advance. How vigorously, almost vehement, temper is put in the context—'I follow after'; t rd k'; and that picturesque '

forth,' or, as the Revised Version gives it, 'stretching
forward.' The full force of the latter word cannot be
given in any one English equivalent, but may be clumsily
hinted by some such phrase as 'stretching oneself out
over,' as a runner might do with body thrown forward
and arms extended in front, and eagerness in every
strained muscle, and eye outrunning foot, and hope
clutching the goal already. So yearning forward, and
setting all the current of his being, both faculty and
desire, to the yet unreached mark, the Christian man
is to live. His glances are not to be bent backwards,
but forwards. He is not to be a 'praiser of the past,'
but a herald and expectant of a nobler future. He is
the child of the day and of the morning, forgetting the
things which are behind, and ever yearning towards
the things which are before, and drawing them to himself. To look back is to be stiffened into a living death;
only with faces set forward are we safe and well.

This buoyant energy of hope and effort is to be the
result of the consciousness of imperfection of which we
have spoken. Strange to many of us, in some moods,
that a thing so bright should spring up from a thing so
dark, and that the more we feel our own shortcomings,
the more hopeful should we be of a future unlike the
past, and the more earnest in our effort to make that
future the present! There is a type of Christian experience not uncommon among devout people, in which
the consciousness of imperfection paralyses effort instead of quickening it; men lament their evil, their
r   and so on, and remain the same y
are sti   to n   t.

view here, which embraces both elements, and even draws the undying brightness of his forward-looking confidence from the very darkness of his sense of present imperfection!

So should it be with us, 'as many as be perfect.' Before us stretch indefinite possibilities of approximating to the unattainable fulness of the divine life. We may grow in knowledge and in holiness through endless ages and grades of advance. In a most blessed sense we may have that for our highest joy which in another meaning is a punishment of unfaithfulness and indocility, that we shall be 'ever learning, and never coming to the full knowledge of the truth.' No limit can be put to what we may receive of God, nor to the closeness, the fulness of our communion with Him, nor to the beauty of holiness which may pass from Him into our poor characters, and irradiate our homely faces. Then, brethren, let us cherish a noble discontent with all that we at present are. Let our spirits stretch out all their powers to the better things beyond, as the plants grown in darkness will send out pale shoots that feel blindly towards the light, or the seed sown on the top of a rock will grope down the bare stone for the earth by which it must be fed. Let the sense of our own weakness ever lead to a buoyant confidence in what we, even we, may become if we will only take the grace we have. To this touchstone let us bring all claims to higher holiness—they who are perfect are most conscious of imperfection, and most eager in their efforts after a further progress in t knowledge, love, and likeness of God in Christ.

III. We have here also distinctly brought out the existence with these characteristics of their oppo

'If in anything ye are otherwise minded,' says

I have already suggested that this expression evidently refers not to difference of opinion among themselves, but to a divergence of character from the pattern of feeling and life which he has been proposing to them. If in any respects ye are unconscious of your imperfections, if there be any 'witch's mark' of insensibility in some spot of your conscience to some plain transgressions of law, if in any of you there be some complacent illusion of your own stainlessness, if to any of you the bright vision before you seem faint and unsubstantial, God will show you what you do not see. Plainly then he considers that there will be found among these perfect men states of feeling and estimates of themselves opposed to those which he has been exhorting them to cherish. Plainly he supposes that a good man may pass for a time under the dominion of impulses and theories which are of another kind from those that rule his life.

He does not expect the complete and uninterrupted dominion of these higher powers. He recognises the plain facts that the true self, the central life of the soul, the higher nature, 'the new man,' abides in a self which is but gradually renewed, and that there is a long distance, so to speak, from the centre to the circumference. That higher life is planted, but its germination is a work of time. The leaven does not leaven the whole mass in a moment, but creeps on from particle to particle. 'Make the tree good' and in time its fruit will be good. But the conditions of are conflict, and these peaceful im impeded

flesh with spirit, and of imagination and heart and
will against the better life implanted in the spirit, are
the lot of all, even the most advanced here, and however a man may be perfect, there will always be the
possibility that in something he may be 'otherwise
minded.'

Such an admission does not make such interruptions
less blameworthy when they occur. The doctrine of
averages does not do away with the voluntary character
of each single act. The same number of letters are
yearly posted without addresses. Does anybody dream
of not scolding the errand boy who posted them, or the
servant who did not address them, because he knows
that? We are quite sure that we could have resisted
each time that we fell. That piece of sharp practice in
business, or that burst of bad temper in the household
which we were last guilty of—could we have helped it
or not? Conscience must answer that question, which
does not depend at all on the law of averages. Guilt
is not taken away by asserting that sin cleaves to men,
'perfect men.'

But the feelings with which we should regard sin
and contradictions of men's truest selves in ourselves
and others should be so far altered by such thoughts
that we should be very slow to pronounce that a man
cannot be a Christian because he has done so and so.
Are there any sins which are clearly *incompatible* with
a Christian character? All sins are *inconsistent* with
it, but that is a very different matter. The uniform
direction of a man's life being godless, selfish, devoted
to the objects and pursuits of time and sense, is incompatible with his being a Christian—but, thank God,
single act, however dark, is so, if it be in contradict
to the main tendency impressed upon the char

and conduct. It is not for us to say that any single deed shows a man cannot be Christ's, nor to fling ourselves down in despair saying, 'If I were a Christian, I could not have done that.' Let us remember that 'all unrighteousness is sin,' and the least sin is in flagrant opposition to our Christian profession; but let us also remember, and that not to blunt our consciences or weaken our efforts, that Paul thought it possible for perfect men to be 'otherwise minded' from their deepest selves and their highest pattern.

IV. The crowning hope that lies in these words is the certainty of a gradual but complete attainment of all the Christian aspirations after God and goodness.

The ground of that confidence lies in no natural tendencies in us, in no effort of ours, but solely in that great name which is the anchor of all our confidence, the name of God. Why is Paul certain that 'God will reveal even this unto you'? Because He is God. The Apostle has learned the infinite depth of meaning that lies in that name. He has learned that God is not in the way of leaving off His work before He has done His work, and that none can say of Him, that 'He began to build, and was not able to finish.' The assurances of an unchangeable purpose in redemption, and of inexhaustible resources to effect it; of a love that can never fade, and of a grace that can never be exhausted—are all treasured for us in that mighty name. And such confidence is confirmed by the mani-t tendency of the principles and motives brought in Christianity to lead on to a condition fection, as well as by the expe have, if of th

and joy, by merciful chastisements dogging our steps
when we stray, by duties and cares, by the teaching
of His word coming even closer to our hearts and
quickening our consciences to discern evil where we
had seen none, as well as kindling in us desires after
higher and rarer goodness, by the reward of enlarged
perceptions of duty and greater love towards it, with
which He recompenses lowly obedience to the duty as
yet seen, by the secret influences of His Spirit of Power
and of Love and of a sound Mind breathed into our
waiting spirits, by the touch of His own sustaining
hand and glance of His own guiding eye, He will reveal
to the lowly soul all that is yet wanting in its knowledge,
and communicate all that is lacking in character.

So for us, the true temper is confidence in His power
and will, an earnest waiting on Him, a brave forward
yearning hope blended with a lowly consciousness of
imperfection, which is a spur not a clog, and vigorous
increasing efforts to bring into life and character the
fulness and beauty of God. Presumption should be as
far from us as despair—the one because we have not
already attained, the other because 'God will reveal
even this unto us.' Only let us keep in mind the caution
which the Apostle, knowing the possible abuses which
might gather round His teaching, has here attached
to it, 'Nevertheless'—though all which I have been
saying is true, it is only on this understanding—
'Whereto we have already attained, by the same let
us walk.' God will perfect that which concerneth you
if—and only if—you go on as you have begun, if you
make your creed a life, if you show what you are. If
so, then all the rest is a question of time. A has been
said, and Z will come in its proper place. Begin with
humble trust in Christ, and a process is commen-

which has no natural end short of that great hope with which this chapter closes, that the change which begins in the deepest recesses of our being, and struggles slowly and with many interruptions, into partial visibility in our character, shall one day triumphantly irradiate our whole nature out to the very finger-tips, and ' even the body of our humiliation shall be fashioned like unto the body of Christ's glory, according to the working whereby He is able even to subdue all things to Himself.'

THE RULE OF THE ROAD

'Nevertheless, whereto we have already attained, let us walk by the same rule.'—PHIL. iii. 16.

PAUL has just been laying down a great principle— viz. that if the main direction of a life be right, God will reveal to a man the points in which he is wrong. But that principle is untrue and dangerous, unless carefully guarded. It may lead to a lazy tolerance of evil, and to drawing such inferences as, 'Well! it does not much matter about strenuous effort, if we are right at bottom it will all come right by-and-by,' and so it may become a pillow for indolence and a clog on effort. This possible abuse of a great truth seems to strike the Apostle, and so he enters here, with this 'Nevertheless,' a *caveat* against that twist of his meaning. It is as if he said, 'Now mind! while all that is perfectly true, it is true on conditions; and if they be not attended to, it is not true.' God will reveal to a man the things in which he is wrong if, and only if, he steadfastly continues in the course which he knows and sees to be right. Present attainments, then, in some sense a standard of duty, and if we honestly and conscientiously observe that standard we shall get light as we journey. In this exhortation of the Apostle's there are many exhortations wrapped up; and in trying to draw them out I venture to adhere to the form of exhortation for the sake of impressiveness and point.

I. First, then, I would say the Apostle means, 'Live up to your faith and your convictions.'

It may be a question whether 'that to which we have already attained' means the amount of knowledge which we have won or the amount of practical righteousness which we have made our own. But I think that, instead of sharply dividing between these two, we shall follow more in the course of the Apostle's thought if we unite them together, and remember that the Bible does not make the distinct separation which we sometimes incline to make between knowledge on the one side and practice on the other, but regards the man as a living unity. And thus, both aspects of our attainments come into consideration here.

So, then, there are two main thoughts—first, live out your creed, and second, live up to your convictions.

Live out your creed. Men are meant to live, not by impulse, by accident, by inclination, but by principle. We are not intended to live by rule, but we *are* intended to live by law. And unless we know *why* we do as well as *what* we do, and give a rational account of our conduct, we fall beneath the height on which G intends us to walk. Impulse is all very well, impulse is blind and needs a guide. The imitatio those around us, or the acceptance of the ap ne of circumstances, are, to some e t. But to be driven me

force of externals is to surrender the highest prerogative of manhood. The highest part of human nature
is the reason guided by conscience, and a man's conscience is only then rightly illuminated when it is
illuminated by his creed, which is founded on the acceptance of the revelation that God has made of Himself.

And whilst we are clearly meant to be guided by the
intelligent appropriation of God's truth, that truth is
evidently all meant for guidance. We are not told
anything in the Bible in order that we may know as
an ultimate object, but we are told .it all in order that,
knowing, we may be, and, being, we may do, according
to His will.

Just think of the intensely practical tendency of all
the greatest truths of Christianity. The Cross is the
law of life. The revelation that was made there was
made, not merely that we might cling to it as a refuge
from our sins, but that we might accept it as the rule
of our conduct. All our duties to mankind are summed
up in the word 'Love one another as I have loved you.'
We say that we believe in the divinity of Christ; we
say that we believe in the great incarnation and sacri-
ficial death and eternal priesthood of the loving Son of
God. We say that we believe in a judgment to come
and a future life. Well, then, do these truths produce
any effect upon my life? have they shaped me in any
measure into conformity with their great principles?
there issue. from them constraining power which
and mould me as a sculptor would a bit of
ds? Am I subject to the G

But we shall not do that without a distinct effort. For it is a great deal easier to live from hand to mouth than to live by principle. It is a great deal easier to accept what seems forced upon us by circumstances than to exercise control over the circumstances, and make them bend to God's holy will. It is a great deal easier to take counsel of inclination, and to put the reins in the hands of impulses, passions, desires, tastes, or even habits, than it is, at each fresh moment, to seek for fresh impulses from a fresh illumination from the ancient and yet ever fresh truth. The old kings of France used to be kept with all royal state in the palace, but they were not allowed to do anything. And there was a rough, unworshipped man that stood by their side, and who was the real ruler of the realm. That is what a great many professing Christians do with their creeds. They instal them in some inner chamber that they very seldom visit, and leave them there, in dignified idleness, and the real working ruler of their lives is found elsewhere. Let us see to it, brethren, that all our thoughts are incarnated in our deeds, and that all our deeds are brought into immediate connection with the great principles of God's word. Live by that law, and we live at liberty.

And, then, remember that this translating of creed into conduct is the only condition of growing illumination. When we act upon a belief, the belief grows. That is the source of a great deal of stupid obstinacy in this world, because men have been so long accustomed to go upon certain principles that it seems incredi to them but that these principles should be true. that, too, is at the bottom of a great deal of intell and noble firmness of adherence to the true man who has tested a principle because he lived upon it has confidence in it that nobody else can have.

Projectors may have beautiful specifications with attractive pictures of their new inventions; they look very well upon paper, but we must see them working before we are sure of their worth. And so, here is this great body of Divine truth, which assumes to be sufficient for guidance, for conduct, for comfort, for life. Live upon it, and thereby your grasp of it and your confidence in it will be immensely increased. And no man has a right to say 'I have rejected Christianity as untrue,' unless he has put it to the test by living upon it; and if he has, he will never say it. A Swiss traveller goes into a shop and buys a brand-new alpenstock. Does he lean upon it with as much confidence as another man does, who has one with the names of all the mountains that it has helped him up branded on it from top to bottom? Take *this* staff and lean on it. Live your creed, and you will believe your creed as you never will until you do. Obedience takes a man up to an elevation from which he sees further into the deep harmonies of truth. In all regions of life the principle holds good: 'To him that hath shall be given.' And it holds eminently in reference to our grasp of Christian principles. Use them and they grow; neglect them and they perish. Sometimes a man dies in a workhouse who has a store of guineas and notes wrapped up in rags somewhere about him; and so they have been of no use to him. If you want to increase, trade with it. As the Lord ve the servants their talents: me.'

of the principles of Christianity, because you have not
lived upon them, nor tried to do it.

And, in like manner, another side of this thought is,
be true to your convictions. There is no such barrier
to a larger and wholesomer view of our duty as the
neglect of anything that plainly is our duty. It stands
there, an impassable cliff between us and all progress.
Let us live and be what we know we ought to be, and
we shall know better what we ought to be at the next
moment.

II. Secondly, let me put the Apostle's meaning in
another exhortation, Go on as you have begun.

'Whereunto we have already attained, by the same
let us walk.' The various points to which the men
have reached are all points in one straight line; and
the injunction of my text is 'Keep the road.' There
are a great many temptations to stray from it. There
are nice smooth grassy bits by the side of it where it
is a great deal easier walking. There are attractive
things just a footstep or two out of the path—such a
little deviation that it can easily be recovered. And
so, like children gathering daisies in the field, we stray
away from the path; and, like men on a moor, we
then look round for it, and it is gone. The angle of
divergence may be the acutest possible; the deviation
when we begin may be scarcely visible, but if you draw
a line at the sharpest angle and the least deviation
from a straight line, and carry it out far enough, there
will be space between it and the line from which it
started ample to hold a universe. Then, let us take
care of small deviations from the plain straight path,
and give no heed to the seductions that lie on either
side, but 'whereunto we have already attained,

There are temptations, too, to slacken our speed.
The river runs far more slowly in its latter course than
when it came babbling and leaping down the hillside.
And sometimes a Christian life seems as if it crept
rather than ran, like those sluggish streams in the Fen
country, which move so slowly that you cannot tell
which way the water is flowing. Are not there all
round us, are there not amongst ourselves instances
of checked growth, of arrested development? There
are people listening to me now, calling themselves
—and I do not say that they have not a right to do
so—Christians, who have not grown a bit for years,
but stand at the very same point of attainment, both
in knowledge and in purity and Christlikeness, as they
were many, many days ago. I beseech you, listen to
this exhortation of my text, 'Whereunto we have
already attained, by the same let us walk,' and continue patient and persistent in the course that is set
before us.

III. The Apostle's injunction may be cast into this
form, Be yourselves.

The representation which underlies my text, and
precedes it in the context, is that of the Christian community as a great body of travellers all upon one road,
all with their faces turned in one direction, but at very
different points on the path. The difference of position
necessarily involves a difference in outlook. They see
their duties, and they see the Word of God, in some
...ly. And the Apostle's exhortation is:
...follow his own insight, and wh...
by

of independent faithfulness to our own measure of
light, as the guide which we are bound to follow.

There is a dreadful want, in the ordinary Christian
life, of any appearance of first-hand communication
with Jesus Christ, and daring to be myself, and to act
on the insight into His will which Christ has given *me*.

Conventional Godliness, Christian people cut after
one pattern, a little narrow round of certain statutory
duties and obligations, a parrot-like repetition of certain words, a mechanical copying of certain methods
of life, an oppressive sameness, mark so much of
modern religion. What a freshening up there would
come into all Christian communities if every man
lived by his own perception of truth and duty! If a
musician in an orchestra is listening to his neighbour's
note and time, he will lose many an indication from
the conductor that would have kept him far more
right, if he had attended to it. And if, instead of
taking our beliefs and our conduct from one another,
or from the average of Christian men round us, we
went straight to Jesus Christ and said to Him, 'What
wouldst *Thou* have *me* to do?' there would be a
different aspect over Christendom from what there is
to-day. The fact of individual responsibility, according to the measure of our individual light, and faithful
following of that, wheresoever it may lead us, are the
grand and stirring principles that come from these
words. 'Whereunto we have already attained,' by that
—and by no other man's attainment or rule—let us wal

But do not let us forget that that same faith
independence and independent faithfulness bec
Christ speaks to us, and we will not let any
voice blend with His, are quite consistent with
in   , de   , the frank recognition of our b

equal right. If we more often thought of all the great body of Christian people as an army, united in its diversity, its line of march stretching for leagues, and some in the van, and some in the main body, and some in the rear, but all one, we should be more tolerant of divergences, more charitable in our judgment of the laggards, more patient in waiting for them to come up with us, and more wise and considerate in moderating our pace sometimes to meet theirs. All who love Jesus Christ are on the same road and bound for the same home. Let us be contented that they shall be at different stages on the path, seeing that we know that they will all reach the Temple above.

IV. Lastly, cherish the consciousness of imperfection and the confidence of success.

'Whereunto we have attained' implies that that is only a partial possession of a far greater whole. The road is not finished at the stage where we stand. And, on the other hand, 'by the same let us walk,' implies that beyond the present point the road runs on equally patent and pervious to our feet. These two convictions, of my own imperfection and of the certainty of my reaching the great perfectness beyond, are indispensable to all Christian progress. As soon as a man begins to think that he has realised his ideal, Good-bye! to all advance. The artist, the student, the man of business, all must have gleaming before them an unattained object, if they are ever to be stirred to to run with patience the race that is set

imperfection, there springs triumphant the confidence
of success.   That will give strength to the feeble
knees; that will lift a man buoyant over difficulties;
that will fire desire; that will stimulate and solidify
effort; that will make the long, monotonous stretches
of the road easy, the rough places plain, the crooked
things straight.   Over all reluctant, repellent duties it
will bear us, in all weariness it will re-invigorate us.
We are saved by hope, and the more brightly there
burns before us, not as a tremulous hope, but as a
future certainty, the thought, ' I shall be like Him, for
I shall see Him as He is,' the more shall I set my face
to the loved goal and my feet to the dusty road, and
'press toward the mark for the prize of the high calling
of God.'   Christian progress comes out of the clash and
collision of these two things, like that of flint and steel
—the consciousness of imperfection and the confidence
of success.   And they who thus are driven by the one
and drawn by the other, in all their consciousness of
failure are yet blessed, and are crowned at last with
that which they believed before it came.

'Blessed are they that dwell in Thy house'—the
prize won is heaven.   But 'blessed are they in whose
hearts are the ways'—the prize desired and strained
after is heaven upon earth.   We may all live a life of
continual advancement, each step leading upwards, for
the road always climbs, to purer air, grander scenery
and a wider view.   And yonder, progress will still
the law, for they who here have followed the Lamb,
sought to make Him their pattern and Comma
will there 'follow Him whithersoever He goeth.'
here we walk according to that 'whereunto we
at   d,' th   re He shall say, 'They will walk
i white, for they are worthy.'

WARNINGS AND HOPES

'Brethren, be ye imitators together of me, and mark them which so walk even as ye have us for an ensample. For many walk, of whom I told you often, and now tell you even weeping, that they are the enemies of the cross of Christ: whose end is perdition, whose God is the belly, and whose glory is in their shame, who mind earthly things. For our citizenship is in heaven; from whence also we wait for a Saviour, the Lord Jesus Christ: who shall fashion anew the body of our humiliation, that it may be conformed to the body of His glory, according to the working whereby he is able even to subject all things unto Himself.'—PHIL. iii. 17-21 (R.V.).

THERE is a remarkable contrast in tone between the sad warnings which begin this section and the glowing hopes with which it closes, and that contrast is made the more striking when we notice that the Apostle binds the gloom of the one and the radiance of the other by 'For,' which makes the latter the cause of the former.

The exhortation in which the Apostle begins by proposing himself as an example sounds strange on any lips, and, most of all, on his, but we have to note that the points in which he sets himself up as a pattern are obviously those on which he touched in the preceding outpouring of his heart, and which he has already commended to the Philippians in pleading with them to be 'thus minded.' What he desires them to copy is his self-distrust, his willingness to sacrifice all things to win Christ, his clear sense of his own shortcomings, and his eager straining towards as yet unreached per-fection. His humility is not disproved by such words, remarkable in them is the clear conscience which Jesus is held forth as an example. Notice, too, how quickly he passes to associate others with him, and to merge the 'Me' into 'Us.' We need not ask who his companions were, since Timothy is associated with him at the beginning of the letter.

The exhortation is enforced by pointing to others who had gone far astray, and of whom he had warned the Philippians often, possibly by letter. Who these unworthy disciples were remains obscure. They were clearly not the Judaisers branded in verse 2, who were teachers seeking to draw away the Philippians, while these others seem to have been 'enemies of the Cross of Christ,' not by open hostility nor by theoretical errors, but by practical worldliness, and that in these ways; they make sense their God, they are proud of what is really their disgrace, namely, they are shaking off the restraints of morality; and, most black though it may seem least so, they 'mind earthly things' on which thought, feeling, and interest are concentrated. Let us lay to heart the lesson that such direction of the current of a life to the things of earth makes men 'enemies of the Cross of Christ,' whatever their professions, and will surely make their end perdition, whatever their apparent prosperity. Paul's life seemed loss and was gain; these men's lives seemed gain and was loss.

From this dark picture charged with gloom, and in one corner showing white waves breaking far o against an inky sky, and a vessel with torn sa driving on the rocks, the Apostle turns with relie the brighter words in which he sets forth the t affinities and hopes of a Christian. They all st fall with the belief in the Resurrection of Chri His present life in His glorified corporeal manhoo

I. Our true metropolis.

The Revised Version puts in the margin as an alternative rendering for 'citizenship' commonwealth, and there appears to be a renewed allusion here to the fact already noted that Philippi was a 'colony,' and that its inhabitants were Roman citizens. Paul uses a very emphatic word for 'is' here which it is difficult to reproduce in English, but which suggests essential reality.

The reason why that heavenly citizenship is ours in no mere play of the imagination but in most solid substance, is because He is there for whom we look. Where Christ is, is our Mother-country, our Fatherland, according to His own promise, 'I go to prepare a place for you.' His being there draws our thoughts and sets our affections on Heaven.

II. The colonists looking for the King.

The Emperors sometimes made a tour of the provinces. Paul here thinks of Christians as waiting for their Emperor to come across the seas to this outlying corner of His dominions. The whole grand name is given here, all the royal titles to express solemnity and dignity, and the character in which we look for Him is that of Saviour. We still need salvation, and though in one sense it is past, in another it will not be ours until He comes the second time without sin unto salvation. The eagerness of the waiting which should characterise the expectant citizens is wonderfully described by the Apostle's expression for it, which literally means to look away out—with emphasis on both prepositions—like a sentry on the walls of a besieged city whose eyes are ever fixed on the pass amongst the hills through which the relieving forces are to come.

It may be said that Paul is here expressing an expectation which was disappointed. No doubt the early Church looked for the speedy return of our Lord and were mistaken. We are distinctly told that in that point there was no revelation of the future, and no doubt they, like the prophets of old, 'searched what manner of time the spirit of Christ which was in them did signify.' In this very letter Paul speaks of death as very probable for himself, so that he had precisely the same double attitude which has been the Church's ever since, in that he looked for Christ's coming as possible in his own time, and yet anticipated the other alternative. It is difficult, no doubt, to cherish the vivid anticipation of any future event, and not to have any certainty as to its date. But if we are sure that a given event will come sometime and do not know when it may come, surely the wise man is he who thinks to himself it may come any time, and not he who treats it as if it would come at no time. The two possible alternatives which Paul had before him have in common the same certainty as to the fact and uncertainty as to the date, and Paul had them both before his mind with the same vivid anticipation.

The practical effect of this hope of the returning Lord on our 'walk' will be all to bring it nearer Paul's. It will not suffer us to make sense our God, nor to fix our affections on things above; it will stimulate all energies in pressing towards the goal, and will turn away our eyes from the trivialities and transie.... that press upon us, away out toward the distance w.... 'far off His coming shone.'

III. The Christian sharing in Christ's glory.

Chapter II., recurs here. The 'fashion' of the body of
our humiliation is external and transient; the 'form'
of the body of His glory to which we are to be assimi-
lated consists of essential characteristics or properties,
and may be regarded as being almost synonymous with
'Nature.' Observing the distinction which the Apostle
draws by the use of these two words, and remembering
their force in the former instance of their occurrence,
we shall not fail to give force to the representation that
in the Resurrection the fleeting fashion of the bodily
frame will be altered, and the glorified bodies of the
saints made participant of the essential qualities of His.

We further note that there is no trace of false
asceticism or of gnostic contempt for the body in its
designation as 'of our humiliation.' Its weaknesses,
its limitations, its necessities, its corruption and its
death, sufficiently manifest our lowliness, while, on the
other hand, the body in which Christ's glory is manifested, and which is the instrument for His glory, is
presented in fullest contrast to it.

The great truth of Christ's continual glorified manhood is the first which we draw from these words.
The story of our Lord's Resurrection suggests indeed
that He brought the same body from the tomb as
loving hands had laid there. The invitation to Thomas
to thrust his hands into the prints of the nails, the
similar invitation to the assembled disciples, and His
partaking of food in their presence, seemed to forbid
the idea of His rising changed. Nor can any suppose
of His glory would be construed
But to

the world was,' as the Shechinah cloud received Him
out of the sight of the gazers below. If this be the
true reading of His last moments on earth, He united
in His own experience both the ways of leaving it
which His followers experience — the way of sleep
which is death, and the way of 'being changed.'

But at whatever point the change came, He now
wears, and for ever will wear, the body of a man. That
is the dominant fact on which is built the Christian
belief in a future life, and which gives to that belief
all its solidity and force, and separates it from vague
dreams of immortality which are but a wish
tremblingly turned into a hope, or a dread shudder-
ingly turned into an expectation. The man Christ
Jesus is the pattern and realised ideal of human life
on earth, the revelation of the divine life through
a human life, and in His glorified humanity is no less
the pattern and realised ideal of what human nature
may become. The present state of the departed is incomplete in that they have not a body by which they
can act on, and be acted on by, an external universe.
We cannot indeed suppose them lapped in age-long
unconsciousness, and it may be that the 'dead in
Christ' are through Him brought into some knowledge of externals, but for the full-summed perfection
of their being, the souls under the altar have to wait
for the resurrection of the body. If resurrection is
needful for completion of manhood, then completed
manhood must necessarily be set in a locality, and
the glorified manhood of Jesus must also now be in a
place. To think thus of it and of Him is not to
vulgarise the Christian conception of Heaven, but to
give it a definiteness and force which it sorely lack
lar t   g. Nor is the continual manhood

our Lord less precious in its influence in helping our familiar approach to Him. It tells us that He is still and ·for ever the same as when on earth, glad to welcome all who came and to help and heal all who need Him. It is one of ourselves who 'sitteth at the right hand of God.' His manhood brings Him memories which bind Him to us sorrowing and struggling, and His glory clothes Him with power to meet all our needs, to stanch all our wounds, to satisfy all our desires.

Our text leads us to think of the wondrous transformation into Christ's likeness. We know not what are the differences between the body of our humiliation and the body of His glory, but we must not be led away by the word Resurrection to fall into the mistake of supposing that in death we 'sow that body which shall be.' Paul's great chapter in I. Corinthians should have destroyed that error for ever, and it is a singular instance of the persistency of the most un-supported mistakes that there are still thousands of people who in spite of all that they know of what be-falls our mortal bodies, and of how their parts pass into other forms, still hold by that crude idea. We have no material by which to construct any, even the vaguest, outline of that body that shall be. We can only run out the contrasts as suggested by Paul in 1st Corinthians, and let the dazzling greatness of the positive thought which he gives in the text lift our expectations. Weakness will become power, all fused into the great light of likeness to the body of His glory; and though that tells us even less, it feeds hope more and satisfies our hearts even whilst it does not feed our curiosity. We may well be contented to acknowledge that 'it doth not yet appear what we shall be,' when we can go on to say, 'We know that when He shall appear we shall be like Him.' It is enough for the disciple that he be as his Master.

But we must not forget that the Apostle regards even this overwhelming change as but part of a mightier process, even the universal subjection of all things unto Christ Himself. The Emperor reduces the whole world to subjection, and the glorifying of the body as the climax of the universal subjugation represents it as the end of the process of assimilation begun in this mortal life. There is no possibility of a resurrection unto life unless that life has been begun before death. That ultimate glorious body is needed to bring men into correspondence with the external universe. As is the locality so is the body. Flesh and blood cannot inherit the Kingdom of God. This whole series of thoughts makes our glorious resurrection the result not of death, but of Christ's living power on His people. It is only in the measure in which He lives in us and we in Him, and are partaking by daily participation in the power of His Resurrection, that we shall be made subjects of the working whereby He is able even to subject all things unto Himself, and finally be conformed to the body of His glory.

Date Due

NOV 1		
JAN 9		
MAR		
JUN 1		
	JUN 1 5 1978	
	JUN 1	
FACULTY JUN 1 5 1992		
OCT		
FACULTY		
MAY 6 '66		
FACULTY APR 3 0 1990		
	PRINTED IN U. S. A.	

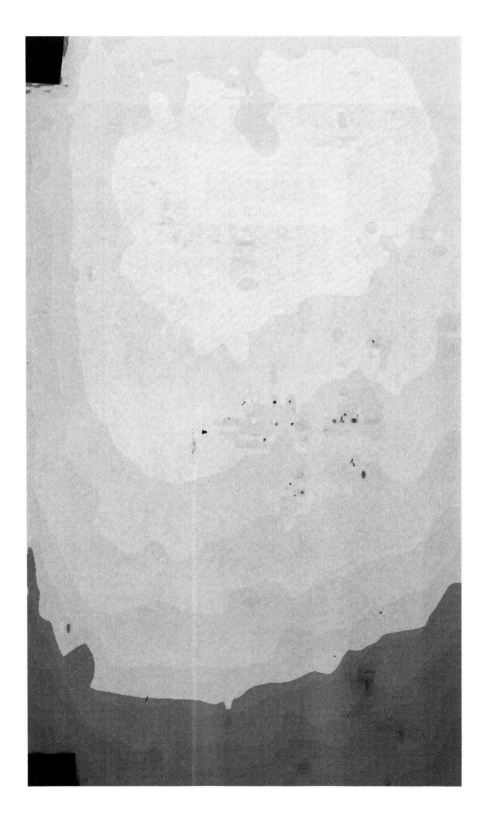